CAN IT HAPPEN AGAIN?
Chronicles of the Holocaust

CAN IT HAPPEN AGAIN?

Chronicles of the Holocaust

EDITED BY ROSELLE K. CHARTOCK AND JACK SPENCER

Published by

Black Dog & Leventhal Publishers, Inc.
151 West 19th Street
New York, NY 10011

Distributed by

Workman Publishing Company
708 Broadway
New York, NY 10003

An earlier edition of this book was published in 1979 by Bantam Books, under the title *The Holocaust Years: Society on Trial*, edited by Roselle K. Chartock and Jack Spencer.

Library of Congress Cataloging-in-Publication Data:
Can it happen again? : chronicles of the Holocaust / edited by Roselle K. Chartock and Jack Spencer.
    p. cm.
Earlier edition was published in 1979 under the title: The Holocaust years: society on trial.
Includes bibliographical references (p.) and index.
ISBN 1-57912-208-6
  1. Holocaust, Jewish (1939–1945)—Personal narratives.   2. Holocaust, Jewish (1939–1945)—Literary collections.   I. Chartock, Roselle. II. Spencer, Jack. III. Holocaust years.

D804.3 .C33 2001
940.53'18--dc21   2001037382

Manufactured in the U.S.A.

ACKNOWLEDGMENTS

"The Death House," from *The Rise and Fall of the Third Reich* by William L. Shirer; copyright © 1959, 1960 by William L. Shirer. Copyright renewed © 1987, 1988 by William L. Shirer. Reprinted by permission of Simon & Schuster, Inc.

"The Final Solution of the Jewish Question" and "The Jews in Hitler's Mental World," from *The War Against the Jews* by Lucy S. Dawidowicz. Copyright © 1975 by Lucy S. Dawidowicz. Reprinted by permission of Henry Holt and Co., Inc.

"The 'Final Solution' in Action: Testimony" from *The Harvest of Hate* by Leon Poliakov; copyright 1954 by Leon Poliakov. By permission of the American Jewish Committee.

"Dehumanization and Starvation" and "The Decent and the Indecent," from *Man's Search for Meaning* by Viktor Frankl. Copyright © 1959, 1962, 1984, 1992 by Viktor Frankl. Reprinted by permission of Beacon Press.

"Flow Chart for 'Operation Reinhard,' Auschwitz, and Majdanek" from *Revolt Amid the Darkness*; copyright © 1993 by permission of The United States Holocaust Memorial Museum.

"We Escaped from Hitler's Germany" by Catherine Noren. Copyright © 1974 by Scholastic Magazines. Reprinted by permission of Georges Borchardt, Inc. for the author.

"Listen to Me!" from *Night* by Elie Wiesel, translated by Stella Rodway. Copyright © 1960 by MacGibbon & Kee. Copyright renewed © 1988 by The Collins Publishing

Contents

I   WHAT HAPPENED?

II.   VICTIMS AND VICTIMIZERS   79

IV. WHAT DOES THE HOLOCAUST REVEAL ABOUT THE INDIVIDUAL AND SOCIETY? 199

Twentieth-Century Man 229

Behavior Under Stress 235

V. AFTERMATH 277

Epilogue

Acknowledgments

This anthology is being re-issued at a time when teaching about the Holocaust has become an integral part of curricula around the country, and at a time when the media have brought this subject into the living rooms of America. When the original edition of the book was published in 1978, however, there had not yet been widespread dissemination of information on the subject; there was not yet a National Holocaust Museum or memorials in cities large and small, not yet a Spielberg film based on a Kenneally book about a Righteous Gentile named Oskar Schindler, not yet a proliferation of novels and memoirs about the Holocaust. In 1978, this anthology was, in its own small way, a pioneering effort. The book was welcomed at that time by thousands of readers, as well as by teachers anxious to incorporate the subject into their courses. And during the time when the book was no longer available, many people repeatedly asked for it and tried to locate copies.

Thus, we are most grateful to J.P. Leventhal, our current publisher, for his revival of this anthology, and for recognizing its continuing educational and humanitarian value. He, too, is aware that, in spite of the increased knowledge on this subject, there is still much ignorance among young and old alike. We appreciate also Mr. Leventhal's belief in this book's potential for stimulating concern for the future of our world, in light of the all-too-similar inhumanities being perpetrated all over the globe today. Moreover, he has been most helpful in our expanding the selections in order to reflect these and other issues.

The added readings include an article about the Holocaust Museum in Washington, D.C.; a powerful poem, "The Hangman;" excerpts from Thomas Kenneally's book, *Schindler's List*, Claude Lanzmann's *Shoah*, and Art Spiegelman's *Maus I*; a piece concerning the movement to deny the Holocaust; one article describing an American town's response to neo-Nazi activities and another describing the recurrence of genocidal behavior in Africa; a flow chart of two concentration camps; an article with details about the medical experiments on twins at Auschwitz; and newspaper accounts from 1943 indicating that there was knowledge of the atrocities both here and abroad; an excerpt from an interview with an embittered adult child who grew up in a Nazi family; references to research that links the music and philosophy of composer Richard Wagner and Hitler himself; and a memorable quote from a noted child psychologist and survivor of the Holocaust.

We have also added a new section to include other groups persecuted by the Nazis, with pieces on the plight of Gypsies and homosexuals. These readings join the original pieces and share the same two-fold mission: to memorialize those who died and to alert the living and those yet to be born of horrors difficult to fathom but all too possible to repeat.

This anthology was originally published by Bantam Books in collaboration with the Anti-Defamation League of B'nai B'rith, and went through four printings from 1978 to 1984. The support provided by Bantam and the ADL enabled thousands of students and others across the country and abroad to learn about a series of events in history which we all agreed should not be forgotten lest they happen again.

With the assistance of a small grant from the National Conference of Christians and Jews and the efforts of its leader, the late Dr. Bernard Olsen, members of the Social Studies Department of Monument Mountain Regional High School in Great Barrington, Mass., John Beacco and Bill Fields, and former member, Larry Webb, devoted many hours to research, reading, and the compilation of related literature.

Following this initial grant, we were assisted by several people at the Anti-Defamation League, including the late Benjamin Epstein, Theodore Freedman, Stan Wexler, and Ruth Routtenberg Seldin. They all deserve our special thanks.

We are most grateful also to the administration and school committee of the Berkshire Hills Regional School District for having the sensitivity to encourage the teaching of this material. And we are especially thankful to the thousands of our students who grappled with this painful subject and thanked us for helping them grow to be "more caring and less prejudiced." These students have always been *our* reason for caring about the future.

We would like to thank Laura Ross and Robert Goff at Black Dog & Leventhal Publishers for their help in this project. They greatly added to the value of this anthology by recompiling, and generally pulling together the manuscript.

In addition to being able to measure the impact of this book on our students' knowledge and attitudes, we have also been able, to a lesser extent, to learn of its effects elsewhere. In an article in *Time* magazine soon after the book's third printing, we read of one of its more dubious distinctions: it was banned at the 1981 Moscow Book Fair.

Finally, we know that all who contributed to this publication feel as we do about the importance of bringing the subject of the Holocaust out in the open for discussion and debate. More than any other subject, the Holocaust teaches us not only about human nature and history, but more important, about ourselves.

ROSELLE K. CHARTOCK
JACK SPENCER

We dedicate this book to all those people,
living and dead, whose lives were
forever defined by this event.

Introduction

If we are to learn from history how to improve the quality of human life, then we must examine both the positive and negative chapters in human history. The readings in this anthology have been excerpted from more than 100 primary (first-hand) and secondary sources so that the reader can begin to learn about the Nazi Holocaust, an example of a negative chapter in history that remains unparalleled. Genocide and racial persecution have always been a part of the past, but never before the Holocaust was such persecution practiced on so large a scale or with such calculated cruelty. The term "holocaust" is formally defined as "the complete destruction of people and animals by fire," and has come to refer specifically to that destruction which was perpetrated on the Jews of Europe during World War II.

"How could the Holocaust have happened?" is the question immediately asked by someone who has just confronted the facts of this grotesque picture of man's inhumanity to man. There are no easy answers to the question of why six million Jews and six million non-Jews were systematically slaughtered in Nazi Germany and elsewhere under the leadership of Adolf Hitler. Nor are there simple answers to the other complex questions raised by this historical phenomenon which defies comprehension, questions such as:

Who were the dead? Why were they killed? Had they tried to escape?

Who were the murderers and their accomplices? How could they commit such acts?

What makes some people resist and others obey authority?

What would I have done under similar circumstances?

Could such a thing happen here—or anywhere—again?

And there are the broader questions:

What can such a catastrophe tell us about human nature?

Are there comparable examples of man's inhumanity?

What is the role and responsibility of the individual in society?

Where does one draw the line between obeying the law and obeying one's conscience?

The readings in this anthology have been selected with these and other disturbing questions in mind. More and more students, and the general public as well, want to know why country after country sat silently by as millions of innocents were murdered. They have asked why this chapter in history was left out of their history books or pushed to the margins of history.

As teachers introducing Holocaust material in classrooms, we have seen students—some for the first time—become seriously interested in reading, research, discussion, and problem-solving, when confronted with ideas that touch their very lives and the lives of everyone in their community. For example, haven't we all had to deal at some time or other with the issues of tolerance and intolerance, obedience and resistance to authority, conformity and individualism, freedom and the repression of freedom, and, of course, good and evil on several levels, within our families, in our roles as citizens of a free country, and as citizens of the world? In addition, we are constantly facing questions of morality—of what is the right or the "good" thing to do in a given situation. Our moral dilemmas obviously don't deal with whether or not to disobey the law by hiding a Jew from the Nazis—a question many Germans faced. Instead, we may have to decide if we'll refuse to pay taxes which we know are going to finance a war we can't morally support, or if we'll speak out against our country's contributions to a totalitarian government, or if we'll do business with a known racist in our community. We may not have to decide whether to obey an authority figure as pervasive as Hitler, but don't all of us have to deal with authority figures? As students, we are often in conflict with parents and teachers. As employees, we must decide how to react to the orders of employers, local officials, even doctors and others whose services we depend on. Thus, a study of the Holocaust goes beyond the specific events of the time period, 1933–1945, by relating these events to the universal and timeless issues of society. By tackling both the unique and universal aspects of the Holocaust, the reader can grapple with a microcosm of history.

In seeking resolution to the difficult, often unanswerable dilemmas raised here, it becomes necessary for the concerned student and citizen to bring to bear on these inquiries as much information as possible from such diverse fields of knowledge as philosophy, literature and poetry, religion, psychology, government, geography, and science. The readings herein are taken from every one of these fields, thus enabling one to see how differing issues actually interrelate; how, for example, an economic depression relates to the generating of fear, prejudice, and eventually violence. By linking these excerpts together there evolves a cohesive foundation for answering the question, "How could the Holocaust have happened?"

No doubt many people will ask while reading this material, "Why is it necessary to paint for the public such a bleak picture of humanity? Isn't it best to sweep this part of history under the rug and forget about it?" It is our emphatic belief that we cannot forget about the Holocaust—for our own sake and the sake of generations to come. Philosopher George Santayana wrote, "Those who do not remember the past are condemned to relive it." It is only through an exploration of both the positive and negative chapters in world history that we can ever expect to learn from the past. What lessons will be gleaned from these selections will depend both on what the reader brings to this anthology, and the desire of the reader to discover the truth about himself and the world. There is, however, one idea all will readily grasp from a study of this subject: that the courage and morality of a society are constantly on trial, and in a crisis, society is often tested to its limits. One student, after being asked if events surrounding the Watergate burglary could ever lead to something of Holocaust proportion, answered: "Could be. Maybe it wouldn't be the Jews again; maybe it would; but if what went on in Auschwitz could happen in a civilized country in 1944, why couldn't it happen in any civilized country at any time if people are really blinded by their own problems and hate?"

This edition of "Chronicles" contains important new material. An excerpt from M. E. Kerr's *Gentlehands* raises the question of how to respond to the realization that Nazi war criminals continue to live often undetected amongst us. Among the many parallels to the Holocaust is the systematic destruction and removal of Native Americans from their land. An eyewitness account of the Wounded Knee Massacre of 1890 recalls that period. And finally, a discussion of Si Lewen's art, along with several of his black and white drawings depicting the horrors of the concentration camps, provide the reader with further evidence of historical events that will forever challenge our comprehension and imagination.

PART I

WHAT HAPPENED?

"Six million were wiped off the face of the earth. And there is the danger that they will also be annihilated from our memories. Are they doomed to a two-fold annihilation?"

ABRAHAM JOSHUA HESCHEL

The Extermination of the Jews

The first three readings in this collection plunge the reader immediately into the physical world of the concentration camp. Be forewarned—much of the material is shocking and ugly, and it is intended to be so, for that is exactly what life in the camps was. The concentration camps were the device invented by German scientific geniuses to carry out the mass murder of millions of "undesirables" with maximum efficiency and as little mess as possible.

To secure cooperative behavior, the Nazis employed outright lies. Those loaded on trains for shipment to the gas chambers were told that they were being "resettled" in labor camps in the east. Outside Germany, few people believed the reports that began trickling out about the existence of extermination camps. The very idea was preposterous.

The first and third readings are from Bernd Naumann's book, Auschwitz. The second reading is from William Shirer's The Rise and Fall of the Third Reich. The first three paragraphs of the Shirer piece are quotations from the testimony of Rudolf Hoess, the commanding officer of Auschwitz.

Auschwitz:
A Concentration Camp

BERND NAUMANN

With every step one took one sank more deeply into the viscous mud. There was practically no water for washing. The prisoners slept on three tiers of wooden slabs, six to each tier, and for the most part without any straw pallets. Roll call twice a day meant that the prisoners had to stand for hours in the wet, cold mud. When it rained the prisoners had to lie on their wooden bunks in their wet garments. No wonder hundreds died daily. The guard towers around Auschwitz I and Birkenau formed the so-called "small guard chain." They were not used during the day; instead, the "big guard chain" encircled a huge perimeter encompassing most of the prisoners working in factories and in the fields, supervised by capos and foremen. Posters decorated with skulls and the warning "Auschwitz Concentration Camp Area—Do not cross this line—Fire will be opened without warning" dotted the big guard chain. But no such warnings were needed to keep civilians from approaching this eery tract, because of the ever-present threat of being suspected of trying to make contact with prisoners or of spying—charges that could land one in the camp. The work details outside the big guard chain were accompanied by as many guards as there were prisoners. At night after all the work details had returned, the guards left the towers of the big guard chain and the small guard went into operation. The returning prisoners were counted by the block leaders at the block leader offices in front of every compound. If a prisoner was missing, the guards of the big chain remained at their posts and a search party was sent out with dogs. Every now and then, however, a prisoner who had managed to steal away from his work detail succeeded in getting through the guards posted 100 feet apart and escaping. When that happened, the other prisoners were kept standing out in the open all night. And next morning, after spending the night in this fashion, they had to go right back to work.

Because of the barbaric sanitary conditions and the completely inadequate diet, combined with the hard labor and other tortures, most prisoners died a miserable death a few weeks or at most a few months after their arrival. Even the women, dressed in Russian blouses and rags, had to perform heavy labor, such as carrying rocks and digging ditches. Only those who managed to become trustees and get assigned to one of the few better details were able to stay alive for longer periods. Auschwitz was an extermination camp, the biggest in all of history. Between two and three million Jews were murdered there in the course of time, as well as thousands of Poles, Russians, Czechs, Yugoslavs, etc.

The Death House

WILLIAM L. SHIRER

We had two SS doctors on duty at Auschwitz to examine the
incoming transports of prisoners. These would be marched by one
of the doctors, who would make spot decisions as they walked by.
Those who were fit to work were sent into the camp. Others were
sent immediately to the extermination plants. Children of tender
years were invariably exterminated since by reason of their youth
they were unable to work.

Always Herr Hoess kept making improvements in the art of mass
killing.

Still another improvement we made over Treblinka was that at
Treblinka the victims almost always knew that they were to be
exterminated, while at Auschwitz we endeavored to fool the
victims into thinking that they were to go through a delousing
process. Of course, frequently they realized our true intentions
and we sometimes had riots and difficulties. Very frequently
women would hide their children under the clothes but of course
when we found them we would send the children in to be exterminated.
    We were required to carry out these exterminations in
secrecy, but of course the foul and nauseating stench from the
continuous burning of bodies permeated the entire area and all of
the people living in the surrounding communities knew that
exterminations were going on at Auschwitz.

The gas chambers themselves and the adjoining crematoria, viewed
from a short distance, were not sinister-looking places at all; it was impossible to make them out for what they were. Over them were well-
kept lawns with flower borders; the signs at the entrances merely said
BATHS. The unsuspecting Jews thought they were simply being taken to
the baths for the delousing which was customary at all camps. And
taken to the accompaniment of sweet music!

For there was light music. An orchestra of "young and pretty girls
all dressed in white blouses and navy-blue skirts," as one survivor remembered, had been formed from among the inmates. While the selection was being made for the gas chambers this unique musical ensemble
played gay tunes from *The Merry Widow* and *Tales of Hoffmann*. Nothing solemn and somber from Beethoven. The death marches at Auschwitz

were sprightly and merry tunes, straight out of Viennese and Parisian operettas.

To such music, recalling as it did happier and more frivolous times, the men, women, and children were led into the "bath houses," where they were told to undress preparatory to taking a "shower." Sometimes they were even given towels. Once they were inside the "shower-room"— and perhaps this was the first moment that they may have suspected something was amiss, for as many as 2,000 of them were packed into the chamber like sardines, making it difficult to take a bath—the massive door was slid shut, locked, and hermetically sealed.

Through heavy-glass portholes the executioners could watch what happened. The naked prisoners below would be looking up at the showers from which no water spouted or perhaps at the floor wondering why there were no drains. It took some moments for the gas to have much effect. But soon the inmates became aware that it was issuing from the perforations in the vents. It was then that they usually panicked, crowding away from the pipes and finally stampeding toward the huge metal door where, as Reitlinger puts it, "they piled up in one blue clammy blood-spattered pyramid, clawing and mauling each other even in death."

Twenty or thirty minutes later, when the huge mass of naked flesh had ceased to writhe, pumps drew out the poisonous air, the large door was opened and the men of the *Sonderkommando* took over. These were Jewish male inmates who were promised their lives and adequate food in return for performing the most ghastly job of all. Protected with gas masks and rubber boots and wielding hoses they went to work. Reitlinger has described it.

> Their first task was to remove the blood and defecations before
> dragging the clawing dead apart with nooses and hooks, the
> prelude to the ghastly search for gold and the removal of teeth and
> hair which were regarded by the Germans as strategic materials.
> Then the journey by lift or rail-wagon to the furnaces, the mill
> that ground the clinker to fine ash, and the truck that scattered
> the ashes in the stream of the Sola.

The Horrors of Daily Life

BERND NAUMANN

Billions of fleas tortured the prisoners in Auschwitz, and those who had shoes gave them away because the vermin prevented the use of this valuable possession. "Those who had only stockings or rags could at least scratch. The bugs didn't get much to eat, but still they were well-nourished.

"In Birkenau we didn't have fleas. Instead we had rats. They gnawed not only at corpses but also at the seriously sick. I have pictures showing women near death being bitten by rats. These animals were bold and impudent; they were not deterred by anything and at night even helped themselves to the bread the prisoners had saved in their pockets from the evening meal because at 'breakfast' there was nothing except a coffee-like brew. Then the prisoners would often accuse each other of having stolen bread from each other, but it was the rats. . . ."

The morning washing up: a row of wooden troughs under an iron pipe with holes through which some water trickled.

"Just enough so that one couldn't say it dripped. Then one hurried to get to the latrine. That was a concrete trough across which lay boards with round holes. There was room for 200 to 300 at one sitting. Latrine details watched to see that no one stayed too long and used sticks to chase the prisoners away. But some couldn't move so quickly, and others weren't through, and because of the strain a portion of the rectum would still protrude. When the latrine detail hit them they would run away and then once more get on line. There was no paper. Those who had jackets with linings would tear off a little piece at a time to clean themselves. Or they would steal a piece from somebody during the night to have some in reserve. The waste water of the washrooms was piped into the latrines to wash away the excrement. But again and again there were major stoppages, especially in places where the water pressure wasn't strong enough. When that happened a terrible stench spread throughout. Then pump details—'shit details'—would come to pump out the mess. . . .

"The people in the camp were so hungry that if a bit of soup spilled over, the prisoners would come running from all sides and like a swarm of wasps converge on the spot, dig their spoons into the mud, and stuff the mess into their mouths. Hunger and extreme want made them into animals."

It is almost impossible to imagine that a government would cold-bloodedly plan to destroy an entire people, innocent and defenseless, and yet that was exactly the intention of Hitler's regime in Germany. All the complex and costly machinery of the concentration camps was used for that purpose. As Lucy Dawidowicz makes clear in this selection from her book, *The War Against the Jews*, the destruction of the Jews was no mere side-effect of the war; it was a carefully planned objective. Hitler's maniacal dream of world domination called for total annihilation of the Jews. In order for Germany to rule the world, he felt he had to first make the German people racially pure, and that required purging it of "internal enemies," chief among whom he listed the Jews.

"The Final Solution of the Jewish Question"

LUCY DAWIDOWICZ

T*he Final Solution of the Jewish Question* was the code name assigned by the German bureaucracy to the annihilation of the Jews. The very composition of the code name, when analyzed, reveals its fundamental character and meaning to the Germans who invented and used it. The term "Jewish question," as first used during the early Enlightenment/Emancipation period in Western Europe, referred to the "question" or "problem" that the anomalous persistence of the Jews as a people posed to the new nation-states and the rising political nationalisms. The "Jewish question" was, at bottom, a euphemism whose verbal neutrality concealed the user's impatience with the singularity of this people that did not appear to conform to the new political demands of the state.

Since a question demands an answer and a problem a solution, various answers and solutions were propounded to the "Jewish question," by foes and even friends, that entailed the disappearance of the Jews as such—abandonment of the Jewish religion or its essential elements, of the Jewish language, Yiddish, of Jewish culture, Jewish uniqueness and separatism. The histories of Jewish emancipation and of European anti-Semitism are replete with proffered "solutions to the Jewish question."

The classic illustration is the "solution" offered by Constantine Pobyedonostsev, chief adviser to Czar Alexander III, in 1881: one-third of the Jews were to emigrate, one-third to convert, and one-third to die of hunger.

To this concept that the National Socialists adopted they added one new element, embodied in the word "final." "Final" means definitive, completed, perfected, ultimate. "Final" reverberates with apocalyptic promise, bespeaking the Last Judgment, the End of Days, the last destruction before salvation, Armageddon. "The Final Solution of the Jewish Question" in the National Socialist conception was not just another anti-Semitic undertaking, but a metahistorical program devised with an eschatological perspective. It was part of a salvational ideology that envisaged the attainment of Heaven by bringing Hell on earth. "The Devil is loose," Friedrich Reck-Malleczewen noted in his diary on October 30, 1942. The most important event of our time, André Malraux said, was *le retour de Satan,* citing the German system of terror.

To attain its heavenly Hell on earth the German dictatorship launched a war that engulfed the whole world. Over 35 million people were killed, more than half of them civilians. On the battlefields one out of every 22 Russians was killed, one out of every 25 Germans, one out of every 150 Italians and Englishmen, and one out of every 200 Frenchmen. The human cost of 2,191 days of war surpassed the losses of any previous war in the world. That war brought death to nearly 6 million Jews, to two out of every three European Jews. Though one-third of them managed to survive, though the Jewish people and Judaism have outlived the Third Reich, the Germans nevertheless succeeded in irrecoverably destroying the life and culture of East European Jewry.

The Final Solution transcended the bounds of modern historical experience. Never before in modern history had one people made the killing of another the fulfillment of an ideology, in whose pursuit means were identical with ends. History has, to be sure, recorded terrible massacres and destruction that one people perpetrated against one another, but all—however cruel and unjustifiable—were intended to achieve instrumental ends, being means to ends, not ends in themselves.

The German state, deciding that the Jews should not live, arrogated to itself the judgment as to whether a whole people had the right to existence, a judgment that no man and no state have the right to make. "Anyone who on the basis of such a judgment," said Karl Jaspers, "plans the organized slaughter of a people and participates in it, does something that is fundamentally different from all crimes that have existed in the past."

To carry out this judgment, designated as the Final Solution, the German dictatorship involved and engaged the entire bureaucratic and functional apparatus of the German state and the National Socialist movement and employed the best available technological means. The Final Solution destroyed the East European Jews. In doing so, it subverted fundamental moral principles and every system of law that had governed, however imperfectly, human society for millennia.

What the Nazis did is fact, history. The evidence exists in eyewitness accounts that fill thousands of pages of testimony. The next two readings are descriptions of actual executions by Germans who were there, on the scene. What these accounts reveal about the behavior of all concerned—the victims, the murderers, and the passive observers themselves—is that a kind of mass hypnosis seems to have had nearly everyone in its grip.

The first account is from the testimony of a Nazi official assigned to work on the gas chambers at a camp in southern Poland. The excerpt is from the book *The Harvest of Hate* by Leon Poliakov.

The "Final Solution" in Action

TESTIMONY

This account is taken from the testimony of one of the Nazi execution-ers responsible for putting into effect Hitler's "final solution" to Germany's race problem. The site of the extermination camp he de-scribes was Belzec, a village in southern Poland. Before this man could be brought to trial, he committed suicide.

Globocnik said: . . . "Your . . . duty will be to improve the work-ings of our gas chambers, which operate on the exhaust from a Diesel engine. We need a more toxic and faster working gas. . . . The Führer has ordered more speed. Dr. Herbert Lindner, who was here yesterday, asked me, 'Wouldn't it be more prudent to burn the bodies instead of burying them? Another generation might take a differ-ent view of these things.' I answered: 'Gentlemen, if there is ever a gen-eration after us so cowardly, so soft, that it would not understand our work as good and necessary, then, gentlemen, National Socialism will have been for nothing. On the contrary, we should bury bronze tablets saying that it was we, we who had the courage to carry out this gigantic task!' " . . .

The next day we left for Belzec. . . .

The following morning, a little before seven there was an announcement: "The first train will arrive in 10 minutes!" A few minutes later a train arrived from Lemberg: 45 cars with more than six thousand people. Two hundred Ukrainians assigned to this work flung open the doors and drove the Jews out of the cars with leather whips. A loud speaker gave instructions: "Strip, even artificial limbs and glasses. Hand all money and valuables in at the 'valuables window.' "

Then the march began. Barbed wire on both sides, in the rear two dozen Ukrainians with rifles. They drew near. Wirth and I found ourselves in front of the death chambers. Stark naked men, women, children, and cripples passed by. A tall SS man in the corner called to the unfortunates in a loud minister's voice: "Nothing is going to hurt you! Just breathe deep and it will strengthen your lungs. It's a way to prevent contagious diseases. It's a good disinfectant!" They asked him what was going to happen and he answered: "The men will have to work, build houses and streets. The women won't have to do that, they will be busy with the housework and the kitchen."

This was the last hope for some of these poor people, enough to make them march toward the death chambers without resistance. The majority knew everything; the smell betrayed it! They climbed a little wooden stairs and entered the death chambers, most of them silently, pushed by those behind them . . . SS men pushed the men into the chambers. "Fill it up," Wirth ordered; 700–800 people in 93 square meters. The doors closed . . . SS Unterscharführer Heckenholt tried to start the motor. It wouldn't start! . . . My stopwatch clocked it all: 50 minutes, 70 minutes, and the Diesel still would not start! . . . The men were waiting in the gas chambers. You could hear them weeping "as though in a synagogue." . . . The Diesel started up after two hours and 49 minutes, by my stopwatch. Twenty-five minutes passed. You could see through the window that many were already dead, for an electric light illuminated the interior of the room. All were dead after 32 minutes! Jewish workers on the other side opened the wooden doors. They had been promised their lives in return for doing this horrible work, plus a small percentage of the money and valuables collected. The men were still standing, like columns of stone, with no room to fall or lean. Even in death you could tell the families, all holding hands. It was difficult to separate them while emptying the rooms for the next batch. The bodies were tossed out. . . . Two dozen workers were busy checking mouths which they opened with iron hooks. "Gold to the left, no gold to the right" . . . Dentists knocked out gold teeth, bridges, and crowns, with hammers. Captain Wirth stood in the middle of them. He was in his element. . . .

From September 1941 until January 1944, Herman Friedrich Graebe was manager and engineer-in-charge of a branch office in Sdolbumow, the Ukraine, of a German building firm. In this capacity it was his job to visit the building sites of the firm. Under contract to an Army Construction Office, the firm had orders to erect grain storage buildings on the former airport of Dubno, the Ukraine.

The Graebe Memorandum

TESTIMONY

On October 5, 1942, when I visited the building office at Dubno, my foreman Hubert Moennikes . . . told me that in the vicinity of the site, Jews from Dubno had been shot in three large pits, each about 30 meters long and three meters deep. About 1,500 persons had been killed daily. All of the 5,000 Jews who had still been living in Dubno before the pogrom were to be liquidated. As the shootings had taken place in his presence he was still much upset.

Thereupon I drove to the site, accompanied by Moennikes and saw near it great mounds of earth, about 30 meters long and two meters high. Several trucks stood in front of the mounds. Armed Ukrainian militia drove the people off the trucks under the supervision of an SS man. The militiamen acted as guards on the trucks and drove them to and from the pit. All these people had the regulation yellow patches on the front and back of their clothes, and thus could be recognized as Jews.

Moennikes and I went directly to the pits. Nobody bothered us. Now I heard rifle shots in quick succession, from behind one of the earth mounds. The people who had got off the trucks—men, women and children of all ages—had to undress upon the order of an SS man who carried a riding or dog whip. They had to put down their clothes in fixed places, sorted according to shoes, top clothing, and underclothing. I saw a heap of shoes of about 800 to 1,000 pairs, great piles of underlinen and clothing. Without screaming or weeping these people undressed, stood around in family groups, kissed each other, said farewells and waited for a sign from another SS man, who stood near the pit, also with a whip in his hand.

During the 15 minutes that I stood near the pit, I heard no complaint or plea for mercy. I watched a family of about eight persons, a man and woman, both about 50, with their children of about one, eight and 10, and two grownup daughters of about 20 to 24. An old woman with snow-white hair was holding the one-year-old child in her arms and singing to it and tickling it. The child was cooing with delight. The couple were looking on with tears in their eyes. The father was holding the hand of a boy of about 10 years old and speaking to him softly; the boy was fighting his tears. The father pointed toward the sky, stroked his head, and seemed to explain something to him. At that moment the SS man at the pit shouted something to his comrade. The latter counted off about 20 persons and instructed them to go behind the earth mound. Among them was the family which I have mentioned.

I well remember a girl, slim and with black hair, who, as she passed close to me, pointed to herself and said, "Twenty-three!" I walked around the mound, and found myself confronted by a tremendous grave. People were closely wedged together and lying on top of each other so that only their heads were visible. Nearly all had blood running over their shoulders from their heads. Some of the people shot were still moving. Some were lifting their arms and turning their heads to show that they were still alive. The pit was already two-thirds full. I estimated that it already contained about a thousand people.

I looked for the man who did the shooting. He was an SS man, who sat at the edge of the narrow end of the pit, his feet dangling into the pit. He had a tommy gun on his knees and he was smoking a cigarette. The people, completely naked, went down some steps which were cut in the clay wall of the pit and clambered over the heads of the people lying there, to the place where the SS man directed them. They lay down in front of the dead or injured people; some caressed those who were still alive and spoke to them in a low voice. Then I heard a series of shots.

I looked into the pit and saw that the bodies were twitching or the heads lying already motionless on top of the bodies that lay before them. Blood was running from their necks. I was surprised that I was not ordered away, but I saw that there were two or three postmen in uniform nearby. The next batch was approaching already. They went down into the pit, lined themselves up against the previous victims and were shot.

When I walked back, around the mound, I noticed another truckload of people which had just arrived. This time it included sick and infirm people. An old, very thin woman with terribly thin legs was undressed by others who were already naked, while two people held her up. The woman appeared to be paralyzed. The naked people carried the woman around the mound. I left with Moennikes and drove in my car back to Dubno.

On the morning of the next day when I again visited the site, I saw about 30 naked people lying near the pit—about 30 to 50 meters away from it. Some of them were still alive; they looked straight in front of them with a fixed stare and seemed to notice neither the chilliness of the morning nor the workers of my firm who stood around. A girl of about 20 spoke to me and asked me to give her clothes and help her escape. At that moment we heard a fast car approach and I noticed that it was an SS detail. I moved away to my site. Ten minutes later we heard shots from the vicinity of the pit. The Jews still alive had been ordered to throw the corpses into the pit—then they themselves had to lie down in this to be shot in the neck.

The effects of prolonged brutal treatment and physical deprivation are vividly drawn in this excerpt from *Man's Search for Meaning* by Viktor E. Frankl. Dr. Frankl, a Viennese psychiatrist, was imprisoned in Auschwitz for three years. He survived, but his wife and most other members of his family perished in the camps.

Dehumanization and Starvation

VIKTOR E. FRANKL

Suddenly there was a stir among my fellow travelers, who had been standing about with pale, frightened faces, helplessly debating. Again we heard the hoarsely shouted commands. We were driven with blows into the immediate anteroom of the bath. There we assembled around an SS man who waited until we had all arrived. Then he said, "I will give you two minutes, and I shall time you by my watch. In these two minutes you will get fully undressed and drop everything on the floor where you are standing. You will take nothing with you except your shoes, your belt or suspenders, and possibly a truss. I am starting to count—now!"

With unthinkable haste, people tore off their clothes. As the time grew shorter, they became increasingly nervous and pulled clumsily at their underwear, belts and shoelaces. Then we heard the first sounds of whipping; leather straps beating down on naked bodies.

Next we were herded into another room to be shaved: not only our heads were shorn, but not a hair was left on our entire bodies. Then on to the showers, where we lined up again. We hardly recognized each other; but with great relief some people noted that real water dripped from the sprays.

While we were waiting for the shower, our nakedness was brought home to us: we really had nothing now except our bare bodies—even minus hair; all we possessed, literally, was our naked existence.

During the latter part of our imprisonment, the daily ration consisted of very watery soup given out once daily, and the usual small bread ration. In addition to that, there was the so-called "extra allowance," consisting of three-fourths of an ounce of margarine, or of a slice of poor quality sausage, or of a little piece of cheese, or a bit of synthetic honey, or a spoonful of watery jam, varying daily. In calories, this diet was absolutely inadequate, especially taking into consideration our heavy manual work and our constant exposure to the cold in inadequate clothing. The sick who were "under special care"—that is, those who were allowed to lie in the huts instead of leaving the camp for work—were even worse off.

When the last layers of subcutaneous fat had vanished, and we looked like skeletons disguised with skin and rags, we could watch our bodies beginning to devour themselves. The organism digested its own protein, and the muscles disappeared. Then the body had no powers of resistance left. One after another the members of the little community in our hut died. Each of us could calculate with fair accuracy whose turn would be next, and when his own would come.

Prison camps of various kinds, well over a hundred by the end of the war, played a key role in the Nazi program to dispose of all people regarded as "undesirable." They were all located in Germany or Poland. In the middle 1930s, the camps were used mainly for internment or "protective custody" of Communists, other political dissidents, homosexuals, the handicapped, and other "non-Aryans." After 1939, many camps were used largely for forced labor: Jews and other prisoners, living at starvation levels, worked in German farms and war factories. Thousands of prisoners died of starvation, exposure, and illness. Countless others were shot to death. Following adoption of the Final Solution plan in 1941, six special camps (those marked with an "X" on the map) were equipped with gas chambers and crematoria. Auschwitz, the largest of these extermination camps, accounted for some two million deaths in a two-and-a-half-year period. A worker at Auschwitz said that "the stench given off by the pyres contaminated the surrounding countryside. At night the red sky over Auschwitz could be seen for miles." Yet people living in the vicinity of these camps claimed to know nothing of their existence.

Flow Chart for "Operation Reinhard," Auschwitz, and Majdanek

This flow chart depicts the operation of two concentration camps, Auschwitz and Majdanek, both in Poland and among those sites expressly designed to be killing factories. The diagram is reminiscent of those used by business and industry to streamline operations and maximize efficiency. In this case, the "production" was centered around the processing and preparation of human beings for death. And the byproducts of the dead, that is, their hair, teeth, eyeglasses, and even their skin were then processed for future use in the manufacture of such household goods as carpets, lampshades, and soap.

Did the men and women who ran these factories consider their "raw materials" as human? Try to imagine, as you follow the chart, what must have been in the minds and hearts of these planners and executioners, most of whom were well-trained technicians but most likely not aware that their skills would someday be applied to operating factories of death.

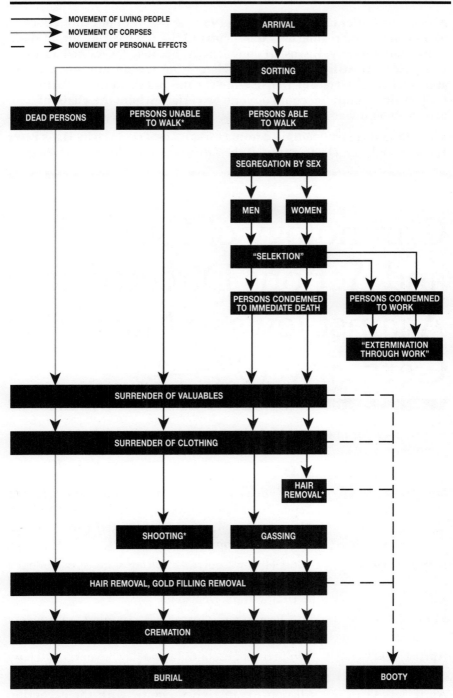

* UNIQUE TO SOBIBOR, TREBLINKA, AND BELZEC

As soon as Hitler came to power in 1933, he began to put into effect various laws and regulations that deprived the Jews, bit by bit, of their rights and property. It was all done legally, because Hitler had absolute power. To stifle protest or criticism, from Jew or non-Jew, armed storm troopers were free to use violence and imprisonment. Particularly at the beginning, could anyone be certain where the chain of actions would lead?

This chronology was compiled from two sources: *Friedrich* by Hans Peter Richter, and *The Destruction of the European Jews* by Raul Hilberg.

Chronology of Laws and Actions Directed Against Jews in Nazi Germany 1933–45

Dates given for laws, decrees, and regulations are dates of public announcement.

1933

January 30, 1933	Adolf Hitler becomes Chancellor of the German Reich. He is the Supreme Leader of the NSDAP (National Socialist German Workers Party) and the SA (storm troopers).
March 5, 1933	Adolf Hitler receives a strong vote of confidence from the German people in the *Reichstagswahl* (parliamentary elections).
March 24, 1933	The Reichstag (German Parliament) empowers Hitler to enact laws on its behalf.
April 1, 1933	Adolf Hitler proclaims a one-day boycott of all Jewish shops.
April 7, 1933	All non-Aryan civil servants, with the exception of soldiers are forcibly retired.

April 21, 1933	Kosher butchering is forbidden by law.
April 25, 1933	Fewer non-Aryan children are admitted to German schools and universities.
June 16, 1933	There are 500,000 Jews living in the Third Reich.
July 14, 1933	German nationality can be revoked—for those considered "undesirable" by the government.

1934

August 2, 1934	Paul von Hindenburg, second president of the German Republic dies.
August 3, 1934	Adolf Hitler declares himself both President *and* Chancellor of the Third Reich.

1935

March 16, 1935	Compulsory military service is reinstituted in Germany in open defiance of the Versailles Treaty.
September 6, 1935	Jewish newspapers can no longer be sold in the street.
September 15, 1935	Nuremberg Laws deprive Jews of German citizenship and reduce them to the status of "subjects"; forbid marriage or any sexual relations between Jews and Aryans; forbid Jews to employ Aryan servants under the age of 35.

1936

March 7, 1936	Jews no longer have the right to participate in parliamentary elections.
	The German army reoccupies the Rhineland.
August 1, 1936	The Olympic Games are opened in Berlin. Signs reading "Jews Not Welcome" are temporarily removed from most public places by order of the Führer—to present a favorable and misleading picture to foreign tourists.

1937

July 2, 1937	More Jewish students are removed from German schools and universities.
November 16, 1937	Jews can obtain passports for travel abroad only in special cases.

1938

March 11, 1938	German troops march into Austria.
July 6, 1938	Jews may no longer follow certain occupations such as broker, matchmaker, tourist guide, real estate agent.
July 23, 1938	As of January 1, 1939, all Jews must carry identification cards.
July 25, 1938	As of September 30, 1938, Jewish doctors can be regarded only as "medical attendants."
July 27, 1938	All "Jewish" street names are replaced.
August 17, 1938	As of January 1, 1939, all Jews must have only Jewish first names. If a Jew has a German first name, "Israel" or "Sarah" must be added to it.
October 5, 1938	Jewish passports are marked with a "J."
October 28, 1938	About 15,000 "stateless" Jews are "resettled" in Poland.
November 7, 1938	Herschel Grynszpan, a Jew, attempts to assassinate the German Attaché, vom Rath, in Paris.
November 9, 1938	Vom Rath dies. Goebbels, recognizing the propaganda value, issues instructions that "spontaneous demonstrations" against Jews are to be "organized and executed" throughout Germany—in retaliation!
	The pogrom begins.
November 10, 1938	Pogrom continues.
November 11, 1938	Jews may no longer own or bear arms.
	Destruction of synagogues in entire Reich.
November 12, 1938	Following the Nazi-organized pogrom, "reparations" of one billion Reichsmarks are imposed on the German Jews, and they must further repair all damages at their own cost.
	Jews may no longer head businesses.
	Jews may no longer attend plays, movies, concerts, and exhibitions.
November 15, 1938	All Jewish children remaining in German schools are removed to Jewish schools.

November 23, 1938	All Jewish businesses are closed down.
November 28, 1938	Jews may no longer be in certain districts at certain times.
December 3, 1938	Local authorities allowed to bar Jews from the streets on Nazi holidays.
	Jews must hand in their driver's licenses and car registrations.
	Jews must sell their businesses, real estate, and hand over their securities and jewelry.
December 8, 1938	Jews may no longer attend universities.

1939

March 15, 1939	German troops march on Czechoslovakia.
April 30, 1939	Rent protection for Jews is reduced.
May 17, 1939	About 215,000 Jews still live in the Third Reich.
September 1, 1939	Germany declares war on Poland.
September 3, 1939	WORLD WAR II BEGINS.
	(Curfew for Jews is instituted: 9 P.M. in summer, 8 P.M. in winter.)
September 21, 1939	Pogroms against Jews in Poland.
September 23, 1939	All Jews must hand in their radios to the police.
October 12, 1939	Austrian Jews are beginning to be deported to Poland.
October 19, 1939	"Reparations" for German Jews are increased to 1.25 billion Reichsmarks and are now payable by November 15, 1939.
November 23, 1939	Polish Jews must now wear yellow stars of David.

1940

February 6, 1940	Unlike the rest of the German people, Jews do not receive clothing coupons.
February 12, 1940	German Jews begin to be taken into "protective custody," that is, deported to concentration camps.
July 29, 1940	Jews may no longer have telephones.
December 24, 1940	Jews to pay special income tax.

1941

June 12, 1941	Jews must designate themselves as "unbelievers."
July 31, 1941	Beginning of the "final solution."
September 1, 1941	Every Jew in Germany must also wear a star of David.
	Jews may no longer leave their places of residence without permission of the police.
October 14, 1941	The large-scale deportation of Jews to concentration camps begins.
October 24, 1941	Friendly relations with Jews prohibited.
December 26, 1941	Jews may no longer use public telephones.

1942

January 1, 1942	Approximately 130,000 Jews now live in the Third Reich.
January 10, 1942	Jews must hand in any woolen and fur clothing still in their possession.
February 17, 1942	Jews may no longer subscribe to newspapers or magazines.
April 17, 1942	A Jewish apartment must be identified as such with a star of David beside the name plate.
April 24, 1942	Jews are forbidden the use of public transportation.
May 15, 1942	Jews are forbidden to keep dogs, cats, birds, etc.
May 29, 1942	Jews are no longer permitted to visit barber shops.
June 9, 1942	Jews must hand over all "spare" clothing.
June 11, 1942	Jews no longer receive smoking coupons.
June 19, 1942	Jews must hand over all electrical and optical equipment, as well as typewriters and bicycles.
June 20, 1942	All Jewish schools are closed.
July 17, 1942	Blind or deaf Jews may no longer wear armbands identifying their condition in traffic.
September 9, 1942	Jews not permitted to institute civil suits.
September 18, 1942	Jews can no longer buy meat, eggs, or milk.
October 4, 1942	All Jews still in concentrations camps in Germany are to be transferred to (extermination camp) Auschwitz.

1943

April 21, 1943	Jews found guilty of crimes are to be conveyed to extermination camps in Auschwitz or Lublin after serving their sentences.
July 1, 1943	Property of Jew to be confiscated after his death.

1944

September 1, 1944	Approximately 15,000 Jews now live in the Third Reich.

1945

January 17, 1945	Soviet troops liberate Warsaw.
February 4–11, 1945	Yalta Conference in the Crimea.
March 5, 1945	American troops reach the Rhine River.
April 11, 1945	American troops liberate Buchenwald death camp.
April 15, 1945	British troops liberate Bergen-Belsen death camp.
April 25, 1945	American and Soviet troops meet at the Elbe River.
April 30, 1945	Hitler commits suicide.
May 7, 1945	Germany surrenders unconditionally. End of the war in Europe.
August 15, 1945	Japan surrenders unconditionally. End of World War II.
November 22, 1945	Nuremberg War Crimes Tribunal commences.

The Nuremberg Trials conclude on October 1, 1946, which happens to be the Day of Atonement (Yom Kippur), with a judgment in which 12 defendants are sentenced to death, three to life imprisonment, four to various prison terms, and three acquitted.

Between the years 1933 and 1938, some 280,000 Jews, or a little more than half the Jewish population of Germany, managed to leave the country, despite enormous difficulties in gaining permission to enter other countries. An American woman here recounts her own family's experiences when Hitler came to power. This family was one of the fortunate ones.

Catherine Hanf Noren is the author of *The Camera of My Family*, a 100-year album of a German-Jewish family.

We Escaped From Hitler's Germany

CATHERINE NOREN

I am a member of a very large German family. On my mother's side alone, there are 30 first cousins. (Her mother was one of eight children. Her father was one of 10 children.) My mother's family name is Wallach. The Wallachs in Germany have been traced back to the 14th century.

There are almost no members of my family left in Germany now. They were all driven out by Adolf Hitler and the Nazis before the Second World War. Those that did not escape from Germany died in concentration camps. The camps were part of Hitler's "final solution"—his plan to murder all the Jews in every land he took over.

Many members of my family did escape. They now live all over the world—in the U.S., Africa, South America, Israel, France, and other nations. For nine years after we left Germany, my parents, my sister, and I lived in Australia.

HITLER MOVES TO OUR TOWN

In 1918, Adolf Hitler was 29 years old. That year, he moved to Munich. Munich was the home of my grandparents and their four children, my mother, my aunt, and my two uncles.

Germany was in a real mess. World War I had just ended. The German government was all in confusion. The people were hungry. The land had been ruined by the war. Even if you had money, there was little to buy. It was the perfect time for a strong man to step in and take over the country.

When Hitler started the Nazi Party in Munich in 1920, it had only seven members. If they were alive today, they would be thought of as the worst kind of vagrants. Hitler himself was a school dropout. He spent his teenage years wandering the streets of Vienna, Austria. He slept in flophouses and did odd jobs from time to time. Once in a while, he sold a painting or two. (He thought of himself as an artist, but he had little talent.)

Hitler, with his tiny Nazi Party, had dreams of power. He decided to try to take over the government of the state of Bavaria in 1923. His idea was to capture 50 important businessmen and city leaders as hostages. He would threaten them with death if the government was not handed over to him.

My grandfather was to be taken as one of Hitler's hostages. My Uncle Rolf remembers that day very clearly. This is how he described it to me recently:

"It was November 8, 1923. First the Nazis took one of the Bavarian leaders at gunpoint. They made him agree to work with them in the new government they were setting up. At nine in the morning, they sent out groups of men to capture 50 hostages. They knew exactly who they wanted, and they sent three or four men to capture each one.

"I was in school that day—high school. They let the whole school out at 11. We were told not to go into the city, but to go straight home. When I got home, a Nazi storm trooper opened the door for me. He had our maid and the mailman in the kitchen. Anybody who came to the door was put into the kitchen so they couldn't warn my father. They had sent people to our apartment and to our father's business.

"After about 15 minutes, the phone rang. The storm trooper took the call. After a while, he told us we could go. They had captured my father at his business. Mother and a friend of hers were walking down the street. They saw people being taken away. They didn't know what was going on. They didn't know that Father had been captured until they got home.

"After the Nazis had all their hostages, they marched into the city. There they were met by the police. The police gave orders to halt, but the Nazis didn't halt. Shots rang out and 19 people—13 Nazis, three policemen, three bystanders—were killed. Hitler threw himself to the ground when the shooting started, and then escaped. The police then went and released the hostages. Father was home again by five o'clock. What would have happened if Hitler was successful? I don't know. But as it was, the whole thing lasted only half a day."

Two days later, Hitler was found hiding in a cupboard at a friend's home. He was arrested and sent to prison. While Hitler was in jail, he wrote a book called *Mein Kampf—My Struggle*. In it, he wrote of his plans to take over the whole German government. He wrote about his hatred of democracy and his hatred of the Jews. He wrote that the Aryans (white, non-Jewish people) were the master race of the world. He wrote that he would lead Germany and make it the greatest empire in the world.

Hitler was released from jail in 1924. The Nazi Party grew larger and stronger. In 1933, less than 10 years after his first takeover attempt, Hitler was named chancellor of all of Germany. As soon as he became chancellor, he started to introduce some of the things he had written about in *Mein Kampf*.

ONLY HALF A BLOCK AWAY

My grandparents and their four children lived only half a block from Hitler in Munich. My Aunt Annelise, one of the four children, told me: "I used to walk home from school. Every once in a while, Hitler and a group of his people passed by in their car. They would honk the horn. Everybody on the sidewalk would stop and salute. Of course, I wouldn't do that. It was quite uncomfortable living so close to him."

Annelise was in junior high during the early 1930s. I asked her whether the hatred of the Jews could be found in the schools as well as in the government. She said that it depended which school you went to and who the teachers were.

"I had only one bad experience," she told me. "It was with my gym teacher who was a real Nazi. I had a friend in that class who was also Jewish. She and I were the best in the gym class. And the teacher was always yelling at the rest of the class, saying, 'You lazy girls! How can you let those two Jew girls be better than you!' "

One of the Nazi laws was that Aryans were not allowed to date Jews. When Annelise was in high school, she had a non-Jewish boyfriend. Wherever they went, they were always scared that they would be caught.

One day, as they were crossing a big square near my grandparents' house, a policemen called her over. "Oh, this is it!" she thought. "Now they've got me."

She walked up to the policeman. "You shouldn't walk on the grass," he said. "You should walk around the square."

A STORM TROOPER KNOCKS

Hitler and the Nazis began to make things very rough for the Jews. My grandfather was also in trouble because of the work he did.

My grandfather was born in a small town in the north of Germany. As he and his brother grew up, they saw that many of the peasant folk traditions of Germany were dying out. As women left their homes and went to work in city factories, they threw away their peasant costumes. Every area of Germany had its own native dress. But this clothing was being forgotten as people wanted to look more modern and sophisticated.

My grandfather and his brother decided to try to save these dying traditions. They opened a folk museum in Munich. The museum had 42 rooms. Each room was designed and decorated with traditional native furniture and folk art of a different area.

Because of this museum, my grandfather was a target for the Nazis. Hitler also wanted to bring back the clothes, furniture, and art of the past. He hated the idea of Jewish people owning this museum. So, the Nazis wanted to get their hands on my grandfather's business. They wanted his collections, his furniture, and his art.

One day in 1937, a Nazi storm trooper knocked on my grandparents' door. My grandmother answered and asked him what he wanted. "I am here to take away all of your cultural objects," he said. "Is there anything that you would like to keep? Is there anything that you particularly love that you would like to save?"

"Yes," my grandmother said. "I want to save these antique pewter containers. I'm saving them for my son Rolf."

The pewter containers were the first things that the Nazi took. He had just wanted to find out what my grandmother treasured the most, so he could be sure and take them. He took a great many other things as well.

My grandparents were among hundreds of thousands of people robbed by the Nazis. During the war, the Nazis stole art treasures from all over Europe. They stashed their loot away in caves and other hiding places. They planned to unpack and enjoy them once they had won the war.

After the war, U.S. and Allied soldiers found these hidden treasures. One of the crates they found was labeled with my grandfather's name—Wallach. They wrote to my grandfather and asked him to list everything the Nazis had taken from him. He sent them the list. All of the stolen property was in the crate, including the pewter containers. My Uncle Rolf got the containers, after all. They are now in his living room in Connecticut. I photographed them a few weeks ago.

CRYSTAL NIGHT

In the late 1930s, the Nazis started to take over all businesses owned by Jewish people. In 1937, an antique dealer named Witte came to see my grandfather. He offered to buy my grandfather's business. But my grandfather said no. The next year, Mr. Witte came again. This time his offer was not an offer at all—it was a threat. Things had changed.

This is what happened: On November 8, a German embassy worker was shot and killed by a Jewish man who hated the Nazis. As revenge, during the next three days, the windows of Jewish stores and synagogues all over Germany were smashed. Thousands of Jewish men and boys were rounded up and thrown into concentration camps. Hitler now had the excuse he needed to start what he called "the final solution"—the murder of all Jews in Germany.

This incident is known as Crystal Night. That's because of the sound of broken glass that was heard throughout the whole country that night. My father was one of the men thrown into jail that night. But he was lucky. He had some money on him. He used it to bribe the guard to let him out of his cell.

A few days after Crystal Night, Witte came back to see my grandfather. He told my grandfather that if he didn't sell, he would be thrown into a concentration camp. So my grandfather sold his business to Witte for a very small sum of money. He put the money in the bank. A few days later, the money was taken by the government. They said it was a tax for being able to leave the country.

GETTING OUT

Many Jewish people had already left Germany. My Uncle Rolf had left, but the rest of my family was still there.

On Crystal Night, right after he was let out of his cell, my father went to the police. He told them that our family had visas to leave the country. He asked if we could go. (I was a tiny baby at that time, and my sister Brigitte was four.) We were given 10 days to get out of the country. Ten days later, we were on a boat to Australia.

My grandparents did not have visas to leave. You had to have a visa from the country to which you wanted to go. They were not easy to get. Hundreds of thousands of people were trying to get out of Europe at that time.

But my Uncle Rolf had come to the U.S. in 1928. He was already a U.S. citizen. And he was able to get visas for my grandparents.

Rolf had come to the U.S. because he was angry. He was 18 in 1928. He had been invited to sit in on my grandfather's business meetings. At his very first meeting, he opened his mouth to say something, and my grandfather told him to be quiet.

Rolf sat silently until the meeting was over. Then he walked out of the room and went to the American Consulate. He applied for a visa to the U.S. A few weeks later, he sailed to America.

Rolf's falling-out with my grandfather turned out to be very lucky. By 1938, he was a U.S. citizen. And he had enough money to be able to sponsor my grandparents, my Uncle Fritz, my Aunt Annelise, and six other members of the family.

Some of my grandparents' sisters and brothers could not get out, though. They couldn't find a sponsor (Rolf was allowed to sponsor only 10 people). And they didn't have enough money to buy their way out. These people—some of my great aunts and uncles and some of their children—died in Hitler's concentration camps. This has been one of the great sadnesses of my family's life.

A NEW LIFE

If my grandfather had been paid fairly for his business, he would have been able to get the rest of the family out of Germany. But he was not. He and my grandmother arrived in New York in 1939 with 10 marks— $2.50 in U.S. money—in their pockets.

My grandparents were starting a new life in New York. And my parents, my sister, and I were doing the same thing in Australia. For the last year of our stay in Australia, I went to public school in Melbourne. The school was very old-fashioned. If you did something wrong or didn't do your homework, the teachers would hit you. The girls were hit with a ruler, the boys got the strap. We used to get rapped over the knuckles for every spelling word we got wrong. To this day, I'm a very good speller!

I loved to draw, and I was always drawing in class. The teacher warned me several times to stop. But one day, a friend asked me to draw a picture of her. Needless to say, I was caught.

The teacher called me up to the front of the class. I was hit 10 times across the back of my knees with a ruler. Then I was sent to stand in the corner with a dunce cap on my head. I stood there, facing the wall, and the tears dripped down my face.

All over the world, the war was going on and people were suffering and dying. But this day in class in Melbourne is one of my most vivid memories from that time.

I will also never forget how happy we all were the day the war ended. We were all set to sail for the U.S. It was very exciting. The journey from Melbourne to New York took six weeks. When we finally arrived, there at the pier waiting for us were my grandparents, my Uncle Rolf, my Uncle Fritz, and my Aunt Annelise.

We were a family again.

In 1943, Elie Wiesel was a boy living in the village of Sighet, in a mountainous region of Hungary. The war had barely touched this remote settlement; the radio was their sole source of information about the fighting. In his novel, *Night*, Wiesel relates how one day all non-Hungarians were expelled from the town. His beloved teacher, Moché the Beadle, was among those rounded up and deported.

"Listen to Me!"

ELIE WIESEL

Several days passed. Several weeks. Several months. Life had returned to normal. A wind of calmness and reassurance blew through our houses. The traders were doing good business, the students lived buried in their books, and the children played in the streets.

One day, as I was just going into the synagogue, I saw, sitting on a bench near the door, Moché the Beadle.

He told his story and that of his companions. The train full of deportees had crossed the Hungarian frontier and on Polish territory had been taken in charge by the Gestapo. There it had stopped. The Jews had to get out and climb into lorries. The lorries drove toward a forest. The Jews were made to get out. They were made to dig huge graves. And when they had finished their work, the Gestapo began theirs. Without passion, without haste, they slaughtered their prisoners. Each one had to go up to the hole and present his neck. Babies were thrown into the air and the machine gunners used them as targets. This was in the forest of Galicia, near Kolomaye. How had Moché the Beadle escaped? Miraculously. He was wounded in the leg and taken for dead. . . .

Through long days and nights, he went from one Jewish house to another, telling the story of Malka, the young girl who had taken three days to die, and of Tobias, the tailor, who had begged to be killed before his sons. . . .

Moché had changed. There was no longer any joy in his eyes. He no longer sang. He no longer talked to me of God or the cabbala, but only of what he had seen. People refused not only to believe his stories, but even to listen to them.

"He's just trying to make us pity him. What an imagination he has!" they said. Or even: "Poor fellow. He's gone mad."

And as for Moché, he wept.

"Jews, listen to me. It's all I ask of you. I don't want money or pity. Only listen to me," he would cry between prayers at dusk and the evening prayers.

I did not believe him myself. I would often sit with him in the evening after the service, listening to his stories and trying my hardest to understand his grief. I felt only pity for him.

"They take me for a madman," he would whisper, and tears, like drops of wax, flowed from his eyes.

Once, I asked him this question:

"Why are you so anxious that people should believe what you say? In your place, I shouldn't care whether they believed me or not. . . ."

He closed his eyes, as though to escape time.

"You don't understand," he said in despair. "You can't understand. I have been saved miraculously. I managed to get back here. Where did I get the strength from? I wanted to come back to Sighet to tell you the story of my death. So that you could prepare yourselves while there was still time. To live? I don't attach any importance to my life any more. I'm alone. No, I wanted to come back, and to warn you. And see how it is, no one will listen to me. . . ."

That was toward the end of 1942. Afterward life returned to normal. The London radio, which we listened to every evening, gave us heartening news: the daily bombardment of Germany; Stalingrad; preparation for the second front. And we, the Jews of Sighet, were waiting for better days, which would not be long in coming now.

I continued to devote myself to my studies. By day, the Talmud, at night, the cabbala. My father was occupied with his business and the doings of the community. My grandfather had come to celebrate the New Year with us, so that he could attend the services of the famous rabbi of Borsche. My mother began to think that it was high time to find a suitable young man for Hilda.

Thus the year 1943 passed by.

Spring 1944. Good news from the Russian front. No doubt could remain now of Germany's defeat. It was only a question of time—of months or weeks perhaps.

The trees were in blossom. This was a year like any other, with its springtime, its betrothals, its weddings and births.

People said: "The Russian army's making gigantic strides forward . . . Hitler won't be able to do us any harm, even if he wants to."

Yes, we even doubted that he wanted to exterminate us.

Was he going to wipe out a whole people? Could he exterminate a population scattered throughout so many countries? So many millions! What methods could he use? And in the middle of the twentieth century!

Besides, people were interested in everything—in strategy, in diplomacy, in politics, in Zionism—but not in their own fate.

Even Moché the Beadle was silent. He was weary of speaking. He wandered in the synagogue or in the streets, with his eyes down, his back bent, avoiding people's eyes.

At that time, it was still possible to obtain emigration permits for Palestine. I had asked my father to sell out, liquidate his business, and leave.

"I'm too old, my son," he replied. "I'm too old to start a new life. I'm too old to start from scratch again in a country so far away. . . ."

The Budapest radio announced that the Fascist party had come into power. Horthy had been forced to ask one of the leaders of the Nyilas party to form a new government.

Still this was not enough to worry us. Of course we had heard about the Fascists, but they were still just an abstraction to us. This was only a change in the administration.

The following day, there was more disturbing news: with government permission, German troops had entered Hungarian territory.

Here and there, anxiety was aroused. One of our friends, Berkovitz, who had just returned from the capital, told us:

"The Jews in Budapest are living in an atmosphere of fear and terror. There are anti-Semitic incidents every day, in the streets, in the trains. The Fascists are attacking Jewish shops and synagogues. The situation is getting very serious."

This news spread like wildfire through Sighet. Soon it was on everyone's lips. But not for long. Optimism soon revived.

"The Germans won't get as far as this. They'll stay in Budapest. There are strategic and political reasons. . . ."

Before three days had passed, German army cars had appeared in our streets.

Anguish. German soldiers—with their steel helmets and their emblem, the death's head.

However, our first impressions of the Germans were most reassuring. The officers were billeted in private houses, even in the homes of Jews. Their attitude toward their hosts was distant, but polite. They never demanded the impossible, made no unpleasant comments, and even smiled occasionally at the mistress of the house. One German officer lived in the house opposite ours. He had a room with the Kahn family. They said he was a charming man—calm, likable, polite, and sympathetic. Three days after he moved in he brought Madame Kahn a box of chocolates. The optimists rejoiced.

"Well, there you are, you see! What did we tell you? You wouldn't believe us. There they are *your* Germans! What do you think of them? Where is their famous cruelty?"

The Germans were already in the town, the Fascists were already in power, the verdict had already been pronounced, yet the Jews of Sighet continued to smile.

The largest single group of people killed by the Nazis were six million European Jews. This number represented one-third of the entire Jewish population of the world at that time. In addition to the six million Jews, the Nazis destroyed an equal number of non-Jews, of various nationalities, during the course of the war.

The chart below is reprinted from *Keeping Posted*.

Estimates of Jewish Losses 1939–45

COUNTRY	ESTIMATED PRE-FINAL SOLUTION POPULATION	ESTIMATED JEWISH POPULATION ANNIHILATED	
		Number	Percent
Poland	3,300,000	3,000,000	90
Baltic countries	253,000	228,000	90
Germany/Austria	240,000	210,000	90
Bohemia/Moravia	90,000	80,000	89
Slovakia	90,000	75,000	83
Greece	70,000	54,000	77
The Netherlands	140,000	105,000	75
Hungary	650,000	450,000	70
SSR White Russia	375,000	245,000	65
SSR Ukraine*	1,500,000	900,000	60
Belgium	65,000	40,000	60
Yugoslavia	43,000	26,000	60
Rumania	600,000	300,000	50
Norway	1,800	900	50
France	350,000	90,000	26
Bulgaria	64,000	14,000	22
Italy	40,000	8,000	20
Luxembourg	5,000	1,000	20
Russia (RSFSR)*	975,000	107,000	11
Denmark	8,000	—	—
Finland	2,000	—	—
Total	**8,861,800**	**5,933,900**	**67**

*The Germans did not occupy all the territory of this republic.

The Nature of Man

We now turn our attention away from the history of the Holocaust, and begin to seek answers to the questions that arise, inescapably, from the foregoing readings. How could this immense tragedy have happened? How could civilized, religious, educated Germans commit acts of such unspeakable bestiality? Were the Nazis unique—or could anyone, we ourselves perhaps, be capable of the same?

The five readings that follow present different perspectives on the nature of man by well-known philosophers and scientists from the 15th century to the present. Each makes reasonably clear its author's beliefs about whether people are fundamentally good or bad.

Niccolo Machiavelli (1469–1527) was an Italian statesman and writer who is regarded as the first political philosopher of modern times. Among his writings are: *The Prince* and *The Art of War.* He believed in government by the people but felt that the Italians of his day were unfit to rule themselves. He was concerned with the use and abuse of power.

The Prince

NICCOLO MACHIAVELLI

This, then, gives rise to the question "whether it be better to be beloved than feared, or to be feared than beloved." It will naturally be answered that it would be desirable to be both the one and the other; but as it is difficult to be both at the same time, it is much more safe to be feared than to be loved when you have to choose between the two. For it may be said of men in general that they are ungrateful and fickle, dissemblers, avoiders of danger, and greedy of gain. So long as you shower benefits upon them, they are all yours; they offer you their blood, their substance, their lives, and their children, provided the necessity for it is far off; but when it is near at hand, then they revolt. And the prince who relies upon their words, without having otherwise provided for his security, is ruined; for friendships that are won by rewards, and not by greatness and nobility of soul, although deserved, yet are not real, and cannot be depended upon in time of adversity.

Besides, men have less hesitation in offending one who makes himself beloved than one who makes himself feared; for love holds by a bond of obligation which, as mankind is bad, is broken on every occasion whenever it is for the interest of the obliged party to break it. But fear holds by the apprehension of punishment, which never leaves men.

It being necessary then for a prince to know well how to employ the nature of the beasts, he should be able to assume both that of the fox and that of the lion; for while the latter cannot escape the traps laid for him, the former cannot defend himself against the wolves. A prince should be a fox, to know the traps and snares; and a lion, to be able to frighten the wolves; for those who simply hold to the nature of the lion do not understand their business.

A sagacious prince then cannot and should not fulfill his pledges when their observance is contrary to his interest, and when the causes that induced him to pledge his faith no longer exist. If men were all good, then indeed this precept would be bad; but as men are naturally bad, and will not observe their faith toward you, you must, in the same way, not observe yours to them; and no prince ever yet lacked legitimate reasons with which to color his want of good faith. Innumerable modern examples could be given of this; and it could easily be shown how many treaties of peace, and how many engagements, have been made null and void by the faithlessness of princes; and he who has best known how to play the fox has ever been the most successful.

Thomas Hobbes (1588–1679) was an English political philosopher whose critical and negative perceptions of man were often unpopular. In his famous work *Leviathan* he was so critical of his government that this work was condemned by the British House of Commons in 1666, and censored. He also wrote *The Elements of Law, Natural and Politic.*

Man Is Evil and Warlike

THOMAS HOBBES

From this equality of ability arises equality of hope in the attaining of our ends. And therefore if any two men desire the same thing, which nevertheless they cannot both enjoy, they become enemies, and in the way to their end, which is principally their own conservation, and sometimes their delectation only, endeavor to destroy or subdue one another. And from hence it comes to pass that where an invader has no more to fear than another man's single power, if one plant, sow, build, or possess a convenient seat, others may probably be expected to come prepared with forces united to dispossess and deprive him, not only of the fruit of his labor, but also of his life or liberty. And the invader again is in the like danger of another.

And from this diffidence of one another there is no way for any man to secure himself so reasonable as anticipation—that is, by force or wiles to master the persons of all men he can, so long till he see no other power great enough to endanger him; and this is no more than his own conservation requires, and is generally allowed. Also, because there be some that take pleasure in contemplating their own power in the acts of conquest, which they pursue farther than their security requires, if others that otherwise would be glad to be at ease within modest bounds should not by invasion increase their power, they would not be able, long time, by standing only on their defense, to subsist. And by consequence, such argumentation of dominion over men being necessary to a man's conservation, it ought to be allowed him.

Again, men have no pleasure, but on the contrary a great deal of grief, in keeping company where there is no power able to overawe them all. For every man looks that his companion should value him at the same rate he sets upon himself; and upon all signs of contempt or undervaluing naturally endeavors, as far as he dares (which among them that have no common power to keep them in quiet is far enough to make them destroy each other), to extort a greater value from his contemners by damage and from others by the example.

So that in the nature of man we find three principal causes of quarrel: first, competition; secondly, diffidence; thirdly, glory.

The first makes men invade for gain, the second for safety, and the third for reputation. The first use violence to make themselves masters of other men's persons, wives, children, and cattle; the second, to defend them; the third, for trifles, as a word, a smile, a different opinion, and any other sign of undervalue, either direct in their persons or by reflection in their kindred, their friends, their nation, their profession, or their name.

Hereby it is manifest that, during the time men live without a common power to keep them all in awe, they are in that condition which is called war, and such a war as is of every man against every man.

John Locke (1632–1704) was an English philosopher who believed in civil liberty, religious tolerance, the power of reason, and the value of experience. His works include: *Essay Concerning Human Understanding; Two Treatises on Civil Government* and *Essays on the Law of Nature.*

Man Is Rational

JOHN LOCKE

The state of nature has a law of nature to govern it, which obliges every one, and reason, which is that law, teaches all mankind, who will but consult it, that being all equal and independent, no one ought to harm another in his life, health, liberty or possessions.

Men living together according to reason without a common superior on earth, with authority to judge between them, are properly in the state of nature.

Man Is Innately Aggressive

ROBERT ARDREY

In the past 30 years a revolution has been taking place in the natural sciences. It is a revolution in our understanding of animal behavior, and of our link to the animal world. In sum, therefore, the revolution concerns that most absorbing of human entertainments, man's understanding of man. Yet not even science, as a whole, is aware of the philosophical reappraisal which must proceed from its specialists' doings.

Assumptions concerning the nature of man, today unquestioned by education, by psychiatry, by politics, by art, or even by science itself, are being eroded by the tiny streams set loose from obscure scientific springs. And few of us, scientists or laymen, know.

That the contemporary revolution in the natural sciences has proceeded thus far in almost total silence must not be regarded as too great a wonder. Other and noisier revolutions have overwhelmed our unquiet time. As compared with the fortunes of the totalitarian state, of nuclear physics, of antibiotics or the long-playing record, the fortunes of the palaeontologist may seem remote from our daily life. And the work of the revolution has been accomplished by such extreme specialists that it has been recorded only in such inaccessible pages as those of the *American Journal of Anthropology* or the *Biological Symposia*. Such heralds gain few hearers in the modern marketplace.

Still more important than the obscurity or specialization of the revolution has been its suddenness. When in 1930 I emerged from a respectable American university as a respectably well-educated young man, no hint had reached me that private property was other than a human institution evolved by the human brain. If I and my young contemporaries throughout the following years wasted much of our fire on social propositions involving the abolition of private ownership, then we did so in perfect faith that such a course would free mankind of many a frustration. No part of the curriculum of our psychology, sociology, or anthropology departments had presented us with the information that territoriality—the drive to gain, maintain, and defend the exclusive right to a piece of property—is an animal instinct approximately as ancient and powerful as sex.

The role of territory in general animal behavior lies today beyond scientific controversy; then it was unknown. We of the Class of 1930 had to emerge into a world of tumultuous evaluation without benefit of this most salient observation. Similarly, we could not know, as we bemused ourselves with the attractions of the classless state, that hierarchy is an institution among all social animals and the drive to dominate one's fellows an instinct three or four hundred million years old. . . .

We, the approximate Class of 1930, today furnish trusted and vital leadership to world thought, world politics, world society and to whatever may exist of world hope. But we do not know that the human drive to acquire possession is the simple expression of an animal instinct many hundreds of times older than the human race itself. We do not know that the roots of nationalism are dug firmly into the social territoriality of almost every species in our related primate family. We do not know that the status-seekers are responding to animal instincts equally characteristic of baboons, jackdaws, rock cod, and men. Responsible though we may be for the fate of summit conferences, disarmament agreements, juvenile delinquents and new African states, we do not know that the first man was an armed killer, or that evolutionary survival from his mutant instant depended upon the use, the development, and the contest of weapons.

We do not know these things, since they are conclusions to be drawn from the contemporary revolution in the natural sciences. We should know, however, that acquired characteristics cannot be inherited, and that within a species every member is born in the essential image of the first of its kind. No child of ours, born in the middle 20th century, can differ at birth in significant measure from the earliest of *Homo sapiens.* No instinct, whether physiological or cultural, that constituted a part of the original human bundle can ever in the history of the species be permanently suppressed or abandoned.

B. F. Skinner (1904–1990) was a professor of psychology at Harvard and a researcher who won several awards for his contributions in the area of human behavior. He is the author of *Walden Two, Science and Human Behavior, Verbal Behavior,* and *Beyond Freedom and Dignity.*

Man Is a Product of His Environment

B. F. SKINNER

Q: Suppose that people who read your book, and take its message seriously, realize that they are controlled. Will they lose their feelings of freedom?

Skinner: I don't know. I certainly believe that my own behavior is entirely a function of three things—my genetic endowment, my past history as an individual (my family, my religious experience, my government, my schooling, the physical environment in which I have lived, and so on), and the present situation. I am absolutely sure that that is all there is in the determination of what I'm going to do at this very moment. But I don't feel discouraged or unhappy about it at all.

Q: You don't feel like a puppet?

Skinner: I don't feel the least bit like a puppet. Operant conditioning is not pulling strings to make a person dance. It is arranging a world in which a person does things that affect that world, which in turn affects him.

Q: When you come into the classroom and make children want to come to school, would you be controlling their behavior?

Skinner: That's right. A girl who teaches in a Kentucky sixth grade told me of a good example. Her students were not doing their homework; they would not sit down and study; they ran around the room and talked a great deal. She decided to try some operant conditioning. Every Friday

76

afternoon she held a lottery, and the child whose name was drawn out of a jar got a prize. Every Monday morning she would put the week's prize on the wall. One week it was a Halloween costume, another a transistor radio. Whenever a pupil brought in his homework, he could write his name on a ticket and drop it in the jar. Whenever he finished an assignment in class, he could do the same. The system changed the girl's life as a teacher completely. Her pupils did all their homework; they sat quietly and listened to her, because something she said might be just the thing they could use to get another ticket with their name in the jar.

Q: A number of your attackers charge that behavior modification is being used in China today, and they are horrified at the very thought that we might apply it that way in this country.

Skinner: Yes, it is said that the word "fascism" surfaces frequently in discussions of my book. The critics are usually good enough to say that I am not fascist, but that I give aid and comfort to fascism. But every fascist state I've heard of uses aversive control. Its citizens behave as the government dictates because they are afraid not to do so. I've spent my life looking for alternatives to punitive control and arguing in their favor. I oppose standard totalitarian techniques and I want people to feel free and enjoy what they're doing. But it may be true that I give aid and comfort to those who want to make any way of life more effective. What worries me is that in some curious way the struggle for freedom and dignity has made it impossible for us to take advantage of what we're discovering about human behavior. If that proves to be the case, there has been a lethal mutation in our culture that may bring it to an end. A fascist way of life might then gain an advantage, but I'm doing what I can to prevent it.

PART II

VICTIMS AND VICTIMIZERS

"And we must not forget that the hate and terror directed against the Jews were greater than against any other group (except, possibly, the Gypsies, who were also marked for genocide). The truth is that quantitative terms like greater, more, additional are irrelevant here; the hostility toward the Jews was different in kind and not in degree. It was abysmal, 'irrational,' groundless in the plain meaning of the word as having no sense, as being beyond sense, not as mere non-sense, for its consequences were dire and dismal, but as non-sense, as having no warrant and no ascertainable 'frame-of-reference.'"

JACOB GLATSTEIN
Anthology of Holocaust Literature

The Jews of Europe

O ne of the striking and puzzling features of the Holocaust is the singling out of the Jews as the main target of hostility. What made them so vulnerable to attack? The next two readings provide some answers to this question. In the first selection, historian Uriel Tal explains that while Jews won equal rights in Germany at the end of the last century, they could never fully integrate into German society. One reason was that the German people believed "German" and "Christian" to be synonymous; a Jew, therefore, could never be considered a "true" German. The selection is from the book Christians and Jews of the Second Reich, 1870–1914.

Christians and Jews in Germany 1870–1914

URIEL TAL

We began our study with a discussion of the double aspiration of the Jews in the Second Reich to integrate into the dominant society and at the same time retain their Jewish identity. This endeavor on the part of German Jews was part of a larger struggle of men to achieve freedom in modern society without forfeiting individuality. This struggle gave rise to a number of concomitant questions: how was this Jewish aspiration regarded by the German Christian society of that day; how did it affect the relations between Jews and Christians on the one hand and the Jew's conception of his role in the modern world on the other; what can we learn from this historical attempt of German Jewry to become an integral part of German society and still retain its Jewish identity, that is, achieve equality without surrendering its freedom; and, finally, what conclusions can we draw from this study concerning the interrelationship between modern Jewish history and the history of mankind or between Judaism and Christianity in the modern era and between the Second and the Third Reich.

Friedrich Paulsen explained in his *System of Ethics*, if one is proud of the fact that he is a Jew and not a German, he has no right to complain that the German people do not accept him as a judge or as a teacher of German children: "To remain a complete Jew and a complete German is impossible." When we recall that Paulsen was a prominent liberal and humanist and an outspoken opponent of anti-Semitism, his words take on added significance as a reflection of Germany's determination not to acknowledge the claims of German Jewry to civil equality while retaining its Jewish identity.

In the Second Reich, as well, religion, albeit in its secular form, occupied an important place. Contrary to the expectations of the Jews and the liberals, religion had not become a private matter limited to the sphere of the individual, nor was it cleansed of its irrational elements in accordance with the principles of the Enlightenment. On the contrary, as a result of the process of religious secularization, Christian and especially Protestant patterns of thought and behavior were impressed on the cultural, social, and political life of the Second Reich. The national movement, the political parties, the social and economic organizations, and some of the principal scientific societies—all of which were an integral part of Germany's rapid process of industrialization—defined themselves explicitly as Christian in essence. The Conservative Protestants and an increasing number of Catholics wished to establish the Second Reich on the principle of a Christian state as it had been formulated in conservative ideology throughout the greater part of the 19th century.

German nationality, contrary to the expectations of the Jews, was not acquired by conscious selection or subjective feelings of the citizen but (according to the romantic school of thought) by belonging to a historic community whose roots went back to ancient tribal and pagan sources or in the more recent past to Lutheran Christian culture or (according to the anthropological school of thought) by belonging to a community whose roots went back to groups of different ethnic, cultural, and even religious origins which, through intermarriage and mutual biological assimilation, had come to constitute the present German nation.

Neither of these two views was favorable to German Jewry in its determined effort to integrate into the dominant society while retaining its identity, the first view because of its exclusive conception of German nationality according to which it was not the conscious acknowledgement of belonging to the nation that determined German nationality, but the objective fact of belonging to an organic ethnic group whose roots went back to the pagan Germanic tribes and to the Germans who became Christians and lived under a feudal system in principalities, duchies, and other traditional social forms in the historical German states; the second view because of its inclusive conception of German nationality according to which the determining factor in nationality was not membership in the nation, but the religious and biological fusion of the various ethnic components of the nation that left no room for particularistic internal groups. This second view was the one accepted by a considerable number of intellectual liberals, including many of the leading opponents of modern anti-Semitism, such as Rudolf von Gneist and Theodor Mommsen, who urged the complete assimilation of Jews into German society and argued that the addition of the Jewish heritage and the personal talents of the Jews would constitute an immense contribution, culturally and biologically, to the growing German nation and would at the same time strengthen the cause of the liberal intellectuals in their struggle against the irrational and pagan elements in German romanticism, potent ingredients in the anti-Semitic ideology of this movement.

Against the background of these conflicting ideologies and political parties within the Second Reich the Jews endeavored to achieve their double goal of complete integration into the social environment without surrendering their identity. Political and racial anti-Semitism during this period failed to exert any appreciable public influence, and whatever effectiveness it had was limited to short intervals and restricted regions. The members of this movement were for the most part recruited from the unstable lower middle class, that is, from the marginal groups within the liberal professions, workers who had migrated from rural to urban areas where they led a precarious existence, and city dwellers of the proletarian working class. Only a small number among these social classes turned to the racial-political anti-Semitic movement, most of them being represented in Christian or socialist political and economic organizations.

As a result of this policy of social reform, in which anti-Jewish propaganda had little part, the anti-Semites in 1893, the year when they first became politically significant, received 263,861 votes in the Reichstag election, or 3.4 percent of the total vote of 7,673,973. In 1898 they reached the high point of their political success when they received 284,250 votes, or 3.7 percent of the total vote of 7,752,693. It is therefore obvious that even in the heyday of their political activity the anti-Semites could not muster enough votes to endorse their policy among their own rank-and-file supporters, who voted instead for the Conservative Protestant and Catholic parties on the one hand and the socialists on the other. This trend continued until the election of 1907 which was preceded by an intensive anti-Semitic campaign in which the anti-Semites sought to strengthen their image as the party of the "small man." The resolutions adopted at the conventions held in Erfurt (1895), in Halle (1896), in Cassel (1898), and in Berlin (1903) reiterated this policy of social reform in favor of the lower middle class, the impoverished farmer, the underprivileged economically and socially, and the embittered and frustrated elements in the large urban centers.

After World War I and during the Weimar Republic the mythological, non-Christian, and anti-Christian character of anti-Semitism grew stronger, thus removing one of the main obstacles to the spread of racial anti-Semitism during the Second Reich and its acceptance by growing masses of the population.

Christian anti-Semitism was not as virulent as racial anti-Semitism. It stigmatized Jewish perfidy, but it permitted the Jew to exist (though not flourish) as the living witness to the truth of Christianity. The Jew must remain to act out his preordained ignominious role as villain in the drama of salvation, at the end of which he would be crowned with glory. But he was always free to abrogate his covenant with Jehovah and accept the benevolent efforts of the church to redeem him. According to racial theory, however, baptism could not penetrate the tainted Jewish seed; the deep stain could only be removed by destroying the source of infection and its bearer, the physical Jew. The Jew must not only be excoriated but eliminated. Christianity, insofar as it had succumbed to Jewish influences, was also culpable since Christian *agape*, love and pity, like Jewish *logos*, law and reason, had alienated man from nature and weakened him in his struggle for existence. However, the Jewish stain could be removed from the Christian cloth, so to speak, by fumigation without destroying the cloth itself.

In the days of the Second Reich these racial theories were not accepted by the great majority of the German people. After World War I and in the period of the Weimar Republic, however, they became increasingly popular, thus removing one of the chief obstacles in the path of the Nazi rise to power. The source of this ideology at the beginning of the Second Reich could be found in the teachings of Naudh-Nordmann, E. Dühring, C. Radenhausen, A. Wahrmund, F. Lange, and P. Förster, which were then transmitted by Theodor Fritsch, H.S. Chamberlain, and members of the anti-intellectualist Rembrandt movement to the leading Nazi ideologists, to such figures as Alfred Rosenberg on the one hand and to the heads of the Deutsche-Christen movement on the other.

Animated by this aggressive mood that sought to deprive the Enlightenment of all its gains, the racial anti-Semites put their faith in the efficacy of blood, the mysterious fountain from which all life flows and which determines the hierarchy of powers that shape history. Apriorism, whether in theology or in critical rational thought, was done away with and blood became the epistemological model whose uniqueness, contrary to the logical structure of rational thought, was that it comprehends both form and content, symbol and reality, the concept and that which is expressed by the concept. Blood became an absolute value because it erases the distinction between the symbol and that which is symbolized, between theory and practice; it attempts to create a total identity between the particular and the general, between the individual sphere and the public domain, between society and the state. It was felt that man's life must be rescued from the anemic ideals of Christianity and restored to its root and anchor in blood. Truth is not within reach of the pretentious intellect nor the reward of holiness, for both remove man from the deep sources of life. When the world demands a courageous response and genuine sacrifice, religion covers its face, unable to sustain the bravest efforts, and the untrustworthy intellect betrays man with its spurious profundities. It is then that blood clamors to be heard, and truth, long repressed, emerges through its cleansing filter. Evangelical Christianity with its morality of humility, selflessness, and excessive self-contempt, reinforced in modern times by democratic social altruism, thus constituted for the racial anti-Semites one of the principal obstructions to man's natural development. By placing spirit above matter, conscience above intuition, and speculative thought above the experience of blood, Christianity poisoned the noblest instincts in man and removed him from his natural roots. The cross is the Christian symbol for the crucifixion of the body and its vital instincts.

It would seem then that racial anti-Semitism and traditional Christianity, although starting from opposite poles and with no discernible principle of reconciliation, were moved by a common impulse directed either to the conversion or to the extermination of Jews. Thus we find that the racial anti-Semites appropriated basic Christian ideas even while reprobating them and adapted them for their own purposes. The Christian doctrine of the Incarnation, for example, whereby God became man, was interpreted by them not in the evangelical sense (John 1:14) nor in the Pauline sense (Colossians 2:9), nor even in Nietzsche's purely mythological sense, but in an empirically political and racial sense. According to the Christian *Heilsgeschichte* the Jews were the theological means to correct evil by acknowledging the principle (John 1:14): "And the Word became flesh and dwelt among us, full of grace and truth; we have beheld his glory, glory as of the only Son from the Father"; and hence the Jews as the children of promise were eligible for salvation "in order that God's purpose of election might continue" (Romans 9:11). According to the racial anti-Semites, however, the Jews could not be the means to correct evil for they themselves were the essence of evil, evil incarnate, and must therefore be exterminated not only in the spirit (as Christianity) but also in the flesh.

When we recall the traditional Christian bias against the Jews— the collective guilt of deicide and the eternal curse of the world that rests upon them because of their unpardonable defection (Matthew 27:22, 25; I Thessalonians 2:15), the official policy of the Church as formulated in such councils as the Synod of Elvira in 306, Clermont in 535, Toledo in 681, or the Third Lateran in 1179 and the Fourth Lateran in 1215, the preachments of Martin Luther against the Jews and his incitement to violence, especially after 1543 when he was disillusioned in his efforts to convert them, the blood libels and accusations in which the persecuted wandering Jew became the symbol of sin and abomination— when we recall all this, we see how Christianity created the patterns of prejudice, hatred, and calumny that could readily provide a rationale to justify organized violence. The anti-Christian elements of racial anti-Semitism were interpreted in such a way that the traditional theological concepts of Christianity were not completely rejected; only their meanings were changed by using a pseudoscientific jargon and applied to the historical realities of that day, without the salutary correction of Christian discipline and belief.

Racial anti-Semitism and the subsequent Nazi movement were not the result of mass hysteria or the work of single propagandists. The racial anti-Semites, despite their antagonism toward traditional Christianity, learned much from it, and succeeded in producing a well-prepared, systematic ideology with a logic of its own that reached its culmination in the Third Reich.

Enormous economic upheavals in Europe, both before and after World War I, served both to weaken the position of Jews and to intensify anti-Jewish feeling, as explained in this reading, excerpted from *The Jewish Catastrophe in Europe*, edited by Judah Pilch. The conditions of Jewish life—social, political, and cultural—in various countries, are also described here. Jews were urbanites and villagers, professors and peasants, religious and secularists, rich and poor.

Jewish Life in Europe Between the Two World Wars (1919–1939)

JUDAH PILCH

GENERAL ECONOMIC AND POLITICAL CONDITIONS

1. Regions of Jewish Settlement

The economic and political conditions of Jewish life in continental Europe varied with each geographic division between East and West. This was the result mainly of the relocation of populations within new boundaries after World War I, when the old empires broke up and many new and old states gained national independence. For purposes of our discussion, Europe will be divided into four geographic regions, as follows:

a. *Eastern Europe:* Poland, Hungary, Rumania; the Baltic countries—Lithuania, Latvia, Estonia, Finland; and the Balkan countries—Yugoslavia, Bulgaria, Greece, and Albania;

b. *The Soviet Union:* White Russia, the Ukraine, the Crimea, and northwest Russia;

c. *Central Europe:* Germany, Austria, and Czechoslovakia;

d. *Western Europe:* France, Luxemburg, Belgium, Holland, Denmark, Norway, and Italy; and those countries that remained neutral in the Second World War—Switzerland, Sweden, Spain, and Portugal.

2. Distribution of the Jewish Population by Region

Both in their actual numbers and in their proportion to the general population, European Jews were more concentrated in the east than in the west. The largest portion lived in Poland—over 3,000,000; the next largest in southwestern Soviet Russia—over 2,000,000; and the third largest in Rumania—some 900,000. Germany's 525,000 constituted almost half of the Jews in central Europe. France's 240,000 and Holland's 157,000 Jews were the bulk of western European Jewry.

In proportion to the general population, too, the five million Jews in eastern Europe (outside Soviet Russia) constituted almost 5 percent of the total population; in the Soviet Union, the Jews made up 1.7 percent of the total, but in the southwestern region, which had two-thirds of Russian Jewry, the figure was over 5 percent of the total. In central Europe the Jewish proportion was 1.8 percent, while in the West it was only 0.5 percent. In the whole of continental Europe the Jews, numbering 9 million, constituted only 2 percent of the total population.

3. The Jews as Major City-Dwellers: Regional Contrasts

The Jews of Europe in modern times have been living mostly in cities rather than in rural areas. By the end of the 19th century they were already concentrated in the metropolitan complexes. In many of the large urban centers, Jews stood out as an ethnic and economic group, and many businesses, professions and other occupations were identified as specifically Jewish. This was not so noticeable in western Europe, where the Jewish population was small in proportion to the general population, even though three-fifths of Western European Jewry lived in 10 of the largest cities. Similarly, in central Europe, while almost all of Austrian Jewry lived in Vienna and half of the German Jews resided in Berlin, their proportion to the general urban population in those two cities and other large centers in western Europe was only 4.5 percent.

The picture changed quite radically in the large cities of eastern Europe and of the Soviet Union. In Polish cities like Warsaw, Lodz, Lublin, Cracow, and Wilno, the Jews comprised between one-fourth and one-half of the inhabitants. . . .

4. Effects of Increased Urbanization

a. Changes in Economic Positions before World War I

As a result of their rapid urbanization in the second half of the 19th century, the Jews gained new and stronger positions than heretofore in the general national economies. In central Europe, notably in Germany, they grew from small shopkeepers and village peddlers (60 percent of their occupations) to big merchants and department store owners, and occupied important places in the professions, the sciences, literature and the press. They also developed a white-collar working class, which had not been in existence before. The small-town peddler and trades-man had practically disappeared by the beginning of the 20th century.

In eastern Europe, too, the Jews moved into the middle and higher urban positions of commerce and industry, having occupied in some areas complete fields of production. Thus, in Lodz in 1900, the textile factories were predominantly in Jewish hands (68 percent)—Jews being owners, technicians, and workers. In tsarist Russia they developed ex-port, import, sugar, and petroleum industries and took an active part in railroad building and some in banking. A large Jewish working class occupied posts in small shops and factories, particularly those produc-ing leather, brush, and confectionary products. In the western countries, where they constituted a small proportion of the general population, the Jews had long occupied positions in commerce and industry and were not dominant in any particular branch of the national economy as a whole, or in any urban occupations as such.

b. Changes in Economic Positions after World War I

In the West, economic positions acquired by Jews during the preceding century remained practically unchanged, but in central and eastern Europe they underwent drastic changes. Two main factors con-tributed to this change: 1) the rising urbanization of the non-Jewish popu-lation, and 2) the breakup of the Russian and Austrian empires after the First World War.

In tsarist Russia, as well as in the Austrian Empire, most Jews lived in compact masses among the minority peoples, who were themselves subjugated by the dominant Great-Russians under the tsars, and by the Germans and Hungarians in Austria-Hungary under the Habsburg em-perors. Toward the end of the 19th and the beginning of the 20th centu-ries, these minority peoples, who were predominantly peasants, began to leave the rural areas in search of new economic opportunities in the cities. There they encountered the already established Jewish merchants, shopowners and professionals with whom they began to compete in their striving to enter the middle and upper economic strata. As long as the central governments were in the hands of the dominant nationalities, the minorities were handled without bias, none receiving any substantial government help. Competition remained on purely economic grounds, and the Jews, more experienced and skilled in the higher occupations, were able to meet the rivalry. Dissatisfaction grew among the subjected minority groups, especially among the Poles, the Ukrainians, and the White Russians, and there was considerable agitation against their Jewish neighbors. In tsarist Russia these anti-Jewish sentiments were often utilized by the central government to instigate pogroms (massacres) and thus to divert the attention of the disgruntled peasants, workers, and small merchants from its own failure to meet their needs.

The situation took a drastic turn for the worse at the end of the First World War, when the western provinces of Russia and the entire Austro-Hungarian Empire were carved up into a number of independent states. Former minority peoples, among whom the Jews had dwelt as just another minority, now became the majorities, dominant nationalities with governmental powers in their own hands. The urban occupations to which they had aspired were now opened to them with the full support of their own governments, and the Jews in those occupations received one heavy blow after another through legislative and financial restrictions or through other economic devices contrived by the ruling authorities.

In Germany and Austria the process of dislodging the Jews from the social and economic status they had achieved had gained great momentum even before the Nazis came to power, and assumed a legal form after they gained control of the government. In Poland, where the Jews had played a determining role in the national economy, the government proceeded more cautiously, for fear of crippling the economic welfare of the country. Similar caution, but to an even greater extent, was exercised in the Baltic states and in Rumania. In Czechoslovakia under President Thomas G. Masaryk (1918–1935), on the other hand, liberal political conditions allowed the Jews to hold on to their own. In the Soviet Union, after the Communist Revolution of October 1917, the economic positions held by the Jews under the tsars were swept away in the general transformation of the social and economic order. Finding their place in the economy of the new system involved more hardship and took longer than it did for the non-Jewish population. In other respects their condition resembled that of other Soviet citizens who became employees of the state-owned enterprises. A considerable proportion of the Jewish population of the small towns resettled in the large cities of the Soviet Union, and a large number of them engaged in professional and managerial occupations.

5. Emigration

As indicated above, the economic conditions of the Jews in central and eastern Europe began to weaken at the beginning of the 20th century and reached a critical stage during the interwar period. In their struggle to retain what they could of their hard-earned status or to make readjustments within the controlled national economies, they encountered ever-increasing obstacles. The general depression, shrinking markets and inflation in the 1920s and '30s, added greatly to their difficulties. While American Jewry, through its Joint Distribution Committee and the ORT, rendered substantial aid in direct relief and in financing and retraining Jews for new occupations, the odds against them in central and eastern Europe were too great. Their impoverishment went steadily from bad to worse. Unable to readjust within their native lands, they chose emigration.

Beginning with the turn of the century, when overseas lands were still wide open to newcomers of every nationality, large numbers of Jews from tsarist Russia (including Poland), Rumania, Austria-Hungary and the Baltic areas, streamed across the Atlantic to the United States; some fled to Canada and Latin America. The period of 1899–1914 witnessed the greatest movement of Jews from eastern Europe to the United States, totalling 1,448,226; of these 70 percent came from Russia and Rumania. Emigration to Palestine was promoted by the emerging Zionist movement which, in the words of the Basel Program adopted by the first Congress of the World Zionist Organization at Basel, Switzerland, in 1897, aimed "at establishing for the Jewish people a publicly and legally secured home in Palestine."

After 1922, American immigration laws sharply reduced Jewish immigration. Average annual immigration of Jews to the United States dropped to 50,000 in 1922–24 and to 11,280 in 1925–30. Many Jews of the former Russian provinces found a haven of refuge in Central and Western Europe, in Germany, Austria, France, Belgium, the Netherlands, and Great Britain, where they succeeded in establishing themselves as permanent residents or citizens. The Zionist Organization directed thousands of Jews to Palestine, especially after the Conference of the Great Powers at San Remo, Italy, in 1920, when Great Britain accepted the Mandate over Palestine with specific responsibility for "the establishment in Palestine of a national home for the Jewish people."

With the advent of Nazi rule in Germany in 1933, the enactment of the notorious Nuremberg Laws in 1935, the annexation of Austria to Germany and the dismemberment of Czechoslovakia in 1938, Jewish emigration from Central Europe turned into flight. Unfortunately, the Western Hemisphere was not open widely enough to welcome the surviving masses of refugees. From 1933 to 1937, the United States admitted only some 30,000 Jewish refugees; Argentina, 63,500; Brazil 64,000; and South Africa, 26,000. The Jewish community of Palestine absorbed 175,000 additional Jews during that period. Up to 1939 a special rescue operation, known as "Youth Aliyah," succeed in bringing to Palestine 4,635 Jewish children from Germany. Numerous other Jewish refugee families were stranded in various countries of the continent, where they later suffered the same fate as the rest of European Jewry. . . .

6. Political Emancipation

a. Individual and Collective Emancipation

"Emancipation" as used in modern Jewish history entails the right of individuals to participate in every phase of political, social-cultural, and economic activities, subject only to the laws governing all citizens of a given country without distinction of race, color, or creed. Specifically, emancipation means the right to reside anywhere in the country, to own property, engage in any legal occupation of one's choice, to receive education in any school or academic institution in the land, to participate in governmental functions that may be available to all citizens, to serve in the armed forces in any rank attainable on merit, and to share in the duties and responsibilities of citizenship on an equal basis with the rest of the inhabitants.

In more than 1500 years of their sojourn on European soil, Jews did not enjoy these rights as individuals until they were formally emancipated, first in western, then in central, and last in eastern Europe. This does not mean that prior to emancipation they were unable to engage in social-cultural, economic, or even political activities. On the contrary, official emancipation came in most instances as the last stage of their cultural and economic integration in the general community: in France and Holland in the 18th century, in other countries of western and central Europe in the 19th century, and in eastern Europe after World War I. But before they were granted political freedom, they did not have a legal right, like all the other inhabitants, to their occupations and positions. The Jews were engaged in varied, yet limited, occupations, holding many positions only by sanction of the ruling authorities, who could grant, withhold or rescind their "privileges" at will or, as one autocrat expressed it, according to "the interests of the exchequer."

Political emancipation, however, also entails not only individual rights but also the rights of groups who constitute an ethnic or national minority within a given country. Such are the rights of minority groups to cultivate their religious and cultural traditions, to educate their children in the ancestral heritage, and generally to form communal associations for the purpose of perpetuating their distinctive form of life and modes of expression. Before emancipation, the Jewish people, as a minority group, enjoyed this "internal freedom" within their own communities in every country in which they lived. Even at times when the ruling authorities sharply curtailed the free exercise of Jewish religious and cultural practices, the restrictions were applied only to the group as a whole rather than to the individual. The individual Jew identified himself with his people as a body, in suffering as well as in joy. The inner structure of the Jewish community remained intact and continued to be governed by its own traditional laws and customs, and it was thus able to overcome external pressures by reorganizing its inner forces or by emigrating to more friendly lands.

This dual position of Jews as individuals within their own community and as an organized body in relation to the general population and to the government changed radically with the advent of their political emancipation. Basically, the political freedom that was granted to them in various stages of the emancipation period meant their right as individuals to participate in the life of the country like all other individual citizens. The freedom of the individual Jew as a citizen also brought with it his freedom to reduce his association with the Jewish community, to sever his relations with it entirely, and to blend or assimilate completely with the non-Jewish majority. This did not take place with the same intensity or speed in every country, for Jewish leaders, concerned with the preservation of Jewish traditional life, resisted political emancipation in the early stage, as for example in the 18th century in Alsace and Holland. What they really sought was not to prevent political freedom as such, but to obtain certain provisions in the acts of emancipation that would guarantee the survival of the Jews as a distinct community and to save them from disappearing within the general population. These guarantees, when achieved, assumed various forms, legal and voluntary, in different countries, depending on the political structure and the general cultural climate of each state. . . .

COMMUNAL, CULTURAL AND RELIGIOUS LIFE

While the internal Jewish "life style" differed from country to country, we present here a picture of the communal, cultural and religious life of Polish Jewry which in 1939 numbered 3,300,000. Eighty-five percent were to be killed by the Nazis.

After World War I, the newly established state of Poland had a Jewish community of 3,300,000, the largest and one of the oldest in Europe and the second largest in the world. It was organized as a *Kehillah*, with power of owning all communal property, such as synagogues, cemeteries, hospitals, and the like, and with authority to direct the communal educational, religious and social-cultural institutions. Each town, large and small, was represented on a Council which was elected by direct, secret ballot. The various organizations found their interests reflected in the bodies of the *Kehillah* through proportional representation.

The greatest achievement of Polish Jewry was its educational system, maintained at its own cost. Here, too, the different Jewish ideological and religious groups maintained their respective types of schools, each with its own language of instruction in Hebrew, Yiddish, Polish, or bilingual. Of the total Jewish school population of 425,000 some 340,000 attended these schools. The Jewish community also maintained teacher training schools, rabbinical academies, trade schools and other cultural institutions, such as museums, libraries, and adult study courses.

In higher general education, Jewish students were greatly handicapped because of discrimination against them by the universities. As many as half of the Jewish trainees in various professions had to seek admission to foreign universities. When they returned home they had great difficulty in gaining permits to practice their professions.

Jewish cultural life of a religious and secular character flourished throughout Poland. There was a large output of books, magazines, dailies and other publications. In higher institutions of Jewish learning, such as the famous *Yeshivoth* of Lublin and Mir, the *Yiddish Scientific Institute* (in Vilna), the *Institute for the Science of Judaism* (in Warsaw), scholars produced many volumes on Jewish subjects and trained students who later spread Jewish knowledge throughout the world. In the Jewish museums of Warsaw, Vilna, and Cracow one could find treasures of the past as well as creations of such contemporary artists as Marc Chagall, Henryk Glicenstein, and Arthur Szyk. A vibrant religious life, centering around thousands of synagogues, courts of hasidic rabbis, and individual homes, endowed the Jews with the strength and courage to live a traditional Jewish life in a non-Jewish world, frequently hostile. The Sabbaths and the holidays, all rites and customs were observed in an atmosphere that glowed with joy and piety.

Jewish communal life also abounded with a variety of political, social, philanthropic, and mutual aid organizations and institutions which helped the Jew to cope with the complexity of problems calling for action. There were organizations aiming to restore to the Jew individual human rights and freedom as well as collective autonomy, and to defend these rights along political lines. Numerous Zionist organizations helped in the rebuilding of Palestine. Agencies were established for health work, as well as a net of philanthropic institutions and youth organizations (upholding divergent religious, secular, Zionist, Yiddishist, and socialist ideologies), most of them aiming at a strong, living Jewish people.

Jews also contributed their full measure to the general culture of Poland in science, art, literature, and music. Among others, Julian Tuwim was considered the foremost contemporary poet of the Polish language, Bruno Winawer was prominent in literature, Bronislaw Huberman in music, and Szymon Ashkenazi in historiography.

The Jewish community of Poland functioned under tremendous hardships of financial limitations and governmental discrimination, which drove large Jewish masses into poverty and migration. The anti-Semitic attitudes of the government and the masses produced economic boycotts and outbreaks of violence against Jews. Nevertheless, the Jews fought their battle for survival with all possible means through internal efforts and with the aid of American Jewry, and they maintained their communal life on a high level to the very end of the interwar period, when the German army overran the country in September 1939.

An Excerpt from *Maus I*

ART SPIEGELMAN

Art Spiegelman has added a unique voice to Holocaust literature in the form of *Maus I,* an award-winning survivors' tale in cartoon form, depicting the story of his father's experiences before, during, and after the Holocaust. Spiegelman's "interviews" with his father, Vladek, act as a kind of catharsis for both father and son. Representing the Jews as mice and the Nazis as cats, Spiegelman, like George Orwell in *Animal Farm* before him, conveys emotions and behaviors by using animals, and in Spiegelman's case, the simplicity of a cartoon format. Unlike *Animal Farm,* however, the actions in *Maus I* are not allegorical but, rather, are historically accurate and biographical, and we can hear the elder Spiegelman's Eastern European voice throughout the story.

In this scene, Spiegelman tells us about the pogrom or attack on the Jews in Germany in 1938, that marks the beginning of the Holocaust. The attack was characterized by physical assaults on Jews and the storming of Jewish-owned shops and synagogues, the result being streets filled with broken glass. Hence, this attack has come to be known as *Kristallnacht,* or "night of broken glass."

SO... ANJA STAYED WITH THE FAMILY AND I WENT TO LIVE IN BIELSKO FOR MY FACTORY BUSINESS AND TO FIND FOR US AN APARTMENT..

BUT SOON IT CAME FROM SOSNOWIEC A TELEPHONE ...

VLADEK! COME HOME RIGHT AWAY— ANJA IS *SICK!*

SHE WAS CRYING AS SOON I CAME IN ...

WHAT'S WRONG, DARLING?

SOB IT DOESN'T MATTER... NOTHING MATTERS.

BUT WHY ARE YOU CRYING?

I DON'T KNOW! I HAVE A GOOD FAMILY...A FINE SON...I SHOULD BE HAPPY...

BUT I DON'T CARE. I JUST DON'T WANT TO LIVE.

HERE, BABY. DRINK THIS AND REST.

I DON'T UNDERSTAND. WHAT'S THE MATTER?

GIVING BIRTH WAS TOO MUCH OF A STRAIN. SHE'S ALWAYS HYSTERICAL OR DEPRESSED...A *BREAKDOWN!*

PLEASE

THE DOCTOR TOLD US ABOUT A SANITARIUM.

...BUT SOMEBODY MUST GO WITH HER...SOMEONE SHE TRUSTS.

EVERYTHING'S ARRANGED—THE CHILD CAN STAY HERE WITH A GOVERNESS.

...AND I'LL WATCH YOUR FACTORY.

SOB

Prejudice and Scapegoating

Prejudice . . . *an important word, a word about feelings and attitudes, a word that has frightening implications.* *"The Germans were prejudiced against the Jews."* *That's one explanation for Nazi behavior. But how did they get that way? Were the Nazis born prejudiced? Why are people prejudiced? The next three readings, taken from the book* Prejudice: The Invisible Wall, *by William Goodykoontz, helps to increase our understanding of this complex subject—as it relates directly to our own lives.*

The Greenies

WILLIAM GOODYKOONTZ

John Doe, Jr., is not born with prejudice against people who have green hair. But from the time he is a small child, he is warned against them. He is not supposed to play with green-haired children. He is told not to talk with them. His parents say, "Stay with your own kind. You'll be bad, John, if you mix with green-haired children."

As John grows older, he learns that his parents, their friends, and neighbors do not want people with green hair to:

attend his church

live in his neighborhood

go to his school, or playground, or camp.

John believes what the adults around him say. And they say that green-haired people should go to church elsewhere, live elsewhere, and go to other schools. As a child, John does not see many people with green hair.

At home, John often listens to his father talk. John Doe, Sr., started out in life with high hopes. But somewhere along the way, John Doe, Sr., did not get the job he wanted or the raise he hoped for. He began to believe that a certain group of people were the cause of his failure and that these people are to blame for everything that is wrong in life. Naturally, the bad ones are the Greenies—the people with green hair!

John Doe, Sr., talks against the people with green hair everywhere he goes—in public and in private. At home, especially, he talks about how dirty, dumb, poor, and evil the people with green hair are. Day after day, he makes jokes about them. He says that they should be thrown out of the community or that they are turning the country over to the enemy. And he always says that no Greenies will ever move into his neighborhood. Complaining about the green-haired people makes John Doe, Sr., forget that he himself is something of a failure. And when he is reminded of his failure, he can easily blame it on the green-haired people.

John Doe, Jr., begins to believe that his father is right. And anyhow he doesn't often talk with green-haired people to see what they're really like. Sometimes he reads about them in newspapers. But since newspapers play up crime, he usually reads about green-haired people who have gotten into trouble with the law. Again John believes his parents are right. Green-haired people do bad things. Even the newspapers say so.

John Doe, Jr., becomes a man. He believes the things he has learned about people with green hair. Then he marries Jane Roe, who has learned the same prejudices against people with green hair. Later they have children. And what do they teach their children? "Don't play with children with green hair. You are bad if you do."

So John Doe, Jr., carries over his prejudices to his children. And his children, too, become infected with the disease called prejudice.

What Is the Difference Between a Prejudice and a Misconception?

WILLIAM GOODYKOONTZ

Herb: Say, did you know that new math teacher is an Armenian?

Lucius: An Armenian! Man, that's terrible. I got him for fourth period. I'm gonna get my schedule changed.

Herb: Take it easy, Lucius. You don't know what he'll be like.

Lucius: What do you mean I don't know? He's Armenian. That's enough for me.

Herb: What's wrong with Armenians?

Lucius: Man, are you dumb! I got an uncle knew some Armenians once. He told me all about 'em. All I need to know. *(Whispers.)* You know what Armenians do? They take people's heads and cut 'em off and shrink 'em real small. And then they wear 'em on watch-chains. Man, they're headshrinkers for real.

Herb: Sure you're talking about Armenians?

Lucius: Sure I'm sure. *(Pauses.)* Well—it was one of those jungle tribes from down there in South America, anyway.

Herb: Armenians don't come from South America.

Lucius: They don't?

Herb: And they aren't a tribe of headhunters, either. You must have them mixed up with somebody else.

Lucius: You sure?

Herb: If you don't believe me, let's go look up Armenians in the library. *(They go to the library and read about Armenians in an encyclopedia.)*

Lucius: Man, they don't sound so bad. That uncle of mine! He don't know from nothing.

Herb: Maybe you got him wrong.

Lucius: Well—maybe. Anyway, I'm glad I don't have to get my schedule changed!

What Should I Do?

WILLIAM GOODYKOONTZ

I'm 16. A boy who has a lot of money has asked me out on a date. I'm ashamed of my family and the poor neighborhood that we live in. How can I go out with him and still not have him know what my family life is like?

There's this one boy who has an ugly face. I like him very much. But I don't know if I *really* like him or if I just feel sorry for him. My friends tell me to quit him. Should I?

We are in a special preparation class. It is not graded the way classes are graded in regular high schools. We don't know what to say when our friends ask us what grade we are in. The grade doesn't really make any difference. It's just the way people act when we say we are in "spec." It takes a lot of courage for us to tell people the kind of class we are in. Can you tell us what to do?

In this excerpt from the book, *Hey, White Girl!* by Susan Gregory, the reader feels acutely the distress of a girl who finds herself a distinct minority of one. All of us can think of situations in which we have experienced similar emotions. Here, the girl is self-conscious about "being different," and she is unsure, perhaps fearful, of what might happen.

Hey, White Girl!

SUSAN GREGORY

"Hey, white girl!" Daddy and I were standing on the curb waiting to cross Jackson when I heard the voice. For a moment I felt a tight knot form in my stomach. But I fought to relax my muscles, look straight ahead, and ignore him. The light changed, and the street became clear. Trying not to feel the eyes I knew were looking me over, I stepped over broken glass and paper. I couldn't help comparing this walk to school with the drive Daddy and I used to take when we lived in Wilmette. For three years, each school day we drove past stately mansions and carefully manicured lawns. We went down Sheridan Road along Lake Michigan. We parked near the school tennis courts and football field. But now we were two pale figures in a sea of black, kicking cans and bottles along the sidewalk like everyone else. And instead of mansions, the streets were lined with squalid tenements, liquor stores, and an occasional empty lot.

John Marshall High School faced an empty lot littered with trash and dressed with one large stand-up billboard advertising the latest thing in Chevrolets. The school's tired red brick walls had a foreboding, prisonlike quality as I stood among the students milling outside the locked front entrance, waiting for the bell on that first day of the fall term.

All new students from outside the Chicago public school system were to meet in Room 129. Never had I seen a quieter group of people. I was the only white student present. Sue, now you'll know, I thought. You'll know what it was like for every Negro who ever integrated a white school alone. As that Negro represented all Negroes to his white fellow students, so you will represent all whites to the Negroes around you. You're on trial now. Yes, really on trial. . . .

There were 5,000 black students, and I had never had contact with so many people before. I was constantly alert to where I was and who I was with and what others' eyes were telling me. I felt most self-conscious in the hall. I tried not to let anyone's glance unnerve me. But sometimes I felt so alone. I couldn't wait to get home, close myself off in our small apartment, get something to eat, and turn on the radio. . . .

Lunch was by far my most difficult ordeal. There was no one to eat with, and I felt tight. I became accustomed to the stares. But was it curiosity or resentment I saw in the eyes of my fellow students? Boys approached me constantly. "Do you feel rich today?" one asked. He wants to borrow money, I thought. He thinks I'm an easy pushover because I'm new and white. "No, never," I shook my head. "What's the matter with everybody? Nobody feels rich . . ." he walked off sadly. . . .

I got lost on the way home that first day. I took a wrong turn and had no idea where I was. I tried to read street signs and watch out for strange people at the same time. I was wary of everyone. By the large Chicago Transit Authority barn I ran into a group of boys. "Hey, girl . . . Hey, white girl . . ." There it was again. I crossed the street as quickly as I could. But there I faced several Puerto Ricans. "Ooooo—I wonder where she goes to school?" I heard one whistle.

The next three excerpts are from *The Nature of Prejudice,* a major work on this subject by psychologist Gordon Allport. Allport has contributed enormously to our understanding of the mechanisms of prejudice. According to his theory, prejudice grows out of personal *frustration*, which in turn generates aggressive feelings. When this *aggression* cannot be directed against the real cause of the frustration, the aggression is *displaced* onto relatively defenseless "scapegoats." This displaced hostility is then rationalized and justified by blaming, projecting, and stereotyping.

The Meaning of Scapegoat

GORDON ALLPORT

The term "scapegoat" originated in the famous ritual of the Hebrews, described in the Book of Leviticus (16:20–22). On the Day of Atonement a live goat was chosen by lot. The high priest, robed in linen garments, laid both his hands on the goat's head, and confessed over it the iniquities of the children of Israel. The sins of the people thus symbolically transferred to the beast, it was taken out into the wilderness and let go. The people felt purged, and for the time being, guiltless.

The type of thinking here involved is not uncommon. From earliest times the notion has persisted that guilt and misfortune can be shifted from one man's back to another. Animistic thinking confuses what is mental with what is physical. If a load of wood can be shifted, why not a load of sorrow or a load of guilt?

Nowadays we are likely to label this mental process *projection*. In other people we see the fear, anger, lust that reside primarily in ourselves. It is not we ourselves who are responsible for our misfortunes, but other people. In our common speech we recognize this failing in such phrases as "whipping-boy," "taking it out on the dog," or "scapegoat. . . ."

Yankees in a conservative Maine community may discriminate socially against the Italians or French-Canadians who live there—but the snobbery is relatively mild, and one can seldom see evidences of actual aggression (true scapegoating). On the other hand, a much more serious problem of antagonism exists in the case of other minorities (Jews, Negroes, Orientals, Mexicans) to whom the dominant majority has said, "We shall never accept you as one of us."

Just as it is impossible to tell clearly when a group is a scapegoat and when it is not, so too we cannot find a clear formula that will cover the selection of scapegoats. The essence of the matter seems to be that different groups are singled out for different reasons. We have already noted the contrast between the accusations made against Negroes and Jews, and have discussed the theory which states that each of these two scapegoats "take away" different *kinds* of guilt.

There seems to be no such thing as an "all-duty scapegoat" although some groups come nearer to this objective than others. Perhaps today Jews and Negroes are blamed for the widest variety of evils. We note that these are *inclusive* social groups consisting of both sexes (and their children), which transmit social values and cultural traits. They are more or less permanent, definite, and stable. By contrast one finds many *ad hoc* scapegoats who are blamed for quite specific things. The American Medical Association or the Soft Coal Miners Union may be much hated by certain portions of society, being blamed for evils in health policy, labor policy, high prices, or some particular inconvenience for which they may or may not be partly responsible. (Scapegoats need not be lily-white in their innocence, but they always attract more blame, more animosity, more stereotyped judgment than can be rationally justified.) . . .

One reason for the popularity of the scapegoat theory is that it is easy to understand. Probably this fact is also an argument for its validity, for the ease of understanding must be related in some way to the commonness of the experience. A storybook for seven-year-olds contains a clear example of the scapegoating theme. The tale runs as follows:

> An enterprising pig with some ducks as companions is aloft in a
> rudderless balloon. A farmer with evil intentions is trying to
> capture the balloon, but the alert piglet pelts the farmer with cans
> of tomato soup. The farmer is spattered by the soup and thor-
> oughly angry. A dirty-faced boy comes out of the barn to help him
> wipe off the soup. But the farmer cuffs the little boy good. He does
> this for three reasons: first, because the balloon had got away; and
> second, because he would now have to take a bath to get the
> sticky soup off him; and, third, because it seemed like a pretty
> good thing to do anyway.

The following case shows how a blend of home and school frustration may lead to prejudice. A college student writes:

> I had honors all the way through school and one double promotion, but I did not have a straight "A" record. I was not happy. My father boasted that he had had only an A and A-plus record when he was in college, and at the same time held down a full-time job. He never let me forget it, and berated me for doing less well than he. I felt utterly frustrated. I wanted to please him but could not succeed. Finally I found comfort in telling myself and other people that it was only the Jewish grinds and cheats who did me out of the top position. (In thinking the matter over I realize that I do not know for a fact that the boys who excelled me in scholarship were Jews, or that they cheated.)

Prejudice

GORDON ALLPORT

The word "prejudice," derived from the Latin noun *praejudicium*, has, like most words, undergone a change of meaning since classical times. There are three stages in the transformation.

(1) To the ancients, *praejudicium* meant a *precedent*—a judgment based on previous decisions and experiences.

(2) Later, the term, in English, acquired the meaning of a judgment formed before due examination and consideration of the facts—a premature or hasty judgment.

(3) Finally, the term acquired also its present emotional flavor of favorableness or unfavorableness that accompanies such a prior and unsupported judgment.

The wording offered by the New English Dictionary recognizes positive as well as negative prejudice: "A feeling, favorable or unfavorable, toward a person or thing, prior to, or not based on, actual experience." While it is important to bear in mind that biases may be *pro* as well as *con*, it is none the less true that *ethnic* prejudice is mostly negative. . . .

It is not easy to say how much fact is required in order to justify a judgment. A prejudiced person will almost certainly claim that he has sufficient warrant for his views. He will tell of bitter experiences he has had with refugees, Catholics, or Orientals. . . .

No one can possibly know *all* refugees, Catholics, or Orientals.

Therefore, any negative judgment of these groups must be based on characteristics that an individual has assumed that all members of an ethnic group possesses. These generalities are known as *stereotypes*.

Why were the Jews the main butt of Hitler's fanatic hatred? Why have Jews been the object of prejudice throughout much of history? Allport suggests five explanations for the Jew's selection as an object of hostility.

The Jew as Scapegoat

GORDON ALLPORT

Anti-Semitism is thought to reach back at least to the fall of Judea in 586 B.C. When the Jews were dispersed, they took with them their relatively rigid and unbending customs. Dietary laws prohibited them from eating with others; intermarriage was forbidden. They were even by their own prophet Jeremiah considered "stiff-necked." Wherever they went their orthodoxy presented a problem.

In Greece and Rome—to mention only two of their new homelands—new ideas were welcomed. The Jews were received as interesting strangers. But the cosmopolitan cultures which they entered could not understand why Jews did not reciprocate the meals, games, and gaiety of their own pagan life. Jehovah could easily be fitted into the galaxy of gods who were worshipped. Why could not the Jews accept the pantheon? Judaism seemed too absolute in its theology, ethnic customs, and rites.

Yet in Ancient Rome it is fairly certain that Christians were persecuted more vigorously than Jews. Tertullian gives a terse record of the scapegoating of Christians. Until the fourth century when Christianity became the officially dominant religion under Constantine, it is probable that the Jews fared relatively better than the Christians. But after that time the Sabbaths were separated, and the Jews became a highly visible group marked off from the Christians.

Since the early Christians were themselves Jews, it took the first two or three centuries of the Christian era for this fact to be forgotten. Then only did the accusation arise that the Jews (as a group) were responsible for the Crucifixion. Subsequently, for centuries it seems that to a large number of people the epithet "Christ killer" was a sufficient cause for scapegoating the Jew on any and all occasions. Certain it is that by the time of St. John Chrysostom (fourth century) elaborate anti-

Semitic homilies were preached, accusing Jews not only of the Crucifixion but of all other conceivable crimes as well.

Some support for anti-Semitism is drawn from straight Christian theological reasoning. Since the Bible explicitly asserts that the Jews are God's chosen people, they must be hounded until they acknowledge their Messiah. God will punish them until they do so. Thus their persecution by Christians is ordained. It is true that no modern theologian would interpret this situation to mean that an individual Christian is justified in acting unfairly or uncharitably toward any individual Jew. Yet the fact remains that God acts in mysterious ways, and apparently His concern is to bring recalcitrant Jews, His chosen people, to acknowledge the New Testament as well as the Old. While modern anti-Semites are certainly not aware that they are punishing the Jews for this particular reason, from the theological point of view their conduct is understandable in terms of God's long-range design.

It is necessary to stress these religious factors in anti-Semitism, for the Jews are above all else a religious group. It may be rightly objected that many (perhaps most) Jews today are not religious. While orthodoxy has declined, there has been no decrease in persecution. Further, it may be objected that in present-day anti-Semitism the sins of the Jews are said to be moral, financial, social; religious deviance is seldom mentioned. All this is true—and yet the vestiges of the religious issue certainly persist. The Jewish religious holidays make for visibility; so too the imposing synagogues in Jewish residential districts.

Still, many people today are indifferent to the specifically religious quarrel between Judaism and Christianity. Many more are able in their own minds to transcend it, realizing well the essential unity of the Judeo-Christian tradition. But, according to a broader interpretation of the matter, each one of us is still affected by the epic quality of spiritual ferment in Jewish culture. Jacques Maritain, the Catholic scholar, expresses the matter thus:

> Israel . . . is to be found at the very heart of the world's structure, stimulating it, exasperating it, moving it. Like an alien body, like an activating ferment injected into the mass, it gives the world no peace . . . it teaches the world to be discontent and restless as long as the world has not God, it stimulates the movement of history.

A Jewish scholar continues the argument: the Jews as a group are no larger than certain unheard-of tribes in Africa. Yet they have provided continuous spiritual ferment. They insist upon monotheism; upon ethics; upon moral responsibility. They insist upon high scholarship;

upon closely knit home life. They themselves aspire to high ideals, are restless, and ridden by conscience. Throughout the ages they have made mankind aware of God, of ethics, of high standards of attainment. Thus—though imperfect in themselves—they have been the mentors of the world's conscience.

On the one hand people admire and revere these standards. On the other hand they rebel and protest. Anti-Semitism arises because people are irritated by their own consciences. Jews are symbolically their superego, and no one likes to be ridden so hard by his superego. Ethical conduct is insisted upon by Judaism, relentlessly, immediately, hauntingly. People who dislike this insistence, along with the self-discipline and acts of charity implied, are likely to justify their rejection by discrediting the whole race that produced such high ethical ideals.

Jews, partly at least because of their religious deviance, were excluded in many countries for long periods of time from owning land. Only transient and fringe occupations were open to them. When the Crusaders needed money, they could not borrow from Christians (whose code did not allow usury). Jews became the moneylenders. In so doing they invited customers but also contempt. Excluded not only from landowning but also from handicraft guilds, Jewish families were forced to develop mercantile habits. Only moneylending, trading, and other stigmatized occupations were open to them.

This pattern has to some extent persisted. Occupational traditions of the European Jews transferred to new lands when Jews emigrated. To some extent the same discrimination barred them from conservative occupations. They were again obliged to develop the fringe activities where risk, shrewdness, enterprise were required. We have seen how this factor led large numbers of Jewish people, especially in New York City, into retailing, theatrical ventures, and professions. This somewhat uneven distribution on the economic checkerboard of the nation made the Jewish group conspicuous; it also intensified the stereotype that they work too hard, make lots of money, and engage in shady dealings in the less stable occupations.

Looking backward once more over the historical course of events, we find another consideration of importance. Lacking a homeland, the Jews were regarded by some as parasites upon the body politic. They had certain attributes of a nation (ethnic coherence plus a tradition of nationhood). But they were, in fact, the only nation on earth without a home. People who distrusted "bi-loyalty" accused them of being less patriotic, less honorable within their adopted land than they should be.

A further factor to be noted is that the insistence upon scholarship and intellectual attainment is a longstanding mark of Jewish culture.

Jewish intellectualism calls to mind one's own defects of ignorance and laziness. The Jews once more symbolize our conscience, against whose pricks we protest.

Surveying such a welter of historico-psychological factors, one naturally wonders whether there is a leading motif that would sum them all up. The nearest approach would seem to be the concept of "fringe of conservative values." The expression, however, must be understood to cover not only deviance in religion, occupation, nationhood, but likewise departure from conservative mediocrity: conscience pricking, intellectual aspiration, spiritual ferment. One might put the matter this way: the Jews are regarded as just far enough *off center* (slightly above, slightly below, slightly outside) to disturb non-Jews in many different ways. The "fringe" is perceived by conservative people to represent a threat. The differences are not great; indeed, the fact that they are relatively slight may make them all the more effectively disturbing. Again we cite "the narcissism of slight differences."

This analysis of anti-Semitism, historically considered, is far from complete. It is intended only to demonstrate that, without historical perspective, we cannot tell why one group rather than another is the object of hostility. The Jews are a scapegoat of great antiquity, and only the long arm of history, aided by psychological insights, can reconstruct the story.

The problem is exceedingly complex, but it will never be solved unless there is at every stage scrupulous regard for factual evidence, concerning both the traits of the Jewish group and the psychodynamic processes of anti-Semites.

Other Voices/Other Victims

There is no question that the Jews were singled out as the main target of Nazi persecution. More than six million Jews were murdered. While anti-Semitism was a key component of the Nazi program, the underlying rationale of "racial purity" was, however, extended to other ethnicities and other political and social groups. Members of these other groups were hounded, rounded up, shipped to concentration camps, and murdered too. It was no secret that those of Slavic origin were deemed sub-Aryan and destined for a fate similar to that of the Jews. The Gypsy population of Europe was also destined for extermination or slave labor. Some estimate that as many as 500,000 Gypsies were killed. Homosexual men were also accorded a special, zealous category of hatred. Other persecuted groups slated for destruction included errant clergy, liberals, communists, the mentally ill, criminals, and "asocials," a category designed to encompass any unclassifiable antifascist or "deviant," from artists to lesbians, who theoretically did not exist in Nazi Germany.

Writings concerning these other groups illuminate an important dimension of the Holocaust; namely, that it was not simply a matter of Aryan against Jew, but of Aryan against any outsider, any threat to conformity. Nazism set out to ensure conformity by eradicating diversity.

The following three pieces can be seen as general testaments to the horror of the Holocaust and the pressure which human relations endured in the camps. But they can also be taken as signposts of the histories of victims not yet fully explored and written. The first is an excerpt from the 1979 play Bent, by Martin Sherman. Max and Rudy are lovers who have just been caught by the Nazis after fleeing Berlin, which, before the Nazi rise to power, had been a center of homosexual life and emancipation.

The second piece is entitled The Juggler, *by Primo Levi. In 1944, 25-year-old Levi, an Italian Jew and a chemist, was arrested by Italian fascists and taken to Auschwitz. He characterized his need to write about both the atrocities and the moments of human compassion at Auschwitz as an "immediate and violent impulse," one which helped bring about his own "interior liberation." Levi returned to his native Turin, Italy, after the war and lived there until his suicide in 1987.*

Like the Jews, the Gypsies were outside the Christian churches' universe of obligation. They have been repeatedly persecuted in Europe. Although the Gypsies are believed to have migrated from India, a homeland of Aryan languages, they were defined in Nazi Germany as non-Aryan and further labelled as asocial. Thus, they could not be assimilated into the race "of pure blood"—the mythical Aryans—which Hitler and Himmler dreamed of creating. And thus, they became legitimate targets for extinction and were the next victims of genocide. The third piece in this section is taken from Accounting for Genocide: National Responses and Jewish Victimization During the Holocaust, *by Helen Fein.*

Bent

MARTIN SHERMAN

ACT ONE

Scene Five

(A train whistle is heard.)

(Sound of a train running through the night. A train whistle again.)

(A circle of light comes up.)

(It is a prisoner transport train. We see one small corner. Five prisoners are in the light—two men in civilian dress, then Rudy *and* Max, *then a man in his 20s, wearing a striped uniform with a pink triangle sewn onto it.)*

(A Guard *walks through the circle of light. He carries a rifle.)*

(Silence.)

*(*Horst *is on lower bunk.* Max *sits at the end of the other bunk.* Rudy *sits on floor at* Max's *left. His first line is to* Max.*)*

Rudy: Where do you think they're taking us?
(Silence.)
(The other prisoners look away.)
(The Guard *walks through the circle of light.)*
(Silence.)
*(*Rudy *slides over to* Horst.*)*
Excuse me. *(To the* Prisoner *next to him)* Did you have a trial?
(The Prisoner *doesn't answer.)*
Max: Rudy!
*(*Rudy *returns to* Max.*)*
(Silence.)
*(*Rudy *and* Max *look at each other. They are both terrified.* Rudy *starts to extend his hand, then withdraws it.)*

(A scream is heard—off, beyond the circle. RUDY *and* MAX *look at each other, then turn away.)*
(Silence.)
*(*OFFICER *enters and crosses left of* RUDY. GUARD 1 *follows him and stands left of him.* GUARD 2 *enters. He pauses halfway down bunk. He rests his right foot on lower right bunk.* RUDY *looks up at* OFFICER *then at* MAX. OFFICER'S *first line is to* GUARD 1 *as he notices* RUDY*'s glasses.)*

OFFICER: Glasses. *(Silence.)*
*(*OFFICER *speaks to* RUDY.*)*
Give me your glasses.
*(*RUDY *hands the* OFFICER *his glasses, looking at* MAX *then the* OFFICER. OFFICER *examines glasses. He shows them to* GUARD 1.*)*
Hornrimmed. Intelligensia.

RUDY: What?
OFFICER: *(Smiles)* Stand up.
*(*RUDY *stands. He is frightened.* OFFICER *puts glasses down.)*
Step on your glasses.
*(*RUDY *looks at* OFFICER *and* MAX.*)*
Step on them.
*(*RUDY, *tentative, steps on glasses.)*
Take him.
*(*OFFICER *indicates to* GUARD 1. RUDY *grabs hold of bunk.* GUARD 1 & GUARD 2 *grab* RUDY *and take him off.* RUDY *fights them.)*

RUDY: Max!

*(*RUDY *looks at* MAX. *The* GUARD *pulls* RUDY *off—out of the circle. The* OFFICER *smiles.)*

OFFICER: Glasses.

*(*OFFICER *kicks glasses toward* MAX. *He exits, glancing at* MAX.*)*
*(*MAX *stiffens. A scream is heard.)*
(Silence.)
*(*MAX *stands and starts around end of bunk.* RUDY *screams again.)*
(The man wearing the pink triangle, HORST, *moves toward* MAX. *He touches him.)*

HORST: Don't.

(He removes his hand from Max *and looks straight ahead.)*
(The Guard *walks through the circle of light.)*
Don't move. You can't help him.
*(*Rudy *screams.* Max *turns away.)*
(Silence.)

Max: This isn't happening.
Horst: It's happening.

*(*Max *notices* Horst. *He crawls to left bunk.)*

Max: Where are they taking us?
Horst: Dachau.
Max: How do you know?
Horst: I've been through transport before. They took me to Cologne for a propaganda film. Pink triangle in good health. Now it's back to Dachau.
Max: Pink triangle? What's that?
Horst: Queer. If you're queer, that's what you wear. If you're a Jew, a yellow star. Political—a red triangle. Criminal—green. Pink's the lowest. *(He looks straight ahead.)*

(The Guard *walks through the circle of light.)*

*(*Rudy *screams.* Max *looks off.)*

Max: *(*Max *covers his head with arms.)* This isn't happening. This can't be happening.
Horst: Listen to me. (Horst *whispers into* Max's *left ear.)* If you survive the train, you stand a chance. Here's where they break you. You can do nothing for your friend. Nothing—
*(*Rudy *screams.* Max *hurls himself against the edge of the right bunk.)*
If you try to help him, they will kill you. If you try to care for his wounds, they will kill you. *(*Horst *leans over edge of bunk and addresses* Max.) *If you even *see*—see what they do to him, *hear*—hear what they do to him—they will kill you. If you want to stay alive, he can not exist.

*(*Rudy *screams.* Max *swings himself around to end of right bunk.)*

Max: It isn't happening.

(Rudy screams.)
Horst: He hasn't a chance. He wore glasses.
(Rudy screams.)
If you want to stay alive, he can not exist.
(Rudy screams.)
It *is* happening.

(Horst lies down, turning to face the wall. On Rudy's scream Max rises, is confused and sits again on end of bunk.)

Max: It isn't happening . . . it isn't happening . . .

(Guard 1 & Guard 2 drag Rudy on. Guard 1 is left of Rudy. Guard 2 is right of Rudy. The Officer follows to stand in front of Guard 2.)

Officer: *(Officer speaks to Max.)* Who is this man?
Max: I don't know. *(Max stops mumbling, looks straight ahead.)*

(Officer looks at Guard 2, smiles then speaks to Max.)

Officer: Your friend?
(Silence.)
Max: No.
(Rudy moans.)
Officer: Look at him.
(Max does not look. He is agitated.)
Look!
(Max looks at Rudy. Officer hits Rudy in chest while looking at Max. Rudy screams and Max looks away at floor.)
Your friend?
Max: No.

(Max continues to focus on floor and closes his eyes. The Officer hits Rudy in chest. Rudy screams.)

Officer: Your friend?
Max: No. *(Max stares straight ahead.)*
Officer: Hit him.
(Max stares at Officer, disbelieving.)
Like this.

(Officer hits Rudy in chest. Rudy screams.
Max stares straight ahead. He shuts his eyes.)

Officer: Hit him.
(Max doesn't move.)
Your friend?
(Officer crosses DR of Max, faces Rudy.)
Your friend?
Max: No.

(Max tentatively rises. He crosses haltingly to Rudy, all the while looking at Officer. He closes his eyes, hits Rudy in chest and dashes back to sit on right lower bunk. He looks at Officer.)

Officer: Open your eyes.
(Max opens his eyes.)
Again.
(Max slowly crosses to Rudy. He looks at Officer and, with eyes open quickly hits Rudy in chest.)
Again!
(Max hits Rudy in chest.)
Again!
(Max repeatedly slugs Rudy in chest.)
Enough.
(Officer pulls Max off. Guard 1 & Guard 2 release Rudy, who falls to floor below right bunk.)
Your friend?
Max: No.
Officer: *(Smiles)* No.

(Guard 1 & Guard 2 exit. There is a pause then Officer exits. Rudy moans and calls for Max. Max sits on right lower bunk. He closes his eyes, grabs edge of bunk and takes a deep breath.)

Max: One. Two. Three. Four. Five. *(Max takes another deep breath.)* Six. Seven. Eight. Nine. Ten.

(Rudy calls Max's name. Max stares ahead. The lights dim on Max, almost to blackout—then, suddenly, they expand, and include the three other prisoners. A morning ray of sunlight.)

(RUDY *lies at* MAX*'s feet.*)

(*The* GUARD *walks through the circle of light.*)

(*Silence.*)

(*As lights come up* OFFICER *enters followed by* GUARD 1. MAX *does not acknowledge them.*)

OFFICER: Stand up.
(MAX *rises.*)
(*Stares at* MAX.) We'll see. (*To* GUARD) Take him.
(GUARD 1 *takes* MAX *and leads him off. The* OFFICER *crosses to* RUDY, *taps him with his boot.*)
Dead.

End of Scene Five

The Juggler

PRIMO LEVI

We called them *"Grüne Spitzen"* (green triangles), common criminals, *Befauer,* from the initials BV with which they were officially designated, and which in turn was the abbreviation of something like "prisoners in preventive detention." We lived with them, obeyed, feared, and detested them, but knew almost nothing about them. For that matter, little is known even now. They were the "green triangles," Germans already held in regular prisons, who had been offered—according to mysterious criteria—the alternative of serving out their sentences in a Camp rather than a prison. As a rule they were scum. A lot of them boasted that they lived better in the Camp than at home, because, in addition to the heady pleasure of command, they were given a free hand with the rations allotted to us. Many were murderers in the narrow sense of the word. They made no secret of it and their behavior showed it.

Eddy (probably a stage name) was a green triangle but no murderer. He had two professions: he was a juggler and, in his spare time, a thief. In June of 1944 be became the vice Kapo of our squad, and he quickly struck us because of his uncommon qualities. Dazzlingly handsome, he was blond, of medium height, but slim, strong, and very agile. He had aristocratic features and skin so light it looked translucent. He could not have been more than 23, and he didn't give a damn about anything or anyone: the SS, work, or us. He had a serene and self-absorbed look that set him apart. The very day of his arrival, he became famous. In the washroom, completely naked, after washing himself carefully with a piece of scented soap, he set it on the top of his head, which was shaved like ours, bent forward and, with imperceptible, practiced, and precise undulations of his back, made the luxurious piece of soap slide little by little from head to neck, then down, down along the entire spinal column all the way to his coccyx, at which point he made it fall into his hand. Two or three of us applauded but he showed no sign of noticing and went off to dress, slowly and abstractedly.

At work he was unpredictable. Sometimes he did the work of 10 men, but even in the dullest tasks he never failed to reveal, suddenly, his professional bent. He would be shoveling dirt and all of a sudden would stop, seize the shovel as if it were a guitar, and improvise a popular song, beating on it with a pebble, now on the wooden handle, now on the iron part. He would be carrying bricks and returning with his dancing, dreamy gait, and all at once he would roll into a fast somersault. Other days he remained huddled in a corner without lifting a finger, but precisely because he was capable of such extraordinary feats no one dared say anything to him. He was not an exhibitionist; doing his tricks he did not pay the least attention to those around him. He seemed instead to be preoccupied with the perfection of his performances, repeating and improving them like a dissatisfied poet who never stops correcting his work. At times we saw him hunting through the scrap metal strewn around the workyard, picking up a hoop, a rod, a snippet of sheet metal, turning it attentively in his hands, balancing it on one finger, whirling it through the air, as though he were trying to penetrate its essence and build a new trick around it.

One day a wagon arrived full of cardboard tubes, like the ones used for rolls of cloth, and our work-squad was sent to unload them. Eddy took me into an underground storeroom, where, below a small window, he set up a wooden chute to be used by my companions for sending down the tubes. He showed me how I had to pile them neatly against the walls, and left. From the little window I could see my companions, happy because of the unusually light work but uncertain and clumsy in their movements, shuttling between wagon and storeroom, carrying 20 or 30 tubes a trip. Eddy carried a few at times and a lot at others, but never haphazardly. Every time he made the circuit he invented new structures and architectures, unsteady but symmetrical as card castles. On one trip he tossed four or five tubes in the air, the way jugglers do with rubber balls.

I was alone in the cellar, anxious to carry through an important operation. I had gotten hold of a sheet of paper and a pencil stub, and for many days I had been waiting for the opportunity to write the draft of a letter (in Italian, of course) which I meant to entrust to an Italian "free" laborer so he could copy it, sign it as if it were his, and send it to my family in Italy. In fact we were strictly forbidden to write, but I was sure that if I could think about it for a moment, I would find a way to devise a message that would be sufficiently clear to the recipients but at the same time innocent enough not to attract the censor's attention. I could not risk being seen by anyone because the fact of writing alone was intrinsically suspect (for what reason and to whom should one of us be writing?), and the Camp and the workyard teemed with informers. After not quite an hour of work on the tubes I felt calm enough to begin writing the letter. The tubes descended from the chute at infrequent intervals, and there was no alarming sound in the cellar.

I hadn't reckoned with Eddy's noiseless step. I noticed him only when he was already watching me. Instinctively—or, rather, stupidly—I opened my fingers. The pencil fell, and the sheet of paper descended slowly to the ground, swaying like a dead leaf. Eddy lunged to pick it up, then slammed me to the ground with a violent slap. But there: as I write this sentence today, and as I am in the act of typing the word "slap," I realize that I am lying, or at least transmitting biased emotions and information to the reader. Eddy was not a brute; he did not mean to punish me or make me suffer. A slap inflicted in the Camp had a very different significance from what it might have here among us in today's here and now. Precisely: it had a meaning; it was simply another way of expressing oneself. In that context it meant roughly "Watch out, you've really made a big mistake this time, you're endangering your life, maybe without realizing it, and you're endangering mine as well." But between Eddy, a German thief and juggler, and me, a young, inexperienced Italian, flustered and confused, such a speech would have been useless, not understood (if nothing else, because of language problems), out of tune, and much too roundabout.

For this very reason, punches and slaps passed among us as daily language, and we soon learned to distinguish meaningful blows from the others inflicted out of savagery, to create pain and humiliation, and which often resulted in death. A slap like Eddy's was akin to the friendly smack you give a dog, or the whack you administer to a donkey to convey or reinforce an order or prohibition. Nothing more in short than a nonverbal communication. Among the many miseries in the Camp, blows of this nature were by far the least painful. Which is equivalent to saying that our manner of living was not very different from that of donkeys and dogs.

Eddy waited for me to get up, then asked to whom I was writing. I answered in my bad German that I was not writing to anyone. I happened to find a pencil and was writing on a whim, out of nostalgia, in a dream. Yes, I knew very well that writing was forbidden, but I also knew that getting a letter out of the Camp was impossible; I assured him I never would have dared to break Camp rules. I knew Eddy certainly would not believe me but I had to say something, if only to arouse his pity. If he were to denounce me to the Political Section, I knew it was the gallows for me, but before the gallows an interrogation—and what an interrogation!—to find out who my accomplice was, and perhaps also to obtain from me the address of the recipient in Italy. Eddy looked at me with a strange expression, then told me not to budge, he'd be back in an hour.

It was a long hour. Eddy came back to the cellar with three sheets of paper in his hand, mine among them, and I immediately read on his face that the worst would not happen. He must have been quite clever, this Eddy, or maybe his tempestuous past had taught him the basics of the sad profession of interrogator. He had looked among my companions for two men (not just one) who knew both German and Italian, and had gotten them separately to translate my message into German, warning them that if the two translations did not turn out to be identical, he would denounce not only me but also them to the Political Section.

He made a speech to me that I find difficult to repeat. He told me that, luckily for me, the two translations were the same and the text was not compromising. That I was crazy—there was no other explanation. Only a madman would think of gambling in such a way with his life, that of the Italian accomplice whom I certainly had, my relatives in Italy, and also his career as Kapo. He told me that I deserved that slap, that in fact I should thank him because it had been a good deed, the kind that earns you Paradise, and that he, *Strassenräuber*, a street-thief by profession, certainly needed to perform good deeds. That, finally, he would not have recourse to denunciation but even he could not exactly say why. Maybe just because I was crazy. But then Italians are all notoriously crazy, good only for singing and getting into trouble.

I don't believe I thanked Eddy, but from that day on, even though I felt no positive attraction to my green triangle "colleagues," I often asked myself what kind of humanity was massed behind their symbol, and I have regretted that none of their ambiguous brigade has, so far as I know, told his story. I don't know how Eddy ended up. A few weeks after this incident he disappeared for several days; then we saw him one evening. He was standing in the passage between the barbed wire and the electrified fence, and around his neck hung a sign on which was written *Urning* (pederast), but he appeared neither upset nor anxious. He watched the re-entry of our work-group with a distracted, insolent, and lazy look, as though nothing that was happening around him concerned him in the slightest.

Extermination of the Gypsies

HELEN FEIN

T he Jews were not the only group in Germany stigmatized as alien, but they were the only stigmatized group of political significance whose elimination had been promised publicly by Hitler 20 years before it began. The Gypsies were also designated for destruction, although scarcely any publicity was devoted to the "Gypsy problem."

Although Gypsies have not played a symbolic role similar to that of the Jews—they cannot be labeled a "middleman minority"—they have been accused of crime and corruption since their entry into Europe, charged with assistance at the Crucifixion, unnatural copulation, cannibalism, necrophiliac activity, and spreading filth and disease. The first response of European states from the 15th to the 18th century was to expel them: 148 such laws were passed by German states alone between 1416 and 1774. Violence was commonly employed for enforcement and deterrence. As late as the 19th century, Gypsy hunts (like fox hunts) occurred in Denmark. Only after drives for expulsion and extermination had failed did states attempt to assimilate them, denying the right of Gypsies to live together, by encouraging settlement and criminalizing the nomads' life. By 1933 police in France, Baden, and Prussia already had files with fingerprinted identification of Gypsies there.

Gypsies were officially defined as non-Aryan by the Nuremberg laws of 1935, which also first defined Jews; both groups were forbidden to marry Germans. Gypsies were later labeled as asocials by the 1937 Laws against Crime, regardless of whether they had been charged with any unlawful acts. Two hundred Gypsy men were then selected by quota and incarcerated in Buchenwald concentration camp. By May 1938, SS Reichsführer Himmler established the Central Office for Fighting the Gypsy Menace, which defined the question as "a matter of race," discriminating pure Gypsies from part Gypsies as Jews were discriminated, and ordering their registration. In 1939, resettlement of Gypsies was put under Eichmann's jurisdiction along with that of the Jews. Gypsies were forbidden to move freely and were concentrated in encampments within Germany in 1939, later (1941) transformed into fenced ghettos, from which they would be seized for transport by the crime police (aided by dogs) and dispatched to Auschwitz in February 1943.

The legal status of Gypsies and Jews, determined irrevocably by the agreement Justice Minister Thierack and SS Reichsführer Himmler on September 18, 1942, removing both groups from the jurisdiction of any German court, confirmed their fate. Thierack wrote, "I envisage transferring all criminal proceedings concerning [these people] to Himmler. I do this because I realize that the courts can only feebly contribute to the extermination of these people."

The Citizenship Law of 1943 omitted any mention of Gypsies since they were not expected to exist much longer. Himmler decreed the transport of Gypsies to Auschwitz on December 16, 1942, but he did not authorize their extermination until 1944. Most died there and in other camps of starvation, diseases, and torture from abuse as live experimental subjects. By the end of the war, 15,000 of the 20,000 Gypsies who had been in Germany in 1938 had died.

The two following pieces are by Alexander Ramati, an American of Polish descent who became interested in the Gypsy holocaust in the early 1980s. The first piece is the introduction to his book, *And the Violins Stopped Playing*. It relates his first meeting with Roman Mirga, a Gypsy survivor of Auschwitz who persuaded Ramati to tell not only his story, but that of his family and of Gypsies during the Nazi regime. The second piece describes the Mirga family's entrance into Auschwitz.

And the Violins Stopped Playing

ALEXANDER RAMATI

INTRODUCTION

I arrived in Göttingen for the session of the World Romany Congress. I checked into a small Central Hotel on Judenstrasse and walked through narrow winding streets to the Stadthalle, a modern three-story Conference Centre, just on the outskirts of the old quarter of the German city. Upstairs, the big hall was filled by 300 delegates from 28 countries, who were listening to the brief speech of welcome by the President, Dr. Jan Cibula. All the delegates' speeches were to be delayed until the next day for, as always with Gypsies, the first order of the conference was entertainment. While the Bhangra Dancers from India were making their way on to the stage to the accompaniment of zithers, I looked around for the man who had invited me to the Congress, Grattan Puxon, the Secretary-General. He was sitting in the front row and as I elbowed my way towards him, we greeted each other. For the past year we had been corresponding, and my arrival in Göttingen was the result of that contact, which had begun when I decided to write a book about the Gypsy holocaust.

I returned to my hotel early, exhausted after my long journey, and was about to retire, when there was a knock on the door of my room and a bellboy brought me a letter. I opened the envelope, believing it would be an invitation to one of the many forthcoming functions. It read: "I am one of the Polish delegates to the Congress. I was told that you are planning to write a book about our wartime persecution. It so happens that I have recorded many events in the life of my family and my tribe during that period. I kept my notes in the hope that some day someone would want to use them, so that the world, especially America which can do so much for us, will know what we have gone through. I was told that you are an American writer of Polish origin, so you will easily be able to read what I have written. I am waiting in the hotel's lobby for your answer."

I walked downstairs. There, in the almost empty hall, I saw a lanky man in his mid-fifties, sitting alone at a small table, a glass of beer in front of him, holding a thick manila envelope. He stood up and extended his hand.

"I am Roman Mirga," he said. He pointed at the envelope. "This will tell you more than all the speeches you'll hear tomorrow, more than all the pamphlets and articles on the subject." I sat down and joined him in a glass of beer.

"Six million Jews were murdered by the Nazis," he continued, "but how many people know that 300,000 Gypsies perished at the same time? The Jews got individual and block compensation; we have received nothing, and discrimination against us continues all over the world. How can we hope to obtain any justice for our cause, to get funds, at least for the education of our children and grandchildren, the survivors of those who died, if the world does not know that they died?"

"I learned about it only a year ago," I said, defensively. "I promise you. . . ."

"The Germans don't even admit that there was a Gypsy holocaust," he interrupted me. "There are memorials in Auschwitz for all the nations whose people died there, except for the Gypsies!"

"I promise you," I went on, "that I will read your material and meet you again tomorrow night."

The man grabbed my hand in both of his. "Thank you," he said. "I always wanted an American writer to write the book. What good would it do, if it were only published in Polish? Until now I have been unable to leave Poland and search for one. What a stroke of luck that you are American and you are Polish, and that you are here." As I was reaching the staircase, he ran after me. "You must do it," he said, "so that I can keep the promise I made to my father. He was a great man, a great leader."

Next day I listened to the speeches of the delegates, their calls for the ending of prejudice, the supporting statements of Jews, such as that of the Nazi-hunter Simon Wiesenthal, and of many Christian sympathizers. I was surprised, however, that no representative of the German government, not even of a provincial government, was present at the Congress.

In the evening I opened the envelope. I was amazed by the writer's painstakingly detailed descriptions. It appeared that he had put down all his recollections shortly after the events had occurred. I began reading at six o'clock in the evening and became so absorbed by Roman Mirga's writing that I was unable to tear myself away. It had all the elements a writer needs—Gypsy lore, drama, characterization. The evening session of the Congress was scheduled to begin at eight. I never went to it. I sat on my bed, reading, utterly fascinated, until I finished some time around 10. Half an hour later a bellboy called to say that a man was waiting for me downstairs.

There he was in the lobby, sitting at the same table as before, having a beer. He got up. "Have you read it?" he asked anxiously. He called the waiter. "Two more beers, please. "

"You were right," I said enthusiastically. "It's all there, just as you said. When did you write it?"

"In 1944," the man answered. "On a Polish farm where I was hiding, in a cellar under the kitchen floor."

"Why don't you write it yourself?" I asked. "It could then be translated into English."

"I am not a writer. And I don't mind how it comes out, so long as it comes out in America, especially in America."

We drank our beers, then had two more. For several days afterwards I saw Roman Mirga a great deal. I made him fill me in on all the details and add more of his recollections. After I left Göttingen I plunged into research on the subject, interviewing scores of eyewitnesses and delving into various archives in order to gather and to cross-check the information. Then I started to write, allowing Roman Mirga to tell his own story and the stories of his family, his tribe, and of the forgotten holocaust of the Gypsy people.

PART ONE

The doors of all the cattle trucks in front of ours were unbolted by armed SS men who were holding German Shepherd dogs on leashes. From our ventilation slat I watched the Jews being ordered out, and those who moved too slowly were helped down the planks by a rifle butt or a snarling attack from one of the dogs.

People lined up, women holding babies in their arms, men and children carrying battered valises or bundles. "Why are they keeping us in the truck?" Franko Zbar asked worriedly. My father kept silent. He and I, glued to our observation spots, watched with apprehension what was happening. A German officer, followed by his aides, was walking alongside the Jews and with a thumb pointing to the left or the right. Soldiers immediately shoved the people to the side directed by their superior. All the old people, those who looked ill, and small children were being sent to the left. There were desperate cries as families were separated. I saw one woman, sent to the right, bolting out of her line and joining her little girl on the left. An SS guard tried to push her away. "I don't want to live any longer!" the woman shouted, clinging to the sobbing child, its little arms clutching her mother's neck. Magnanimously the SS officer waved the guard off. *"Lassen sie da!* Leave her there!"

Suddenly our door was flung open. The SS men shouted, *"Raus, Zigeuner!"* A plank was thrown down and we descended, all of us, our dark Gypsy faces ashen from fear in the broad daylight. The thick stench of unwashed human bodies and sweat wafted sourly in the air.

Two trucks were coming towards us. The soldiers ordered us to climb on to the vehicles. A young SS lieutenant asked who our leader was. "I am," my father answered in German.

"You are going to *Zigeunerlager,*" the officer said. "The Gypsy camp, the family camp. You'll like it there."

"What will happen to us?" my father's voice wavered.

"What do you mean? Nothing. You are not Jews, you are Aryans, like us." These were exactly the words that Colonel Krüger had uttered in Brest Litovsk at Mikita Kowal's birthday party.

"But this is a . . . concentration camp." I knew from the pause my father made that he wanted to say a different word, perhaps 'extermination,' but thought better of it.

"You'll work. We need all the manpower we can get, to help us in our effort to crush the Bolsheviks." Again the familiar words of Colonel Krüger. "In that camp you'll find Sintis, some of them officers and soldiers of the Wehrmacht." He smiled indulgently, keeping up the conversation as a few of the soldiers boarded the vehicles with us and the others closed up the rear. *"Gute Reise!"* he added. "Have a good journey!"

Where were we going, I wondered. Suddenly the spirits of those around me rose. Auschwitz had been just a stop on our way to discharge the Jews. People need to believe in the best, not the worst. The men of our kumpania had not seen the execution of the Gypsies on the road to Lukov, had not seen the flames of Sobibor as I had.

The trucks started. We drove on a road alongside a branch railway line that was being built, with scores of men working on it in the striped uniforms of the camp. On our right stretched a forest, with farmhouses dotting its edges. The countryside waking up to the spring looked peaceful and pastoral—contrasting sharply with the emaciated band from the camp working on our left. All the time, preoccupied with what was happening to us, I scarcely felt Zoya's hand in mine. But now I squeezed it with feigned reassurance, before I looked at my father, an old habit, one of 18 years. His face remained grim in spite of what he had heard from the SS lieutenant. I turned to my mother. She was drying the tears which she had shed for my sister. "We shall find her," I said to her, leaning forward and kissing her cheek. "When the war is over." My voice trailed off. I could hardly believe what I was saying.

Abruptly the barbed wire and the watch-towers on the left of our road came to an end. The people in my truck smiled with relief. Even when a new camp and new barbed wire came into view, their mood did not change. "This is the other camp—for us," my grandfather Sandu said. "A work camp."

We passed through a gate with armed sentries guarding the entrance. A huge complex of wooden barracks with a few brick buildings stretched in front of us. "Birkenau," an SS man explained helpfully. We rode past a men's camp and a women's camp, but as I saw that the prisoners had the Star of David sewn on to their jackets, a cold shiver ran down my spine. We *were* in another camp, but Jews were there, too. And where there were Jews, nothing good could be in store for us. The German lieutenant had deceived us. But then suddenly another part of the camp came into view. Incredibly, I saw groups of old women chatting among themselves, old men smoking pipes or playing harmonicas, children dancing and laughing. Everyone around me was peering out eagerly. "They are our people!" Gregory Mular shouted jubilantly. Gypsies in the camp waved to us.

"The officer did not lie!" my grandfather said spiritedly.

We stopped at the last barrack. "Sauna!" the SS guard volunteered. "*Entlausung*—disinfection!"

From the barrack a fatherly looking SS sergeant rushed out to meet us. "Only the men may come down!" he shouted. "Women wait!" As we began to climb down from the truck, he added reassuringly, "You're dirty after the trip. You'll take showers and change your clothes." Again I looked at my father. He nodded slightly as if agreeing with the sergeant. I turned to Zoya still on the truck, her eyes following me, and gave her a nod like my father had done.

We trudged into the building. There was a long table manned by Gypsy prisoners in blue and white striped trousers and jackets, supervised by SS guards. "Undress!" the sergeant ordered. "And hand over your clothes." We did as instructed, one after another handing over what

135

we had. I tried to keep my gold watch, but the sergeant said, "Everything! You must keep nothing. It will be given back to you!" The prisoner behind the table asked in perfect German, "What's your name?" He must be a Sinti, I decided. I answered and saw him scribbling my name on a tag and pinning it to my clothes. My father held his fiddle tight to himself. "It will be given back to you," the SS guard said to him. "All Gypsies get their instruments back. Get into the sauna."

But the next room to which we were sent, naked as the day we were born, was not the sauna. I saw several Jewish prisoners here, each behind a chair, each holding hairclippers in his hand. I sat between my father and my uncle Rudolf. The prisoners, I guessed, were professional barbers, brought from another part of the camp for the occasion. They all looked very thin, their bones protruding, their eyes sunk deep, wearing a perennially sad, resigned expression. My hair was being swiftly cut off, and I watched it falling down, the only blond locks on the floor among dark Gypsy hair. "Ready?" the SS guard asked me. "Go, take a shower!" He pointed at a door, in front of which I noticed another Jewish prisoner with a huge pile of towels and a basin filled with cakes of soap. I was handed a bar and a towel and passed through the door.

I saw several rows of showers. "Hell!" I heard Franko Zbar hiss his disgust. "When I wash, I feel dirty. I no longer feel like a man." But in he went and so did all of us. For me it was not a problem. I had always taken showers in Warsaw. The water was icy cold. I dried myself and came out. Our clothes had already gone; the hair, swept up from the floor, was being packed into sacks. Three sacks bore labels in German, 'Foreign currency,' 'Jewellery,' 'Watches.' My heart turned over. I was certain my gold watch was in that last sack.

The same prisoners we had seen before had striped uniforms ready, piled up for us on the table. Each of us was handed a set and also a pair of wooden shoes picked up from baskets on the floor. "I have two left ones," I heard Antoni Puma complain. "Mine are too big," Bora Natkin protested. "Mine too small," Leon Kwiatek said. "This is not a shoe shop," the SS sergeant intervened. "No exchange is allowed. Be quick, your ladies are waiting."

We were led out of the back door and, slushing through the mud, reached an alleyway running parallel to the main one. We could not see our women, nor they us. With a heavy heart I thought of my wife's beautiful long raven hair about to land on the floor, put into a sack, and then probably taken by train on the way to Germany. I hardly noticed I was entering a barrack or being ushered to a long table behind which sat another group of Sinti prisoners, again under the supervision of SS guards. "Stand in line!" an SS man said. I could no longer see the sergeant. He had apparently chosen to stay with the women.

We formed a queue. While my father-in-law and my uncle were exchanging their shoes behind me, I heard a guard ordering, "Bare your arms!" I did not understand why, but the first of the prisoners behind the table was dipping a needle into an inkpot and tattooing the capital letter 'Z' and a four-digit number on my father's forearm.

When my turn came I was passed on to another man who opened a folder and wrote on top of it, 'Auschwitz II-BII E.' Birkenau, I realized, was part of the big Auschwitz complex of camps. The man was filling in the questionnaire with the answers to my name, age, place of birth, tribe, and other particulars. He wrote German and spoke German.

When our registration was over, we were all taken to another barrack. The SS sergeant was coming across the camp towards us. "This is where you'll live," he said amiably. "Welcome! By the way, my name is Otto Fürst. This barrack is mine."

We entered. The place was partly filled with Gypsies, old people and children, the latter wearing oversized adult camp clothing with sleeves that hid their hands, and trousers that swept the floor. They all surged towards us, talking at once in Polish, Czech, German, and various Romany dialects.

"Stand back!" The sergeant raised his hand to them. "Let the new arrivals settle first, you can talk later." I saw bunks with straw mattresses and a single blanket, three in a group, one on top of another, awaiting us. The barrack had two doors, on its left and right, a tall stove, and two tables in the middle where, surprisingly, stood vases with fresh-cut flowers. "From our own nurseries," the sergeant said. "Welcome!" Then he amiably patted the head of one of our little boys who had just taken off his huge jacket, trying to figure out how to shorten it. "Hey, where is your number?" the sergeant asked. The boy pulled down his trousers and showed his little buttocks and the number tattooed there. His forearm had been too narrow to accommodate the letter and four digits.

Some of the men burst out laughing, which the sergeant chose to ignore, but at this moment our women entered. They wore prisoners' striped uniforms and their heads were shaven. My eyes darted towards Zoya. She was trying to hide the crown of her head with her hand, and so was my mother who was right behind her. My heart went out to them both. My father closed his eyes tight as if he could not bear the humiliation.

Exhausted from the ordeal, we all lay down. Our family took one triple-tier bunk, each narrow bed for two people. My grandparents took the bottom bunk closest to the floor, my parents the middle one, and

Zoya and I had the top one. We had to climb up, but at least we also had most of the fresh air from the cracks in the roof.

"I'm sorry," my wife said.

"Sorry for what?"

"My hair." She kept her distance, unsure of my reaction, her hands still trying to cover her bare head.

"My God!" I said and took her into my arms. "I love you, for yourself, not for your looks." She burst into uncontrollable crying. "I mean," I added quickly, "It doesn't matter, your hair, besides it will grow back. Haven't you seen the others? They allow the hair to grow back. They shave it just the one time, for hygiene."

"How long will it take? For my hair to grow back."

My lovely Zoya. All she was concerned about in this concentration camp was her looks, so that she could again be her beautiful self for her husband. "A few months."

"I must get a scarf," she said. "From somewhere, but I must."

Suddenly a gong sounded. A large container was being wheeled in by other Gypsy prisoners. "Come and eat!" they shouted in Polish. We clambered down. There was now a stack of tin cups and plates and aluminium cutlery on the table. Sergeant Fürst was in charge. "Take a set," he ordered, "and keep them. Remember, it's the property of the Third Reich. Don't lose them. Get in line."

We did so. We got real Gypsy soup made from nettles, and bread. Our family shared a whole loaf—part oats, part potatoes, part sawdust. The soup was good and warm and we did not mind what the bread was made from. This was to be our daily bread from now on, to fill our empty stomachs, and we blessed the heavens for it.

Although it was daytime, we settled down on our bunks to get some sleep after all the time and travelling since being caught on the road in Hungary. Zoya, more confidently, cuddled into my shoulder and, when I kissed her, she eagerly, as if almost disbelieving it, smothered me passionately with kisses. I made love to her, not because I really felt like it or had a strength to, but because it was the only thing I could do to convince her that I loved her even without her hair, and at the same time to reassure ourselves that we were both alive in Auschwitz.

Later in the afternoon we were awakened by the gong. Sergeant Fürst and the SS guards were calling us to get into line. They were being helped by some Sinti kapos who were better treated than anyone else because they assisted the Nazis. Across the same muddy ground we were marched to the same barrack where we had been tattooed and had had files opened on us.

This time three officers were sitting behind the table, our documents in front of them. They began assigning jobs—young men to laying water pipes in the hard ground, young women to levelling muddy ground. Those who were past middle age were directed to cleaning latrines or to carrying the food containers. Like all the families we stood together, my parents, grandparents, Zoya and I. I noticed that one of the officers was dressed differently from the others. He wore jodhpur boots and white gloves, as if he had been called on duty just before going out riding.

Slowly our turn came. The officer wearing the gloves picked up my father's file, then looked up, his eyes squinting as if searching his memory. What struck me about him was not just his swarthy, almost Gypsylike complexion, but a large cleft between his upper teeth that somehow looked familiar. The German raised his forefinger. "I know you," he said, pointing it at my father.

A flash of recognition dawned on my father and me at the same time. "Fukier's Wine Cellar," my father said.

"Of course! In Warsaw Old Town."

"You asked me to play Brahms and Liszt. You're a doctor, from Bavaria."

"Correct! Doktor Josef Mengele. Do you have your fiddle with you?"

"They took it away in the sauna."

"You'll get it back. Immediately!" Excitedly the officer leaned towards the one sitting next to him and whispered something in German that we could not hear. His colleague nodded approval. "You'll play in a Gypsy orchestra," Mengele said.

"Orchestra?" my father asked, bewildered.

"Of course. What kind of a Gypsy camp would it be without an orchestra?"

He quickly made a note on my father's file and the captain next to him, apparently the head of the commission, signed it 'Hauptsturmbannführer Perry Board.' Dr. Mengele added his signature, 'Hauptsturmbannführer Doktor Josef Mengele.'

"My son, my wife, you remember them?" Father said. "They were playing with me that same night at Fukier's. And my daughter-in-law, she is a dancer, a very good dancer."

"It's a string orchestra," Mengele said. "And you're the only one of your family who plays violin. Remember, I invited you to come to my home-town for an engagement?" He chuckled. "Well, I have kept my promise. Auschwitz is now my home-town." Again he consulted his colleagues, then looked at the files. "Your women will get jobs in the kitchen—your parents won't work—too old. As for the young man, well, he looks good and strong . . ."

"My son finished high school in Warsaw," my father said quickly. "He speaks perfect German."

"So do all the Sinti."

"But they don't speak Polish. He speaks perfect Polish, too."

"*Dolmetscher*, eh? Translator. Well, we do have a number of Polish Gypsies here . . ." He pointed again with his finger. "Because you are an artist, who plays real Gypsy music, and because he is your son, I will take him to my office. As *Dolmetscher* he will be useful."

"Thank you, sir," my father said and gave me a nudge.

"Thank you," I repeated.

We walked out of the barrack. Almost immediately some of the Elders who were in our barrack before us, joined us and began asking where we came from. Were there still Gypsies travelling the roads? What was happening at the front? However, we were even more eager than they to ask questions, to find out about the camp. Most of them came from Poland, from the Bialystok area. They had been here for months. Only recently, they said, had they been given striped camp uniforms; before that they had worn their own clothes. There had also been a canteen where they could buy cigarettes, sausage, razor blades. But their money had been taken from them, for their own protection. Gypsies steal even from Gypsies, they had said. And then of course they closed the canteen.

"How many people are in the Zigeunerlager?" my father asked.

"Six thousand at present. Some have been sent to other camps. Still, life is bearable. In the other parts of the camp, where the Jews are, there is only one end in sight. Some SS men joke that they come here through the gate and get out through the chimneys. The chimneys of the crematoria."

"Where are the crematoria?"

"There," an old man with a wizened face pointed. "Among the trees. Four brick buildings, 300 meters behind you."

"I don't see any smoke coming out of the chimneys."

"Closed for repairs. Just for a day or two."

Suddenly my father took a step forward. "That man there, isn't that Janusz Kwiek, king of the Kelderari?"

"Yes," a number of people answered at once. My father shook his head painfully. I looked at the stooped old man surrounded by others, standing in a group. He felt my father's glance on him and came forward.

140

"Are you Kelderari, the group that came in today?"

"No, we are Polska Roma, the Lowland Gypsies. But I played at your coronation in Warsaw. I played violin."

The old man waved his hand. "Just a memory."

"It was a splendid affair. The Polish primate, the archbishop of Gniezno, anointed your Majesty. And I remember your speech. You said," my father talked excitedly, "that it is our duty to educate our sons and daughters, so that one day the Gypsy nation may take its rightful place as a member of the League of Nations."

Kwiek smiled. "July 4, 1937. Only seven years ago. Seems an eternity. Are there any Gypsies free outside?"

"Oh, yes. In Hungary, at least."

"Not for long, not for long." He looked at me and Zoya. "Sooner or later we will share the fate of the Jews. But you, you younger ones, try to escape if you can. Save yourselves. Have children and educate them." He blinked his eyes, then rubbed them. "I'm tired, I must lie down."

And he walked away. We watched in silence as the lonely, bent figure of the king of the Gypsies, in the striped uniform of the camp, receded into the distance on the Lagerstrasse of Auschwitz.

PART III

HOW AND WHY?

"I also want to speak very frankly about an extremely important subject. Among ourselves we will discuss it openly; in public, however, we must never mention it. . . .

"I mean the evacuation of the Jews, the extermination of the Jewish people. This is something that is easy to talk about. 'The Jewish people will be exterminated,' says every member of the party, 'this is clear, this is in our program: the elimination, the extermination of the Jews: we will do this.' And then they come to you—80 million good Germans—and each one has his 'decent' Jew. Naturally, all the rest are pigs, but this particular Jew is first-rate. Not one of those who talk this way has seen the bodies, not one has been on the spot. Most of you know what it is to see a pile of one hundred or five hundred or one thousand bodies. To have stuck it out and at the same time, barring exceptions caused by human weakness, to have remained decent: this is what has made us tough. . . .

"This is a glorious page in our history which never has and never will be written."

SS Reichsführer Heinrich Himmler
Speech to a meeting of SS generals in Posen on October 4, 1943

The Third Reich

This brief history examines the reasons for the failure of democracy in Germany, and describes the means by which Hitler came to power. As you read, note these key concepts which help to explain why Germany was fertile ground for a dictatorship: extreme nationalism, idealization of the military, little experience of democracy, humiliating defeat in World War I, economic depression, unemployment.

The Third Reich in Perspective

GERTRUDE NOAR

M odern German history is the history of the failure of German democracy. The roots of Nazism lie in that history of failure.

Until late into the 19th century, long after most western peoples were united, the word "Germany" did not refer to a single nation, but to a Central European patchwork of over 100 German states ranging in size from minuscule to middling. Each was more or less independent and under the autocratic rule of a petty prince or—in the case of larger ones like Prussia and Bavaria—a king. In the Middle Ages every attempt to impose a central authority upon the German lands had proved abortive, the Holy Roman Empire being more a fiction than a fact. In the 16th century, the Lutheran Reformation had tremendous effects which still affect our lives today, but it too failed to bring about the unification of Germany.

The world-shaking French Revolution, at the end of the 18th century, with its ideals of liberty, equality, and fraternity expressed politically in rule by Parliament, failed to inspire the German people to similar effort. The aristocracy and landed gentry fought all attempts to establish a parliament based on democratic suffrage. When a great wave of revolution swept Europe in 1848, democratic uprisings also took place in Berlin, the capital of Prussia, and in other German states. The German liberals, supported by most of the middle class and peasantry, came to power for the first time. But they lacked resolution and compromised with the Prussian military autocracy and the German princes. In the end many were forced to flee Germany for England or America.

Until 1848 democracy and nationalism had more or less gone hand in hand in Germany, as they had in western Europe and America. But after the failure to institute liberal reforms in 1848, this situation changed. Prussia—the strongest of the German states, thanks to a powerful army commanded by a military elite—set about uniting Germany under its own rule. Prussia's Prime Minister, Otto von Bismarck, used a policy of intimidation and conquest to bring about the unification.

The union was completed on January 18, 1871, when the Prussian King was proclaimed Kaiser of the German Reich (Emperor of the German Empire) after the defeat of France in the Franco-Prussian War. Thus, Germany did not unite voluntarily on the basis of a democratic parliamentary system, which was the pattern in western Europe and America; rather did Prussia unite the German people by conquering them. From the alliance between German nationalism and Prussian militarism there followed all those sinister events of modern German history which culminated in the catastrophe of Nazism.

William L. Shirer writes: "Bismarck's unique creation is the Germany we have known in our time . . . in which first this remarkable man and then Kaiser Wilhelm II and finally Hitler, aided by a military caste . . . succeeded in inculcating a lust for power and domination, a passion for unbridled militarism, a contempt for democracy and individual freedom and a longing for authority. . . ."

Bismarck announced the future course of Prussian Germany in 1862 by declaring: "The great questions of the day will not be settled by resolutions and majority votes—that was the mistake of the men of 1848— but by blood and iron."

The policy of blood and iron, of war and conquest and empire, led Imperial Germany into World War I, which, after years of enormous slaughter, ended with her ignominious surrender and the abdication and flight of Kaiser Wilhelm II. The revolution that broke out in November 1918 again presented Germany with an opportunity to reconstruct herself on democratic foundations, and again she failed, although the failure did not become apparent at once.

The Weimar Republic proclaimed by the Social Democrats at the end of 1918 was established quite half-heartedly, as it were, by default. It was born out of defeat in war and not out of a triumph of democratic sentiment. And indeed the old Junker landowning and military class remained very much alive and powerful. Although the Weimar Constitution was a model liberal and democratic *document*, the Republic rested on shaky foundations so long as it failed to disarm and defeat all those hostile classes and groups which were biding their time and merely tolerating a democratic regime: the feudal Junker landlords and upper castes, the General Staff and military caste, the industrial magnates, and the heads of the Prussian bureaucracy.

The Social Democrats, or Labor party, who were the largest single political organization, vacillated. Instead of moving energetically to destroy these hostile elements, they compromised with them, just as German liberalism had compromised with the autocracy in the 19th century. Later these same reactionary elements, in spite of their dislike for Hitler as a vulgar demagogue, would finally install him in power.

The Weimar period from 1918 to 1933 was just such a time of turmoil and disorder as was needed to spawn the Nazi movement. Almost immediately after the end of the war, reactionary groups began to clamor that the army had not been defeated by the Allies at the front, but had been "stabbed in the back" at home by democrats and socialists. They said this even though they knew the General Staff had compelled the Imperial government to sue for an armistice long before there was any revolutionary disturbance, by informing it that the army could not carry on the war any longer.

Armed bands of terrorists and freebooters assassinated liberals, democrats, and socialists, and supported attempts to overthrow the government. The humiliating Versailles Treaty was laid at the door of the Weimar democrats. The mark began to fall. By 1923 it was worth four billion to the American dollar. The savings of the middle class, the principal depositors, were wiped out and there was general impoverishment and desperation.

When the crash of 1929 ushered in the worldwide Depression, factory production declined drastically, businesses closed, and millions were thrown out of work. Conditions bred fear and despair, which in turn, bred violent hatreds. Adolf Hitler knew how to play on these feelings and enlist them in the service of nationalist delirium, hatred of democracy, and the drive for military domination and conquest—which, for all his talk of a Nazi "revolution," were the more or less traditional features of Prussian Germanism.

Adolf Hitler was born on April 20, 1889, in the Austrian town of Braunau-on-the-Inn, across the border from Bavaria. Austria was then a part of the Austro-Hungarian Empire. The Austrians spoke German and many, like Hitler, thought of themselves as German and looked with contempt on the other, mostly Slavic, nationalities that made up the Empire. The youthful Hitler wished passionately to become an artist, but was rejected by the Vienna Academy of Fine Arts as lacking talent. He spent four crucial years, 1909–13, in Vienna, most of the time as a down-and-out tramp shunning regular employment. During these years, Hitler crystallized his own brooding hatreds and resentments into a philosophy. Its cornerstones were: glorification of war and conquest; exaltation of the Germans as the Master Race; hatred of the Jews; contempt for democracy.

In 1913 Hitler went to Munich and when World War I broke out enlisted in the German army. After the war he stayed in the army and was assigned to spy on political parties in Munich which the military considered dangerous. One such party was the tiny German Workers party, which turned out to be violently nationalist. Hitler, instead of reporting it to the authorities, was the seventh man to join it, in 1919. The name of this party was changed to the National Socialist German Workers party in 1920 ("Nazi" is an abbreviation of the first part of the German title). Under Hitler's frenzied leadership it grew from a tiny group to a mass organization with millions of members. Eventually it became the only political party in Germany.

Hitler built the Nazi party in frank emulation of the mass party of the Social Democrats; in Vienna he had been impressed by the great demonstrations of Viennese Social working men, their popular press, and their oratory. But the Social Democratic party was democratic—what did Hitler see in it to serve his dictatorial purpose? Hitler had appreciated very early that in the modern age, German militarism and nationalism could no longer rule by means of the traditional aristocratic minorities and elites, but required the support of the "masses."

To win the mass support of unemployed factory workers, small farmers lacking land, threadbare and underfed office clerks and civil servants, shopkeepers on the verge of ruin, and disinherited middle class people, to whom the Communist party was also appealing, the Nazis needed to promise more than anti-Semitism and anti-Communism, nationalism and militarism. They needed to pretend that they would carry out a social revolution. (Hence the word "Socialist" in the party name. The Nazi "social" aims were dropped soon after the party came to power.)

At the very first public meeting of the Nazi party in 1920, Hitler's talents as a demagogue and orator had marked effect. His pounding fists, burning eyes, hoarse cries, and hysterics aroused his audience to a fever pitch. He outlined a 25-point program, which became the party's official platform, that promised everything to everybody. Among other things he promised a larger "living space" (i.e., more territory) for Germany; full citizenship only for people of "German blood"; confiscation of war profits; old age pensions; low rentals to small businessmen; anti-Communism, and abolition of interest on land and mortgages.

By 1923 the party membership had grown from the handful of 1920 to some 17,000, most of it concentrated in and around Munich. In November of that year, Hitler enlisted the support of General Erich von Ludendorf and attempted to carry out what has since come to be known as the "Beer Hall Putsch": he proclaimed the outbreak of the "national revolution" in a Munich beer hall and announced that the Bavarian and Reich governments were dissolved. A few shots fired by the authorities sufficed to rout the Nazi "revolutionaries." The Nazi party was banned. He was released after less than a year, at the end of 1924—the Weimar judges, for the most part the old judiciary of Kaiser Wilhelm days, being always tolerant of treason when committed by nationalists. Hitler seemed defeated and discredited.

After completing his autobiography, *Mein Kampf* (My Battle), which openly revealed his sinister political intentions, Hitler set out to re-build the National Socialist party. No more "putsches" from now on; he had learned his lesson. Now he would capture power legally. "We shall have to hold our noses and go into the Reichstag," he said.

In the years from 1925 to the end of 1928, the Nazi membership was scarcely more than 100,000, in spite of active campaigning. But in 1929 the Depression struck Germany. In the hunger, despair, and chaos that it brought, Hitler at last found his chance; millions of Germans began to listen to the promises and threats he vociferated daily. Where the Nazis had polled 810,000 votes in 1928, in the fall of 1930 they polled six-and-a-half million, increasing their seats in the Reichstag from 12 to 107. They were now second only to the Social Democrats.

Meanwhile the Nazi party had grown into a vast apparatus orga-nized down to the street and block level, and complete with special sections for children, youth, women, professional groups, and labor or-ganizations. It published innumerable newspapers and magazines. The party itself was organized like the government and became a state within a state. The brown-shirted Storm Troopers (*Sturm Abteilungen*—SA), the Nazi armed force, were bands of thugs who conquered the streets for Hitler by beating and killing opponents and breaking up their meetings. Everywhere the Nazi emblem of the swastika, the crooked cross which so perfectly expressed the sinister spirit of Hitlerism, was in evidence.

With a powerful mass organization and an electoral following of millions, Hitler now began to look to the top. In the spring of 1932, he ran for president (head of the state; the chancellor was head of the gov-ernment) against the incumbent, Field Marshal Paul von Hindenburg. He failed, and Hindenburg was re-elected, but the Nazi party had in-creased its vote to 13.5 million. In two Reichstag elections in 1932 Hitler tried to win a majority of Germans to his party so as to become chancel-lor and form a government of his own. The Nazis won nearly 14 million votes in the first, and became the largest German party, but still they fell short of a majority. In the second election the Nazi vote fell off by two million.

At this point a union of the anti-Nazi forces could have stopped Hitler. But the Communists were attacking the Social Democrats as "social fascists" and looking to the victory of Hitler as a stage along the way to their own capture of power. They denounced the Weimar Repub-lic as violently as the Nazis.

The conservative and reactionary groups, the ever-powerful Prussian Junkers, army and big business, who had only tolerated the Republic, were now prepared to bury it. Using Hitler as their tool, they hoped eventually to restore the Hohenzollern monarchy. Through Franz von Papen they made a deal with Hitler agreeing to back him for chancellor. In return for this they would retain the preponderance of power for themselves, including the vice-chancellorship and most of the cabinet posts. On January 30, 1933, President von Hindenburg appointed Adolf Hitler Chancellor of Germany.

The Nazi leader had no intention of serving as the Junkers' tool. In only a few months he became dictator. He used the occasion of the Reichstag fire in February 1933, which the Nazis almost certainly started themselves but which they blamed on the Communists, to attack and drive out of existence not only the Communist party but the democratic anti-Nazi parties.

In spite of the Nazi reign of terror which was now backed up by the power of the state, Hitler still failed to capture a majority of the vote in the last free elections in March 1933. At this point the Nazis simply refused to seat the Communist delegates who had been elected, threatened other delegates with the same fate, and thus secured the two-thirds majority by which the Constitution was amended, to place all legislative functions in Hitler's hands. Now he and he alone made the laws, as well as executed them.

By the summer of 1933 the Nazis were the only party in Germany. They proceeded to nazify German life completely (their word for this process was *Gleichschaltung*), bringing it under the total domination of the political religion (ideology) of National Socialism. They nazified the Christian churches as well, and even made efforts to replace them with an outright pagan racist ("Nordic") ritual. "Totalitarianism" is the term we have coined to describe the total control of a nation's life by a mass political movement. Concentration camps, that dreadful invention of the 20th century, were set up in which to lock up opponents of the regime: liberals, radicals, Jews, religious leaders, and intellectuals.

These descriptions of individual Germans, what their lives were like, and their feelings, breathe life into the dry facts of history. The vignettes reveal Germans, in the year 1930, in every stratum of society, suffering the consequences of the Treaty of Versailles, which imposed harsh terms on the German vanquished. The mood of the country was one of growing bitterness and dissatisfaction.

This material is reprinted from *The Shaping of Western Society* by Edwin Fenton and John Goode.

Seven Case Studies

EDWIN FENTON AND JOHN GOODE

CASE 1

Hermann Struts, a lieutenant in the German army, has been a lieutenant since World War I when he fought bravely on the western front. Coming from a long line of military officers and having graduated from the German military academy, Hermann is proud of Germany's military tradition. His pride is personal, because his family had been part of that tradition, and it is general, because Germany had always boasted a fine army that had secured the nation's well-being and leadership.

Yet Hermann has not been promoted for more than 10 years. Because the German army had been so drastically reduced by the Treaty of Versailles, there have been relatively few promotions. In the old army, Hermann would have been at least a captain by now, because he is a resourceful officer. He probably would have been a major. Hermann resents the Versailles Treaty, which forced Germany to give up its military tradition. He believes this has forever injured Germany's honor, and his honor as a soldier. He feels that if the present government had vetoed the treaty and allowed the German army to resist it, neither Germany nor he would be in their present position.

CASE 2

Karin Hauptmann works in a textile factory in Berlin. Although her trade union has actively worked for better conditions and higher wages, it has not made many gains, primarily because the 1923 inflation and the present depression have weakened the entire economy. However, Karin believes that the union would succeed if the economy were stable. As it is, the union has kept her unemployed. When many of her friends were laid off, Karin's union persuaded the company managers to keep the senior employees. Factories where unions are weak kept only the younger employees, because the company managers say they are more productive.

Karin has been worried by the ideas many of her fellow workers have expressed recently. They have said that the greediness of the factory owners causes business cycles and that when the owners are forced to cut back production, they take it out on the workers. These fellow workers think the only way to end the Depression is to let the workers control the factories and the government. Karin still believes that the workers get fair treatment as long as there are strong unions. Moreover, she thinks that managing the factories and the government should be left to people who understand these complicated jobs.

CASE 3

Eric von Ronheim, chief executive of an electric motor factory in Frankfurt, is extremely concerned about the present economic Depression. Reduced production means lower profits for his company. If Germany had not been treated so harshly at Versailles, the nation would have enough resources to produce goods for consumption, and conditions would be far better. But the government had had to impose heavy taxes in order to pay the reparations the Allies had demanded. Indeed, much of his own profits are going into these taxes. Moreover, the overtaxed Germans have little money to spend on German goods, and so demand is dangerously low. Since other countries are also suffering from Depressions, there is almost no foreign market for German goods. Even if Germany were to come out of the Depression, Eric knows taxes would be increased to finish paying the reparations.

Eric is also worried about the menacing number of Communists in Germany who wish to organize the same kind of government as the Soviet Union has. If the Communists succeed, the capitalists would receive no mercy from the workers. And Germany would be controlled by its old enemy, the Soviet Union.

CASE 4

Karl Schmidt is a steelworker in the rich, steel-producing Ruhr Valley. But like so many people in the Ruhr, he is out of work. The Depression has forced many steel mills to shut down until there is a market for their goods. On the day Karl's mill closed, the owners announced that shrinking profits made it impossible to keep the workers on their jobs. Yet, Karl reasons, the owners still live in big houses and drive expensive automobiles. Why are the owners protected from this economic slump while the workers suffer? The government is helping the workers somewhat with unemployment compensation, but the payments are hardly enough to support Karl, his wife Anna, and their two children. Moreover, the government has declared that it has little money left, and it cannot continue the payments much longer.

As far as Karl understands, if the government would stop paying the reparations, perhaps it could help Germany recover. But Karl also knows that if the government stops its payments, the French might again occupy the Ruhr Valley, as they had in 1923. What is needed, Karl believes, is a government that listens to the workers—perhaps even one that is run by the workers, as some of his friends argue. And he feels Germany needs a government that can deny France and the other nations the reparation payments.

CASE 5

Lotte von Kohler, a prominent attorney who attended the University of Bonn, has a strong sense of the German cultural, literary, and historical traditions. She believes that the great gifts her people have contributed to western civilization have been ignored. Lotte dreams of a newly created republic uniting all the German democratic traditions and leading the way to a totally democratic Europe. She is upset by the unfortunate methods the Weimar Republic often uses to repress the parties of the extreme left more cruelly than those of the extreme right.

However, Lotte's sense of justice is more outraged by the demeaning attitude with which the Allies, particularly the French, view the German republic. She, and others like her who believe in Germany and human dignity, would like to prove to these countries that the Germans are a great race.

CASE 6

Wilhelm Schultz is a peasant who works with his parents on their farm in East Prussia. His aunt and uncle live just a few miles away, in the area of East Prussia that the Versailles Treaty had sectioned off as the Polish Corridor. They send reports describing how the Poles mistreat the Germans. Wilhelm's grandparents live nearby in Danzig, but their relatives never visit them. Going to Danzig means crossing into Poland which has many travel restrictions. Wilhelm's schooling had taught him great love for the German heroes like Siegfried, and he was dismayed that his government had signed a treaty that put many Germans, like his aunt and uncle, under Polish rule. Then again, he watches people who violate basic Prussian values rise to respected positions in the government. He sees that these people are often drunk and rowdy. This is not the way Prussians should behave, Wilhelm thinks.

Wilhelm and his parents are finding times hard. The thriving port of Danzig had once been the market for his parents' goods. Now it is difficult to ship goods there because they have to cross the Polish Corridor. Besides, the Poles have opened a rival port to take business away from Danzig. Moreover, the Depression does not make things easier. Finally, the Communists nearby in the Soviet Union are a constant threat to Wilhelm and his parents because they support the end of private property. Wilhelm and his parents are proud to call their land their own, for this gives them an added dignity. Communists want to take this land and this dignity from them—the last rewards the world seems to offer.

CASE 7

Gerda Munchen is the owner of a small Munich grocery store started by her parents. For years her parents had saved to send her to the university. But Gerda chose not to go to the university, and the money stayed in the bank. In 1923 Gerda had a good use for it. Her two daughters were both brilliant; one wanted to be a doctor, and the other hoped to be a lawyer. The money in the bank would have paid for their education. But that same year inflation had hit Germany because the government had printed so much money to pay the reparations. Since the money was not backed by anything economically solid, it had become nearly worthless. Two weeks before her older daughter was to leave for the university, the bank had called to say that her savings were worth only enough to buy three postage stamps. This was certainly a blow to Gerda, but it was more of a blow to her daughters whose futures hung in the balance. They asked her what kind of faith they could put in a system that ruined hardworking people.

Now in 1930, there seems little to be done to regain the losses. People are not making any money and, therefore, cannot buy as many groceries as they had before. And the competition from the big department and chain stores makes it difficult for Gerda to compete. Again Gerda's economic difficulties are not her fault. Her daughters once more question the system that has brought these hardships to their mother and to them.

The Communists offered one answer for Germany's problems, but most Germans rejected it. Hitler gave them what they were most hungry for—pride in being German, as well as hope for economic improvement. This is explained by Herr Damm, an "ordinary" German, to Milton Mayer, from whose book *They Thought They Were Free* the selection is taken.

Herr Damm

MILTON MAYER

" . . . I was a tobacco salesman," said Herr Damm, who had risen to be office manager of the Party headquarters in Kronenberg, "but I was let out when the state tobacco tax was raised 100 percent in 1930. I reported to the Labor Office immediately and wrote applications for every job, but I got no work. At first I drew unemployment compensation, but then, since I was still single, I was told I could go back home to the village and live on my father's farm, which, when my father died, my oldest brother would get. That's the way it was in the spring of 1932, when the National Socialists from Kronenberg held a recruiting evening in the village *Bierstube*. Only one member of each household was allowed to sign up, and my family all agreed that I was the one. I agreed, too. Why not? And, by the way, Herr Professor, it was the *only* political party that had ever held a recruiting meeting in our village as far back as anyone could remember. . . .

"Hitler was a simple soldier, like millions of others, only he had a *feeling* for masses of people, and he could speak with passion. The people didn't pay any attention to the Party program as such. They went to the meetings just to hear something new, anything new. They were desperate about the economic situation, 'a new Germany' sounded good to them; but from a deep or broad point of view they saw nothing at all. Hitler talked always against the government, against the lost war, against the peace treaty, against unemployment. All that, people liked. By the time the intellectuals asked, 'What is this?' it had a solid basis in the common people. It was the *Arbeiter, Sozialist* Party, the Party of *workers controlling the social order*; it was not for intellectuals.

"The situation in Germany got worse and worse. What lay underneath people's daily lives, the real root, was gone. Look at the suicides;

look at the immorality. People wanted something *radical,* a real change. This want took the form of more and more Communism, especially in middle Germany, in the industrial area, and in the cities of the north. *That* was no invention of Hitler; *that* was real. In countries like America there is no Communism because there is no desire for *radical* change.

"Hitlerism had to answer Communism with something just as radical. Communism always used force; Hitlerism answered it with force. The really absolute enemy of Communism, always clear, always strong in the popular mind, was National Socialism, the *only* enemy that answered Communism in kind. If you wanted to save Germany from Communism—to be *sure* of doing it—you went to National Socialism. The Nazi slogan of 1932 was, 'If you want your country to go Bolshevik, vote Communist; it you want to remain free Germans, vote Nazi.'

"The middle parties, between the two millstones, played no role at all between the two radicalisms. Their adherents were basically the *Bürger,* the bourgeois, the 'nice' people who decide things by parliamentary procedure; and the politically indifferent; and the people who wanted to keep or, at worst, only modify the status quo. . . ."

All 10 of my friends, including the sophisticated Hildebrandt, were affected by this sense of what the Germans call *Bewegung,* movement, a swelling of the human sea, something supraparty and suprapolitical, a surge of the sort that does not, at the time, evoke analysis or, afterward, yield to it. These men were victims of the "Bolshevik" rabies, to be sure. They were equally victims of economic hardship and, still worse, of economic hopelessness, a hopelessness that they suffered more easily by identifying it with their country's. But they were seekers, too, and affirmers—agents, not just patients.

Their country was torn to pieces from without, of course, but still more cruelly from within. Germans had been at one another's throats since 1918, and dissension grew shriller and more bitter all the time. In the course of the decomposition, the principle of *being German,* so newly won under Bismarck and so preciously held for fear of its slipping away, was indeed being lost. The uniting of the country, of all of its people, was possible only on this one principle of *being German,* and my 10 friends, even including the old fanatic Schwenke, onlookers at the disruptive struggles of the old parties and the old party politicians, at the process of shredding the mystical fabric which supported this principle, asked, "Where is Germany?" Nazism—Hitler, rather—knew this and knew that nothing else mattered to my friends so much as this, the identification of this Germany, the community again, in which one might know he belonged and, belonging, identify himself. This was the movement which any non-German might see at once for what it was; and this was the movement which restored my friends as the sight of home restores the lost child; or as the sight of the Lorelei Maiden, seen sitting high above the Rhine, combing her golden hair with a golden comb in the surprising late sunshine, bewitches the sailor, who overlooks the rocks beneath the river.

National Socialism was a revulsion by my friends against parliamentary politics, parliamentary debate, parliamentary government—against all the higgling and the haggling of the parties and the splinter parties, their coalitions, their confusions, and their conniving. It was the final fruit of the common man's repudiation of "the rascals." Its motif was, "Throw them all out."

My friends wanted Germany purified. They wanted it purified of the politicians, of *all* the politicians. They wanted a representative leader in place of unrepresentative representatives.

Against "the whole pack," "the whole kaboodle," "the whole business," against *all* the parliamentary politicians and *all* the parliamentary parties, my friends evoked Hitlerism, and Hitlerism overthrew them all. . . .

"Yes," said Herr Damm, "our family were always great anti-Semites. My father and grandfather were followers of Dr. Böckel, who founded the Anti-Semitic Party in Hesse, way back in the '80s. We used to have the Party flag, with the anti-Semitic inscription on it, 'Freedom from Jewry,' but the Americans took it away."

"Did you ever have any dealings with Jews?" I said.

"Always," he said. "We had to, in the country. Before the farmers' credit union was founded by Dr. Böckel—it was anti-Semitic, to save the farmers from the Jews—we were at the mercy of the cattle dealers. They were all Jews, and they all worked together."

"How do you know that they all worked together, Herr Damm?"

"They always do. They held us in the palm of their hand. Do you know what one of them once did? He bought a calf from my father and took it to town and sold it to my father's cousin, *at a profit.*"

"Yes," I said, "but that is just the profit system. You believe in the profit system, don't you? You're certainly no Communist!"

"Of course," he said, "but only think—to my father's own cousin! If my father had known his cousin wanted the calf, he could have sold it to him himself, without the Jew."

"Well—" I said.

"Look, Herr Professor, a Jew buys a cow. When he buys it, it's terrible, everything's wrong with it, he wouldn't have it for a gift. So he pays a few marks for it. Then he goes to the next farmer with it, to sell it, and it's the most wonderful cow in the world. Do you see what I mean?"

"I think so," I said, wreathed, internally, with a smile as I thought of "the American Way," "but don't Germans," that is, non-Jews, "buy as low and sell as high as possible?"

"Yes, but that's just it. Look, Herr Professor," he went on, patiently, "Germans couldn't trade with one another. There was always a Jew between them. All Jews are *Händler*, traders, never workers or farmers. Every child knows this. All trade was in the hands of the Jews. What could we poor Germans"—he was speaking of what Hitler calls, in *Mein Kampf*, the "genius-race"—"do?"

I liked Herr Damm. He was a professional clodhopper—he had been used for Party work among the farmers, whose "language," that is, whose mind, he spoke—but he was still a clodhopper. On another occasion, he was visiting me in town; or, rather, since it was to be our last talk together, I was his host at a one-dollar deluxe dinner at Kronenberg's best restaurant. I brought the talk back to one of our first conversations, in which he had told me that he was the only *Kreisamtsleiter* in our whole *Gau* who had refused to leave the Church. "I told them I was born in the Church," he had said, "and I would die in it, and not in the 'German Church,' but the Christian Church."

"Now," I said, as we were lighting up after dinner, "what many Christians in America cannot understand is how you Christians in Germany could accept the persecution of the Jews, no matter how bad they were. How could you accept it as *Christians*?"

It was the first time I had taken the initiative on the subject. "The Jews?"—he said—"but the Jews were the *enemies* of the Christian religion. Others might have other reasons for destroying them, but we Christians had the *Christian duty* to. Surely, Herr Professor, you know how the Jews betrayed our Lord?"

These excepts from William Allen's *The Nazi Seizure of Power* shed further light on German willingness to follow Hitler. The author provides information about some of the ingenious means by which the Nazis won support.

The Hitler Youth movement was formed for the express purpose of creating loyal subjects to the state. By 1935, over three million boys and girls aged 10 and older were enrolled. "We were born to die for Germany" was one of their popular slogans. In addition to a strenuous physical fitness program, they received training in the use of weapons and heard lectures on Nazi ideology.

Why I Joined the Hitler Youth

WILLIAM ALLEN

There was no pressure put on me by my father or anyone else to join the Hitler Youth—I decided to join it independently simply because I wanted to be in a boy's club where I could strive towards a nationalistic ideal. The Hitler Youth had camping, hikes, and group meetings. I was number nine in the Thalburg group when I joined in 1930. There were boys from all classes of families though mainly middle class and workers. There were no social or class distinctions, which I approved of very much. There was no direct or obvious political indoctrination until later—after Hitler came to power. Without really trying to get new members, the Thalburg Hitler Youth grew rapidly. I think most of the other boys joined for the same reason I did. They were looking for a place where they could get together with other boys in exciting activities. It was also a Depression time and there were many such influences abroad from which decent boys wished to escape. In any event, I don't think the political factor was the main reason boys joined. We did march in parades and hated the SPD, but that was all general, not specific—it was all a part of it. We weren't fully conscious of what we were doing, but we enjoyed ourselves and also felt important.

A Town Goes Nazi

WILLIAM ALLEN

T he factors that brought Thalburg to the brink of the Third Reich with a three-fifths Nazi majority (almost double the national average) were not numerous, but they were complexly interrelated. Paramount among them was the Depression. Though only the working class suffered physically in the three-year crisis, the town's middle class was more decisively affected through fears that an ultimate catastrophe would thrust upon it the same fate as the "shelterless," or that social revolution would destroy its status. More important than the actual misery caused by the Depression was the constant flow of news items stressing that misery.

There were only 17 bankruptcies in Thalburg in the entire Depression era, 11 of which befell small, marginal shopowners, and the other six for causes dissociated from the Depression. But the bankruptcies were strung out over a long period of time and each involved lengthy and dolorous legal proceedings, all faithfully reported in the press. At the high point of unemployment, in April 1932, only eight percent of the townspeople were unemployed, but the constant protests, fights, demonstrations, and the endless stream of gray-faced workers coming to the District Employment Office kept unemployment uppermost in the minds of the town's middle class. Nazi agitation drew upon this mood and intensified the unsettled atmosphere.

Thalburg was a nationalistic town long before 1930, though as the Depression wore on, commitment to nationalism and militarism increased. Outside forces contributed to this, as did Nazi propaganda, but by manipulating the symbols of patriotism the NSDAP in Thalburg associated itself with an important tradition. The same applied to the Nazis' exploitation of religious feelings, especially their use of Lutheran pastors as speakers in Thalburg.

A further factor which aided the rise of Nazism in Thalburg was politicalization. The yearnings and needs created by the Depression, class antagonisms, and resurgent nationalism all seemed capable of political solution. Constant elections meant constant campaigning and each campaign spurred bitterness and radicalism. From the local elections of November 1929, to the Reichstag elections of November 1932, there were nine major campaigns, five in 1932 alone. Thalburgers voted heavily in all of these. This followed the pattern of the whole electoral district, which had the second highest voting participation record of Germany's 35 electoral districts. In Thalburg, between 94 percent and 97 percent of those eligible voted in each of the major elections. Since registration was automatic, only the sick and feeble-minded stayed home. The rest were involved in politics, which is to say that political passion pervaded almost all areas of human existence in Thalburg.

Nazi propaganda efforts in Thalburg went beyond pure activism. Persistent, imaginative, and driving effort was coupled with a shrewd appreciation of what was specifically suitable for Thalburg, and for each element in the town. Aside from general speeches on nationalism, Jews, and "Marxists," there were meetings devoted to artisans, businessmen, civil servants, pensioners, and workmen. Thalburg's local peculiarities were taken into account; there was little real anti-Semitism in the town, hence this was soft-pedaled. But the townspeople were strongly religious and this was exploited to the hilt. When there was no specific group to be appealed to, the Nazis relied on pageantry, "evenings of entertainment," film showings, plays, acrobatic acts, lotteries, dances, sport exhibitions, military displays, recitals by children, and other expedients from a seemingly inexhaustible bag of tricks. They drew the tortured masses into the mammoth meetings where one could submerge oneself in the sense of participating in a dynamic and all-encompassing movement geared towards radical action in fulfillment of every need. The enemy was defined in similar terms: he was the Jew, the Socialist, the godless one, or, if one preferred amorphous generalities, the System which was to blame for everything from the collapse of the Enterprise Bank to the Treaty of Versailles.

In Their Own Words

What motivated the Nazis themselves, especially those in the SS and the Gestapo who organized the transports, ran the camps, and participated in the mass slaughter? Four Nazis, two of them near the top of the hierarchy, two of them rank-and-file secret police, offer explanations of their behavior. Rudolf Hoess was commandant of Auschwitz; Albert Speer was the Minister for Armament and War Production.

These selections are taken from the following sources: Commander of Auschwitz by Rudolf Hoess; Nuremberg Diary by G. M. Gilbert; Auschwitz by Bernd Naumann.

Commander of Auschwitz

My task was not an easy one. In the shortest possible time I had to construct a transit camp for 10,000 prisoners, using the existing complex of buildings which, though well-constructed, had been completely neglected, and were swarming with vermin. . . .

It was clear to me from the very beginning that Auschwitz could be made into a useful camp only through the hard and untiring efforts of everyone, from the commandant down to the lowest prisoner.

If I wanted to get good and useful work out of the prisoners, they must be given better treatment. . . .

I had complete confidence in these assumptions. Nevertheless, within a few months, I might even say during the first weeks, I became bitterly aware that all goodwill and the best intentions were doomed to be dashed to pieces against the human inadequacy and sheer stupidity of most of the officers and men posted to me. . . .

I must emphasize here that I never personally hated the Jews. It is true that I looked upon them as the enemies of our people. But just because of this I saw no difference between them and the other prisoners, and I treated them all in the same way. I never drew any distinctions. In any event the emotion of hatred is foreign to my nature. But I know what hate is, and what it looks like. I have seen it and I have suffered it myself. . . .

When in the summer of 1941 Himmler gave me the order to prepare installations at Auschwitz where mass exterminations could take place, and personally to carry out these exterminations, I did not have the slightest idea of their scale or consequences. It was certainly an extraordinary and monstrous order. Nevertheless the reasons behind the extermination program seemed to me right. I did not reflect on it at the time. I had been given an order, and I had to carry it out. Whether this mass extermination of the Jews was necessary or not was something on which I could not allow myself to form an opinion, for I lacked the necessary breadth of view.

Hoess Explains Why He Killed The Jews

I asked him if he had ever considered whether the Jews whom he had murdered were guilty or had in any way deserved such a fate. Again he tried patiently to explain that there was something unrealistic about such questions because he had been living in an entirely different world. "Don't you see, we SS men were not supposed to think about these things; it never even occurred to us.—And besides, it was something already taken for granted that the Jews were to blame for everything." I pressed him for some explanation of why it was taken for granted. "Well, we just never heard anything else. It was not just newspapers like the *Stürmer* but it was everything we ever heard. Even our military and ideological training took for granted that we had to protect Germany from the Jews. . . . It only started to occur to me after the collapse that maybe it was not quite right, after I heard what everybody was saying.—But nobody had ever said these things before; at least we never heard of it. Now I wonder if Himmler really believed all that himself or just gave me an excuse to justify what he wanted me to do.—But anyway, that really didn't matter. We were all so trained to obey orders without even thinking that the thought of disobeying an order would simply never have occurred to anybody and somebody else would have done just as well if I hadn't. . . . Himmler was so strict about little things, and executed SS men for such small offenses, that we naturally took it for granted that he was acting according to a strict code of honor. . . . You can be sure that it was not always a pleasure to see those mountains of corpses and smell the continual burning.—But Himmler had ordered it and had even explained the necessity and I really never gave much thought to whether it was wrong. It just seemed a necessity."

Other Gestapo Men Explain

WILHELM BOGER, FORMER MEMBER OF THE CAMP GESTAPO:

During the reign of National Socialism I knew only one mode of conduct: to carry out the orders of superiors without reservation. I did not ask to be stationed in Auschwitz. Today I realize that the idea I believed in spelled disaster and that it was wrong. It has been said here that I conducted rigorous interrogations as ordered. But what I saw at the time was not Auschwitz as a terrible extermination site of European Jewry but the fight against the Polish resistance movement and Bolshevism.

HANS STARK, FORMER MEMBER OF THE CAMP GESTAPO:

I took part in the murder of many people. I often asked myself after the war whether I had become a criminal because, being a dedicated National Socialist, I had murdered men, and I found no answer. I believed in the Führer; I wanted to serve my people. Today I know that this idea was false. I regret the mistakes of my past, but I cannot undo them.

Albert Speer Speaks

I should have and actually did realize it sooner, but kept playing at this hypocritical game until it was too late—well, because it was easier. . . .

That was the kind of weakness and hypocrisy I accuse myself of, because I had begun to realize even then that Hitler was playing havoc with German lives and resources; but I put the thought away. It was too dangerous. It is easy to rationalize things—patriotism in war, and all that. That is my guilt, and I don't deny it.

Hitler's Theories

Hitler articulated his system of beliefs and ideas in his book Mein Kampf ("My Struggle") in 1923, 10 years before he came to power. Part autobiography and part manifesto, it was written when he was in his mid-30s and just beginning his political activity. Accepting and building on theories of innate differences between "races" which were current at that time, Hitler preached the superiority of the Aryan (Indo-European) races, specifically the German people. The Jews, in Hitler's view, were members of a distinct "race," all having the same blood. Not only was this race inferior, it was the antithesis of everything noble and enlightened that distinguished the German "master race."

The first two selections are from Mein Kampf; the third is from The War Against the Jews by Lucy Dawidowicz.

On the Aryan

ADOLF HITLER

All the human culture, all the results of art, science, and technology that we see before us today, are almost exclusively the creative product of the Aryan. This very fact admits of the not unfounded inference that he alone was the founder of all higher humanity, therefore representing the prototype of all that we understand by the word "man." He is the Prometheus of mankind from whose shining brow the divine spark of genius has sprung at all times. . . .

Thus, for the formation of higher cultures the existence of lower human types was one of the most essential preconditions. . . . It is certain that the first culture of humanity was based less on the tamed animal than on the use of lower human beings. Only after the enslavement of subject races did the same fate strike beasts. For first the conquered warrior drew the plow—and only after him the horse. Hence it is no accident that the first cultures arose in places where the Aryan, in his encounters with lower peoples, subjugated them and bent them to his will. . . . As long as he ruthlessly upheld the master attitude, not only did he remain master, but also the preserver and increaser of culture.

About the Jew

ADOLF HITLER

The Jewish people, despite all apparent intellectual qualities, is without any true culture, and especially without any culture of its own. For what sham culture the Jew today possesses is the property of other peoples, and for the most part it is ruined in his hands.

Thus, the Jew lacks those qualities which distinguish the races that are creative and hence culturally blessed.

The Jew never possessed a state with definite territorial limits and therefore never called a culture his own. . . .

He is, and remains, the typical parasite, a sponger who like a noxious bacillus keeps spreading as soon as a favorable medium invites him. And the effect of his existence is also like that of spongers: wherever he appears, the host people dies out after a shorter or longer period.

Thus, the Jew of all times has lived in the states of other peoples, and there formed his own state, which, to be sure, habitually sailed under the disguise of "religious community" as long as outward circumstances made a complete revelation of his nature seem inadvisable. But as soon as he felt strong enough to do without the protective cloak, he always dropped the veil and suddenly became what so many of the others previously did not want to believe and see: the Jew.

The Jews in Hitler's Mental World

LUCY DAWIDOWICZ

T he Jews inhabited Hitler's mind. He believed that they were the source of all evil, misfortune, and tragedy, the single factor that, like some inexorable law of nature, explained the workings of the universe. The irregularities of war and famine, financial distress and sudden death, defeat and sinfulness—all could be explained by the presence of that single factor in the universe, a miscreation that disturbed the world's steady ascent toward well-being, affluence, success, victory. A savior was needed to come forth and slay the loathsome monster. In Hitler's obsessed mind, as in the delusive imaginings of the medieval millenarian sectarians, the Jews were the demonic hosts whom he had been given a divine mission to destroy.

All his life Hitler was seized by this obsession with the Jews. Even after he had murdered the Jews, he had still not exorcised his Jewish demons. At 4:00 A.M. on April 29, 1945, the last day of his life in the Berlin bunker, he finished dictating his political testament. His last words to the German people were: "Above all I charge the leaders of the nation and those under them to scrupulous observance of the laws of race and to merciless opposition to the universal poisoner of all peoples, international Jewry."

For the victims living in the ghettos, camps, and forests, music and song were healing forces, one of the links to the life from which they had been torn. Music also provided strength to survive and to hope. The victimizers, on the other hand, put music to evil purposes. For Hitler, music became a major propaganda tool for stirring up emotions of hate and unhealthy nationalism, and after a busy day of killing or ordering others to kill, music gave comfort to Nazi officials, many of whom loved Mozart and Beethoven.

The next reading, by one of the editors of this anthology, primarily targets the music and thought of German composer Richard Wagner, who, though dead some 50 years before Hitler's rise, nevertheless served Hitler in a number of ways. Ironically, the passionate strains of Wagner's compositions became powerful weapons for spreading anti-Semitism and belief in German superiority.

Politics and Music: Wagnerian Music and Thought in the Third Reich

ROSELLE K. CHARTOCK

Music and politics have always mixed. From "Yankee Doodle" and the "Star Spangled Banner" to "We Shall Overcome" and the huge rock concerts of the 1980s, music has served to arouse emotions and inspire followers of a variety of causes. This mixture of music and politics, of course, transcends American culture. In the realm of nationalism and patriotic music, dangerous situations have arisen, situations in which healthy patriotism became unhealthy and music became the instrument for spreading fanatical pride and destruction.

Such was the case during the Nazi Holocaust, the period during which three-quarters of European Jewry and millions of others were destroyed during World War II by Adolph Hitler and his followers. Beautiful music, the noble product of human creativity that has lifted the human spirit for centuries was, during the Holocaust, used for the most diabolical purposes by sadistic Nazis, both to torment and tease their victims and to pacify and deceive them about their impending extermination. Music helped to establish the illusion of well-being as victims marched into the "showers," or gas chambers. In addition, music was played for hospitalized victims before they were taken to be gassed. Nazi doctors, most notably Dr. Josef Mengele, used music so they could observe how the insane, manipulated like guinea pigs, would react to musical and other stimuli. Then music would be played for the murderers to help them relax after a hard day's "work."

Hitler's anti-Jewish beliefs and his theory that a superior Aryan race existed and should be cultivated were presented in his book, *Mein Kampf (My Struggle)* which he wrote while in Landsburg Fortress Prison in 1923, after his failure to seize power from the Weimar Republic. Ironically, the source of the Third Reich and many of its racist and anti-Semitic ideas can be found in the life, music, and prose of Richard Wagner (1813–1883), one of the world's greatest composers. Though 50 years separated Wagner's death (1883) and the establishment of the Third Reich (1933), Wagner's art, in the minds of many, is synonymous with Nazism. Hitler, quite simply, worshipped Wagner. He was Hitler's favorite composer.

But is it fair to hold Wagner accountable in any way for what happened in Germany 50 years after his death? Historical evidence and a look at Wagner's use of myth can shed light on the question.

It was in Linz, Austria, that Hitler, in his teens, discovered both Wagner's music and the composer's ideology in his fiercely anti-Semitic writings, *Judaism in Music* and *Decay and Regeneration.* For Hitler, Wagner's music represented his own world view: "Die Meistersinger," a musical symbol of power; "Walkure," a hymn to violence and war; "Siegfried," a celebration of Nazi youth and strength; and "Parsifal," an expression of his racist beliefs. Wrote Hitler, "Whoever wants to understand National Socialist Germany must know Wagner."

The composer had developed in his music and journalism the idea of a de-Judaized Germanic religion in which pagan Teutonic elements merged with Christianity. "Emancipation from the yoke of Judaism appears to us the foremost necessity," wrote Wagner. He believed that one of the purposes of his music was to further German nationalism. Portraying the Jew as evil was in his mind one of the ways to inspire that nationalism.

Hitler loved to reminisce about all of the times he had heard the great Wagnerian works, of what they had meant to him, and of the inspiration he had derived from them. In October 1923, Hitler went to Bayreuth, the theatre-opera festival created by Wagner in 1876, and the location since 1905 of the Bayreuth Festival. At Bayreuth, Hitler met an English anti-Semite, Houston Stewart Chamberlain, who lived there with his wife, Wagner's daughter. He also met Cosima, Wagner's wife and mistress of Bayreuth; Siegfried, the weak son and heir, composer, director, and preserver of the great musical tradition and Winifred, his English-born wife, who for a while was one of Hitler's most revered friends. At their home Hitler felt happy and at ease. He thoroughly impressed the aging Chamberlain, who predicted that Hitler would be the Savior of Germany and its purifier.

"What joy each of Wagner's works has given me!" Hitler exclaimed on the evening of January 24, 1942, soon after the first disastrous German defeats in Russia, as he spoke to his generals in the depths of an underground shelter in East Prussia. "I remember my emotions the first time I entered Wahnfried [the composer's home]. To say I was moved is an understatement. At my worst moments they [Wagner's family] never ceased to sustain me. . . . The ten days of the Bayreuth season were always one of the blessed seasons of my existence. And I rejoice at the idea that one day I shall be able to resume the pilgrimage!"

According to William Shirer, author of *The Rise and Fall of the Third Reich*, Wagner's towering operas inspired Hitler's fanatical nationalism and hatred of the Jew. These operas, by recalling so vividly the world of German antiquity with its heroic myth, provided Hitler and the Nazis the justification they needed to perpetuate their own myths.

In fact, most of Wagner's operas were based on German mythology, which he considered the ideal vehicle for the poet because it has its roots in "the People." He believed that myth contained eternal truth and had the power to lift the People above the ordinary plane and to portray their deepest urges and aspirations. "The People," or *Volk*, were exalted by the Nazis, who defined the *Volk* as a people of unmixed racial origins who were mystically bound together in a primitive community of blood and soil without boundaries.

Though Hitler believed that "Tristan and Isolde" was "Wagner's masterpiece," it is the stupendous "Nibelungen Ring," a series of four operas inspired by the great German epic myth, "Nibelungenlied," that gave Germany and especially the Third Reich so much of its primitive Germanic "mythos."

In "The Ring," Wagner depicts his youthful hero, Siegfried, winning the Nibelung's treasure from the dragon and awakening the warrior-maiden, Brunnhilde, from her magic sleep. His own hatred of the problems caused by money and his belief that the Jew dominated that world of money led Wagner to consider the idea of the legendary Nibelung's Hoard as a symbol of all that was evil in politics and economics and modern capitalism. The fateful ring of the Nibelungs, a tribe of dwarfs, takes the form of a stockbroker's wallet, the stockbroker being the Jew. He viewed his historical king, Friedrick Barbarossa, as a rebirth of the pagan Siegfried, the god-like figure of light, capable of redeeming the evil Hoard. Siegfried, in turn, was identified with Christ.

In many cases a nation derives its identity from its mythology, and many modern Germans liked to identify themselves with Siegfried and Kriemhild, Brunnhilde and Hagen, ancient heroes and heroines in a primitive and demonic world. These elements were always "in the people's soul," declared Max Mell, a contemporary poet who wrote a modern version of the "Song of the Nibelungs." In that German "soul" could be felt the struggle between the spirit of civilization and the irrational, barbaric spirit of the Nibelungs; and, during the time period with which this article is concerned, the latter seemed to gain the upper hand. "It is not at all surprising that Hitler tried to emulate Wotan, (King of the gods and father of Siegfried), when in 1945, he, like the mythical Wotan, willed the destruction of Germany (Valhalla) so that it might go down in flames with him."

The pagan myth of Siegfried helped Hitler to justify his diabolical plans for genocide, euthanasia, and Lebensborn, his systematic breeding program established for the purpose of literally bringing about a pure Germanic race. In the myth, Wotan is visited by spirits who tell him the mission of Siegfried will be to give birth to a race of supermen. Interestingly, but incorrectly, philosopher Frederich Nietzsche's work (1844–1900) has been targeted with influencing Hitler's theories of Germanic racial superiority and his eventual plans for genocide and Lebensborn. Nietzsche, in *The Will to Power*, prophesies that an elite will come to rule the world and from this elite will spring the supermen. This prophecy is similar to the pagan myth. But unlike Wagner, and later Hitler, Nietzsche did not interpret this ideal superman to be Aryan German. It was actually Nietzsche's sister, Elizabeth, who, after his death, attempted to politicize Nietzsche's work with the intent of translating his ideal man into an Aryan. In fact, Nietzsche had contempt for nationalism. Nor was he an anti-Semite. He eventually broke off his friendship with Wagner because he believed Wagner's philosophical and musical scope was narrow and limited by his nationalism and intense prejudices.

After the break between them, Nietzsche wrote two short books criticizing Wagner's baser Germanism, his anti-Semitism, and the darker aspects of his art and writing. Author Derek Watson paraphrased the essence of Nietzsche's argument in one of those works, *The Wagner Case* (1888). In this book Nietzsche explains that the musician can redeem corrupt society and that music is the means whereby man transforms this base world into a better place to live. Wagner's great fault, according to Nietzsche, was to abuse his gifts by resorting to romantic fantasy and Christian ideology and by turning his back on life. Wagner, he said, demanded unquestioning belief; it was a crime to be scientific or skeptical. "Wagner was not a man but a disease which made music sick." "His disease," said Nietzsche, "is symptomatic of a decaying civilization." These descriptions could, indeed, apply to Hitler as well.

Before 1954, Nazi ideologists had used Nietzsche for their own ends. But with Karl Schlecter's edition of Nietzsche's works in 1954, the degree of Elizabeth's influence was fully revealed. (Elizabeth remained a disciple of Wagner's teachings and, in fact, went to Paraguay with her husband in 1886 and founded Neueva Germania to put into action Wagner's teachings about racial purity and vegetarianism.)

Because Hitler believed that National Socialist ideology should be expressed in musical terms, he insisted in 1938 that Wagner's *Rienzi* be played at the ceremonial opening of the Nazi Party Rallies at Nuremberg. Hitler chose Nuremberg as the location for his yearly week-long rallies because Wagner had set his drama and opera, "Die Meistersinger," in Nuremberg, an ancient city that Wagner considered to be an ideal seat for German art, for a music school, and for his operas. The story behind *Rienzi* is relevant here. Produced first in Dresden in 1842, and based on a novel by Bulwer-Lytton (1832), *Rienzi* is the story of a Roman tribune (Rienzi) filled with pride of birth and country who dreamed of releasing his native city from the hands of nobles and making it once again the leader of the world. Said Hitler, "Listening to this blessed music as a young man . . . I had the vision that I too must someday succeed in uniting the German Empire and making it great once more." Rienzi sees his dream as patriotic and religious and his duty becomes passion. His efforts ultimately fail and end in Rienzi's death.

William Shirer, then a reporter, attended a Nuremberg Rally in 1943, and observed the following:

> Hitler's arrival was dramatic. The band stopped playing. There was a hush over the 30,000 people packed in the hall. Then the band struck up the "Badenweiler March," a very catchy tune and used only when Hitler makes his big entries. Hitler appeared in the back of the auditorium, and, followed by his aides Goering, Goebbels, Hess, Himmler, and the others, he strode slowly down the long center aisle while 30,000 hands were raised in salute. . . .

> Then an immense symphony orchestra played Beethoven's
> *Egmont Overture.*

According to Albert Speer, Hitler's chief architect and advisor, Hitler also took an active role in designing sets for Wagner's operas during the Third Reich. One time, he gave the Reich Stage Designer a series of sketches for all the scenes of *The Ring.* "We must bring the masses illusions," he once said in 1938. According to Speer, the bombing of an opera house pained Hitler more than the destruction of inhabited homes.

A number of current critics insist that Wagner's posthumous role in the Third Reich *must* be acknowledged. According to George Kren and Leon Rappoport *(The Holocaust and the Crisis of Human Behavior),* in Wagner's operatic world superior love justifies any and all absurdities, or violations of moral law. Thus, it is no surprise that Hitler attempted to show that rationally he must destroy the Jew in the name of his love for the German people.

Beate Ruhm von Oppen, in writing about German intellectual resistance during the Holocaust, stated that ". . . in a nation as musical as the German, the chief corrupter came by the vehicle of music. His name was Richard Wagner." Von Oppen added, "Whatever Wagner served up as language in his operas and writing cast its destructive spell on the educated elite." For example, the excessively unattractive foster father of Siegfried in *The Ring* is the operative equivalent of the "Jew," who Wagner wrote was "incapable of human speech and therefore also of music . . ." Von Oppen believes that those who cannot translate Wagner's librettos but listen instead only to music "know not what they hear."

In *Judaism in Music* (1850) and other tracts, Wagner expressed the greatness of the German spirit and attacked Jews as anti-German. Like Hitler he blamed them for all he thought wrong with the world. In *Know Thyself,* he hints that the only hope for mankind is the elimination of the Jews. And in still another article, *Public and Popularity,* Wagner argues that the identification of Jesus with Jewish roots is "one of the most terrible confusions in all world-history." In reference to these anti-Semitic traits, biographer Derek Watson writes, "That such inflated claptrap could be regarded by many as the highest wisdom and that Wagner could draw men of no small intelligence into the orbit of his own absurd self-delusions, is truly mysterious."

One of the strongest condemnations of Wagner's role as precursor to Hitler appears in Robert Gutman's book, *Richard Wagner, The Man, His Mind and His Music.* Gutman views "Parsifal" as an allegory of racism purely on the evidence of its text and in light of Wagner's racial theories as expounded in his essays. For Gutman, the darkest interpretation of "Parsifal" is as 'the gospel of National Socialism,' a drama depicting the redemption of the Aryan race from its sin of mixing with the blood of inferior races through annihilation of the Jews and the regeneration of Aryan blood. It is, for Gutman, an anti-Christian work: cruel, depraved and demonic, though none of his criticism touches upon the music itself which Gutman concedes to be among Wagner's greatest.

Whatever conclusions the reader draws in regard to Wagner's responsibility for the Third Reich, it must nevertheless be said that at least in the music we can observe strength and humanity, and while much of Wagner's inspiration was racist, the music itself remains singularly outstanding. Zubin Mehta, Conductor of the New York Philharmonic Orchestra and a popular conductor in Israel, chose to play Wagner a few years ago in Israel before an audience which knew better than most about the inspiration behind Wagner's music. Many were offended, shouted out, or were angered to the point of throwing things. Others simply walked out. But there were those who defended Mehta because they believed the music should be judged apart from its creator's beliefs.

Whatever blame Wagner must bear for National Socialism remains for us to ponder, but, that music and myth played a political role during the Third Reich is beyond doubt.

On a more positive note, I attended a concert at Tanglewood a few years back and read the program notes for a work by Russian composer Dmitri Shostakovich. In contrast to the racist sentiments in some of Wagner's operas, Shostakovich wrote his Thirteenth Symphony to recall the Holocaust and to protest against repression of Jews in his own country and of other peoples all over the world.

In 1962, Shostakovich (1906–1975) completed his Symphony No. 13 in B-flat Minor to poems of Russian poet Yevgeny Yevtushenko during the "thaw" brought about by Nikita Khrushchev's campaign of de-Stalinization and denunciation of anti-Semitism. One of these poems, "Babi Yar," recalls the massacre of Russian Jews by the Nazis and Russian collaborators. The poet wrote it after he visited the ravine of Babi Yar, on the outskirts of Kiev, where Nazi troops machine-gunned more than 70,000 and perhaps as many as 90,000 Jews in 1941, in the 10 days from Rosh Hashanah to Yom Kippur. However, the Communist authorities, believing the "thaw" to have gotten out of hand, fiercely attacked the poem and began to refer to the symphony as the "Jewish Symphony." When the time came for its premiere in 1962, no one knew if it would actually take place; it did, and with an overwhelming response. Shostakovich is said to have considered the completion of the Thirteenth Symphony as one of the two greatest events in his life as a composer.

The following is an excerpt from the poem, "Babi Yar," which the composer set to music for solo and choral voices:

And I myself am one long soundless cry
Above the thousand thousands buried here.
I am every old man here shot dead.
I am every child here shot dead.
Nothing in me will ever forget this.

The "Internationale"—let it thunder
When forever will be buried
The last of the anti-Semites on earth.

There is no Jewish blood in mine,
But I am adamantly hated
By all anti-Semites as if I were a Jew.
That is why I am a true Russian!

Music continues to play a powerful political role, nationally and internationally, and will most certainly continue to do so.

The Nazi Program

T he concepts of racial and national superiority were given practical expression in the very first Nazi party platform, adopted in 1920. Though the party did not come to power for another 13 years, many of the proposals remained unchanged and were eventually put into effect. The "socialist" planks, however, were essentially propaganda aimed at winning the support of the workers, and were never taken seriously by party leaders.

The document is reprinted from National Socialism, published by the U.S. Department of State.

The Nazi Program

The National Socialist German Workers' Party, at a great mass meeting on February 25th, 1920, in the Hofbrauhaus-Festsaal in Munich, announced their Program to the world.

In section 2 of the Constitution of Our Party this Program is declared to be inalterable.

The Program of the German Workers' Party is limited as to period. The leaders have no intention, once the aims announced in it have been achieved, of setting up fresh ones, merely in order to increase the discontent of the masses artificially, and so ensure the continued existence of the Party.

1. We demand the union of Germans to form a Great Germany on the basis of the right of the self-determination enjoyed by nations.

2. We demand equality of rights for the German People in its dealings with other nations, and abolition of the Peace Treaties of Versailles and St. Germain.

3. We demand land and territory [colonies] for the nourishment of our people and for settling our superfluous population.

4. None but members of the nation may be citizens of the State. None but those of German blood, whatever their creed, may be members of the nation. No Jew, therefore, may be a member of the nation.

5. Anyone who is not a citizen of the State may live in Germany only as a guest and must be regarded as being subject to foreign laws.

6. The right of voting on the State's government and legislation is to be enjoyed by the citizen of the State alone. We demand therefore that all official appointments, of whatever kind, whether in the Reich, in the country, or in the smaller localities, shall be granted to citizens of the State alone.

We oppose the corrupting custom of Parliament of filling posts merely with a view to party considerations, and without reference to character or capability.

7. We demand that the State shall make it its first duty to promote the industry and livelihood of citizens of the State. If it is not possible to nourish the entire population of the State, foreign nationals [non-citizens of the State] must be excluded from the Reich.

8. All non-German immigration must be prevented. We demand that all non-Germans, who entered Germany subsequent to August 2nd, 1914, shall be required forthwith to depart from the Reich.

9. All citizens of the State shall be equal as regards rights and duties.

10. It must be the first duty of each citizen of the State to work with his mind or with his body. The activities of the individual may not clash with the interests of the whole, but must proceed within the frame of the community and be for the general good.

We demand therefore:

11. Abolition of incomes unearned by work.

12. In view of the enormous sacrifice of life and property demanded of a nation by every war, personal enrichment due to a war must be regarded as a crime against the nation. We demand therefore ruthless confiscation of all war gains.

13. We demand nationalization of all businesses which have been up to the present formed into companies [Trusts].

14. We demand that the profits from wholesale trade shall be shared out.

15. We demand extensive development of provision for old age.

16. We demand creation and maintenance of a healthy middle class, immediate communalization of wholesale business premises, and their lease at a cheap rate to small traders, and that extreme consideration shall be shown to all small purveyors to the State, district authorities and smaller localities.

17. We demand land-reform suitable to our national requirements, passing of a law for confiscation without compensation of land for communal purposes; abolition of interest on land loans, and prevention of all speculation in land.

18. We demand ruthless prosecution of those whose activities are injurious to the common interest. Sordid criminals against the nation, usurers, profiteers, etc., must be punished with death, whatever their creed or race.

19. We demand that the Roman Law, which serves the materialistic world order, shall be replaced by a legal system for all Germany.

20. With the aim of opening to every capable and industrious German the possibility of higher education and of thus obtaining advancement, the State must consider a thorough reconstruction of our national system of education. The curriculum of all educational establishments must be brought into line with the requirements of practical life. Comprehension of the State idea [State sociology] must be the school objective, beginning with the first dawn of intelligence in the pupil. We demand development of the gifted children of poor parents, whatever their class or occupation, at the expense of the State.

21. The State must see to raising the standard of health in the nation by protecting mothers and infants, prohibiting child labor, increasing bodily efficiency by obligatory gymnastics and sports laid down by law, and by extensive support of clubs engaged in the bodily development of the young.

22. We demand abolition of a paid army and formation of a national army.

23. We demand legal warfare against conscious political lying and its dissemination in the Press. In order to facilitate creation of a German national Press we demand:

(a) that all editors of newspapers and their assistants, employing the German language, must be members of the nation;

(b) that special permission from the State shall be necessary before non-German newspapers may appear. These are not necessarily printed in the German language;

(c) that non-Germans shall be prohibited by law from participating financially in or influencing German newspapers, and that the penalty for contravention of the law shall be suppression of any such newspaper, and immediate deportation of the non-German concerned in it.

It must be forbidden to publish papers which do not conduce to the national welfare. We demand legal prosecution of all tendencies in art and literature of a kind likely to disintegrate our life as a nation, and the suppression of institutions which militate against the requirements above-mentioned.

24. We demand liberty for religious denominations in the State, so far as they are not a danger to it and do not militate against the moral feelings of the German race.

The Party, as such, stands for positive Christianity, but does not bind itself in the matter of creed to any particular confession. It combats the Jewish-materialist spirit within us and without us, and is convinced that our nation can only achieve permanent health from within on the principle: THE COMMON INTEREST BEFORE SELF.

25. That all of the foregoing may be realized we demand the creation of a strong central power of the State. Unquestioned authority of the politically centralized Parliament over the entire Reich and its organizations; and formation of Chambers for classes and occupations for the purpose of carrying out the general laws promulgated by the Reich in the various States of the confederation.

The leaders of the Party swear to go straight forward—if necessary to sacrifice their lives—in securing fulfillment of the foregoing Points.

A logical extension of the Nazi racial philosophy was the two-pronged movement to improve the German stock: on the one hand, to add as many "pure" Germans as possible to the population, and, on the other, to rid the German people of undesirable elements. How these goals were implemented, with characteristic efficiency, is described in these selections from the book *Hitler's SS* by Richard Grunberger. It is important to note here that protests against euthanasia succeeded in bringing the program to a halt.

The Lebensborn Movement

RICHARD GRUNBERGER

All the pieces in Himmler's eugenic jigsaw—infertile couples, Germanized Slavs, "procreation assistants," unmarried mothers—were moved into place by "Lebensborn" (Foundation of Life), an SS foundling hospital-cum-adoption society established in 1936. According to the Lebensborn report for 1938, "832 valuable German women decided despite their single state and the sacrifice entailed, to eschew abortion and present the nation with a child." Assessing each German's life contribution to the economy at 100,000 Reichsmark, Lebensborn claimed to have enriched the country by 83 million Reichsmark.

Eventually thousands of Lebensborn wards were placed with childless Nazi couples; more importantly, in wartime the original objective—delivering and fostering illegitimate German children—was superseded by the genetic spoliation of Eastern Europe.

During his first inspection tour of occupied Poland, Himmler had been deeply stirred by the Nordic appearance of many Slav children and this may have started a train of thought culminating in his war aim "to enlarge Germany's existing blood basis of 90 million to 120 million." Kidnapped children—snatched from orphanages or alleged resistance families—were taken to Lebensborn homes dotted across occupied Europe; after a processing period during which the bewildered children were drilled in rudimentary German and denied any contact with their compatriots, they went off to the Reich already bearing the names of their designated foster parents.

Germanization was by no means confined to children nor were all Germanized Slavs necessarily outright victims of force. In Poland, where Poles and Germans had long intermarried, Polish nationals of part-German ancestry could apply for Reich citizenship which—given the situation of Poles under Nazi occupation—many were quite eager to do.

But volunteers could never meet Himmler's need for genetic reinforcements, and two special SS agencies—the Volksdeutsche Liaison Office and the Race and Settlement Office—scoured Europe to select human specimens considered suitable for Germanization. Besides abduction, the tasks of RUSHA, the Race and Settlement Office, ranged from conscription of slave labor, the infliction of (frequently capital) punishment on East Europeans guilty of intimacy with German women, to the clearance of Slavs from regions earmarked for German settlement.

One such region was the Warthegau in western Poland. The Warthegau "plantation" involved clearing one and a half million Poles and Jews out of a large area to make room for half a million *Volksdeutsche* from eastern Poland, Rumania, and the Baltic States. Himmler, newly styled "Reich Commissioner for the consolidation of German folkdom," ordered the clearance during the Arctic winter of 1939–40, and thus caused a heavier death toll than resulted from Hitler's concurrent directive to decapitate the Polish nation by liquidating its intellectuals and priests.

Euthanasia

RICHARD GRUNBERGER

A related aim—that of purifying the gene pool of the German race—lay behind the Euthanasia Campaign of 1940–41. In September 1939 Hitler ordered the "mercy-killing" of the feeble-minded and incurables throughout the Reich—on grounds both of eugenics and wartime economy in food, accommodation, and medical personnel. The first liquidation center became operational before the end of the year; another five, one of them situated at the well-known psychiatric clinic of Hadamar, came into operation early in 1940. The man placed in overall charge of the program was Christian Wirth, the former superintendent of the Criminal Investigation Department in Stuttgart.

Wirth initially disposed of his victims by shooting them in the neck. After some time he switched over to gassing them in specially constructed chambers—and thus qualifies as co-originator of the mass-extermination methods subsequently used in the so-called "Final Solution of the Jewish Question."

In each euthanasia establishment a room camouflaged as a shower room was hermetically sealed. This was connected by a system of pipes to cylinders of carbon monoxide. The patients, before being taken in groups of 10 or 15 into this gas chamber, were generally made drowsy with the aid of morphine (or scopolamine) injections or drugged with soporifics. Each center housed a crematorium; families were informed of patients' deaths on preprinted forms attributing death to heart failure or pneumonia.

The steep increase in fatalities, reported under conditions of ill-concealed secrecy—palls of smoke above the crematoria were visible for miles, and at Hadamar the village children would greet incoming hospital buses with cries of "here come some more to be gassed"—prompted mounting disquiet in the country. Among many rumors in circulation was one which alleged that even badly wounded soldiers were being "mercy-killed" at military hospitals.

In August 1941 the Catholic Bishop Galen denounced the euthanasia killings in a sermon from the pulpit of his cathedral at Münster, Westphalia. This turned out to be the most successful single act of resistance ever undertaken in the Third Reich: the systematic killing of institution inmates (which had thus far cost approximately 100,000 lives) ceased almost immediately.

Nor was any retaliatory action taken against the bishop, although the Gestapo soon afterward beheaded three parish priests who had distributed his sermon in leaflet form. Such glaring discrepancy of punishment was the fruit of Machiavellian calculation: while the death of anonymous parish priests would go unremarked in the surrounding welter of violence and confusion, persecution might have elevated the well-known prelate to the status of a national resistance figure.

Medical experiments performed on twins in the concentration camps stand out as some of the most bizarre and grotesque of the abuses perpetrated on Jews, in part, because the abusers were doctors, whom we presume are dedicated to the preservation of human life. Used as guinea pigs, many of the subjects died or, according to the next reading, were left scarred both physically and mentally for the rest of their lives.

Reporter Jon Nordheimer also records the contradictory roles Dr. Josef Mengele played in the minds of his subjects. While some died in the course of the experiments, others, ironically, were kept alive because of their usefulness to this "Angel of Death."

This article from the April 14, 1991, *New York Times* presents only one aspect of the medical experiments performed on humans. Castrations and amputations were also common. Interestingly, a debate has evolved that concerns the question of whether or not doctors of today should use the research that remains from these experiments, or whether this research should be rejected because the subjects were human beings *forced* to undergo gruesome operations.

For Twins of Auschwitz, Time to Unlock Secrets

JON NORDHEIMER

They are surviving members of what Irene Hizme calls "the most exclusive club in the world": Jewish twins hand-picked by the Nazi physician Josef Mengele at the Auschwitz-Birkenau death camp to be guinea pigs, in her words, "for experimentation to develop a master race."

She was six years old, and for years afterward she thought she would carry her awful secret to the grave. "To talk about it," she said last week, "is a descent into darkness."

Eva Kor of Terre Haute, Ind., could not bring herself to describe the scenes of horror to her children. "The pain was too great," she said.

FIGHTING A NIGHTMARE

Peter Somogyl, a New Jersey businessman, says he has put the nightmare behind him. But his wife says his cries of torment still awaken him in a cold sweat.

Nearly half a century after they entered the gates of Auschwitz, the Mengele twins are being heard as never before. *Children of the Flames,* a book by Lucette Matalon Lagnado and Sheila Cohn Dekel, describes the blighted histories of twins who have come forward in recent years. Some, like Mrs. Hizme, who lives in Oceanside, L.I., are forcing themselves to speak in public for the first time.

Mengele selected about 1,500 sets of twins—Jews, Gypsies, and others—for projects conducted at his genetics laboratory. Many died in the research; at the end of the war, fewer than 200 individuals were alive.

In the experiments, many had blood drained and transfused in research that was said to be connected with Mengele's search for ways to increase the fertility and birth rates of German women. He also tried to find ways to change eye color. Mengele worked on one twin and used the other for comparison.

Twenty-seven known survivors of the experiments live in the United States, most of them in the New York metropolitan area. Six are in Canada and about 100 in Israel and elsewhere.

SOME MAINTAIN THE SECRECY

Some survivors say they believe there are others still living who have allowed their past to remain locked in secrecy, too anguished by the experiments performed on them to speak out. Some who were toddlers when Mengele and his staff subjected them to radical tests and surgical procedures might have concentration camp tattoos and unexplained scars, but no conscious memory of the ordeal.

Little of the research exists. It is thought that after the war Mengele either destroyed his records and tissue samples or carried them into hiding, first in Europe and then in South America. In more than 40 years, his death has been reported many times. In 1985 his son and some experts identified the remains of a man who drowned near São Paulo, Brazil, in 1979 as his.

"On the surface we enjoy normal lives, but we have never escaped the long, dark shadow of Mengele," said Mrs. Hizme, a 53-year-old mother of two. "If I push it out of my day, it returns."

Mrs. Hizme was speaking of her memories before a hushed audience at Congregation Ohab Zedek on West 95th Street in Manhattan at an observance of Holocaust Memorial Week.

The memory that never ages haunts the survivors even as they grow old. In interviews last week, they said they carried a burden that other survivors of the camps do not: that their selection for Mengele's experiments spared their lives. Their families died at Auschwitz. So did children who were not selected for the research.

'WHAT KIND OF FOUNDATION?'

"If childhood is the foundation of a human being's life," said Mrs. Kor, who was nine in 1944, when she arrived at Auschwitz, "then what kind of foundation can we have if our memories are filled with the smell of burning flesh and chimneys belching the black smoke of our families?"

There was one other difference, and for the twins it is the hardest to explain.

Mengele, known as the "Angel of Death" for his role in choosing who would live and who would die, was also, for them, Mengele the protector.

As long as he required them for his research, they were spared the gas chamber. Giving blood samples and submitting to X-rays and injections were daily options to death, even though most of the twins would eventually die painful deaths, as did those who entered the crematorium on their first day in Auschwitz.

Even the young ones, like Irene Hizme, understood the deadly game they played. Her parents had taken their children and fled from their native Germany to Czechoslovakia to escape Hitler, but all were rounded up in 1943 and transported to Auschwitz.

Given special status, the twins lived in their own barracks, separated by sex. They got an extra ration of food once or twice a week and were given the medical care denied to tens of thousands of others.

'SAVIOR AND DEMON'

"Savior and demon," was the way Mrs. Hizme described the dichotomy about Mengele in young minds. Even today survivors describe him as kindly and avuncular. They say he gave them candy and kissed them.

"Some of the older girls thought he was handsome and had a crush on him," Mrs. Kor said.

On his first day at Auschwitz, Mr. Somogyl recalled, the SS guards at the railway unloading dock walked among the masses of arriving Jews shouting, "Twins! Twins!" like buyers in a fish market. As they did so, Mengele surveyed those who answered the call, whistling Mozart as he selected who lived and who died.

Ms. Lagnado, who spent seven years tracking down surviving twins for her book, said they told her they felt shame that they had survived, "not because they were strong, but because of a freak of nature."

After Auschwitz was liberated by Russian soldiers on Jan. 27, 1945, Eva Kor and her twin, Miriam, returned to their home in Transylvania, only to learn that 117 relatives had perished in the war.

Mrs. Hizme was plucked from Auschwitz by a peasant, who kept her until a rescue committee organized by American Jews found her a year later. She was reunited with her twin brother, Rene, in the United States in 1950.

LISTENING TO THE PAST

Rene Slotkin, Mrs. Hizme's twin, was sitting in the rear of Temple Ohab Zedek while his sister spoke. He winced at each word. Mrs. Hizme has multiple sclerosis and is in a wheelchair. Slotkin said, "I can't help but think of the experiments. Mengele experimented on one twin and kept the other for a control. I was the control. Irene got the injections. There's no records of what they put into her young body."

Mr. Somogyl was also in the temple. Later, he said that he, too, after all these years cannot reconcile his experiences. In his long daily trip between work in New Jersey and his home in Pleasantville, N.Y., when he is alone with his thoughts he listens to classical music tapes in the car.

But no Mozart; only Italian operas, mostly Verdi.

PART IV

WHAT DOES THE HOLOCAUST REVEAL ABOUT THE INDIVIDUAL AND SOCIETY?

"Though the German people who gave active or passive support to Hitler must of necessity carry the main burden of guilt for what was done, there are many others who must share it with them: the men and women of other nations who joined the SS and helped to staff the camps; the countries, such as Rumania and Hungary, who in the end persecuted their Jews with a savagery no less possessed than that of the Nazis; in fact, when the truth of the matter was gradually revealed to the Allied nations and to the world outside Germany by those who risked their lives to bring the facts from the secret places of extermination, everyone who refused to take heed of this authenticated knowledge and made no attempt to prevent the further torture and death of these innocent people must, on however relative a scale, share in the great burden of guilt which still lies heavily on the conscience of us all."

ROGER MANVELL AND HEINRICH FRAENKEL
The Incomparable Crime

In situations of moral conflict, we must choose a course of action. Even if we are only bystanders, we will choose whether to look away—or to involve ourselves. Everyone whose life was touched in some way by the Nazis had to make a choice: to look away, to cooperate, or to resist. In the next four selections, we meet four individuals: two who were actively involved in killing prisoners in the camps; two who could have remained completely untouched, but who chose, freely and consciously, to involve themselves.

In this first selection taken from his memoir, *Auschwitz*, Dr. Miklos Nyiszli, a Jewish physician, is tortured by the memories of his participation in Nazi medical experiments.

A Doctor for the Nazis Remembers

DR. MIKLOS NYISZLI

S ick at heart, and physically ill, I started my long voyage homeward. The trip was not a pleasant one: everywhere I looked I saw, where flourishing cities and towns had once stood, nothing but gutted ruins and the collective, white-crossed graves of the dead.

I dreaded the truth, fearing to return to an empty, plundered home, a home where neither parents nor wife, daughter nor sister would be waiting to greet me with warmth and affection. Persecution and sorrow, the horrors of the crematorium and funeral pyres, my eight months in the *kommando* of the living dead, had dulled my sense of good and evil.

I felt that I should rest, try to regain my strength. But, I kept asking myself, for what? On the one hand, illness racked my body; on the other, the bloody past froze my heart. My eyes had followed countless innocent souls to the gas chambers, witnessed the unbelievable spectacle of the funeral pyres. And I myself, carrying out the orders of a demented doctor, had dissected hundreds of bodies, so that a science based on false theories might benefit from the deaths of those millions of victims. I had cut the flesh of healthy young girls and prepared nourishment for the mad doctor's bacteriological cultures. I had immersed the bodies of dwarfs and cripples in calcium chloride, or had them boiled so that the carefully prepared skeletons might safely reach the Third Reich's museums to justify, for future generations, the destruction of an entire race. And even though all this was now past, I would still have to cope with it in my thoughts and dreams. I could never erase these memories from my mind.

At least twice I had felt the wings of death brush by me: once, prostrate on the ground, with a company of SS trained in the art of summary execution poised above me, I had escaped unharmed. But 3,000 of my friends, who had also known the terrible secrets of the crematoriums, had not been so lucky. I had marched for hundreds of kilometers through fields of snow, fighting the cold, hunger, and my own exhaustion, merely to reach another concentration camp. The road I had traveled had indeed been long.

Now, home again, nothing. I wandered aimlessly through silent rooms. Free, but not from my bloody past, nor from the deep-rooted grief that filled my mind and gnawed at my sanity. And the future seemed just as dark. I walked like my own ghost, a restless figure in the once familiar streets. The only times I managed to shake off my state of depression and lethargy was when, mistakenly, I thought for a fleeting second that someone I saw or briefly encountered on the street was a member of my family.

One afternoon, several weeks after my return, I felt chilly and sat down near the fireplace, hoping to derive a little comfort from the cheerful glow that filled the room. It grew late; dusk was falling. The doorbell roused me from my daydreams. Before I could get up to answer it my wife and daughter burst into the room!

They were in good health and had just been freed from Bergen-Belsen, one of the most notorious of the extermination camps. But that was as much as they were able to tell me before breaking down. For hours they sobbed uncontrollably. I was content just to hold them in my arms, while the flood of their grief flowed from their tortured minds and hearts. Their sobs, a language I was well familiar with, slowly subsided.

We had much to do, much to relate, much to rebuild. I knew it would take much time and infinite patience before we could resume any sort of really normal life. But all that mattered was that we were alive . . . and together again. Life suddenly became meaningful again. I would begin practicing, yes. . . . But I swore that as long as I lived I would never lift a scalpel again. . . .

This Auschwitz physician, not Jewish, appears to have been more concerned with the menu for lunch than with his activities in the camp. Hans Hermann Kremer joined the Nazi Party in 1932 and the armed SS in 1941. On August 29, 1942, he was ordered to Auschwitz to substitute for another physician who had fallen ill. The diary excerpts are reprinted from *Human Behavior in the Concentration Camp* by Elie Cohen.

From a Doctor's Diary

HANS HERMANN KREMER

September 2, 1942: First time present at a *Sonderaktion*. [The most spectacular of the mass atrocities were called *Sonderaktionen*. One of these, which was practiced particularly in Auschwitz, was the burning of live prisoners, especially children, in pits measuring 20 by 40 to 50 meters, on piles of gasoline-soaked wood.]

September 5, 1942: This afternoon present at a *Sonderaktion* from the female concentration camp (Muselmanner): The most horrible of horrors. Hschf. Thilo, doctor of the troops, is right when he told me this morning that we are at *anus mundi*. In the evening at approximately 9:00 hours again present at a *Sonderaktion* from the Netherlands. Men all want to take part in these actions because of the special rations they get then, consisting of a fifth of a liter of schnapps, five cigarettes, 100 gram sausage and bread. Today and tomorrow on duty.

September 6, 1942: Today, Sunday, excellent lunch: tomato soup, half a hen with potatoes and red cabbage (20 gram fat), sweets and marvelous vanilla ice. . . . In the evening at 8:00 hours a *Sonderaktion*.

September 9, 1942: This morning I got the most pleasant news from my lawyer Prof. Dr. Hallermann in Münster, that I got divorced from my wife on the first of this month. (Note: I see colors again, a black curtain is drawn back from my life!) Later on, present as doctor at a corporal punishment of eight prisoners and an execution by shooting with small-calibre rifles. Got soap flakes and two pieces of soap. . . . In the evening present at a *Sonderaktion*, fourth time.

September 10, 1942: In the morning present at a *Sonderaktion* (fifth time).

September 20, 1942: Listened to a concert of the prisoners' band this afternoon in bright sunshine. Bandmaster: conductor of the Warschauer Staatsoper. Eighty musicians. For lunch we had pork. . . .

A young man who joined the resistance movement in Denmark was captured by the Nazis and sentenced to be executed. In this letter to his mother, he explains why he is glad he chose to live by his ideals. The selection is from *Dying We Live: The Final Messages and Records of the Resistance.*

Kim, Cabin Boy and Seaman

KIM MALTHE-BRUUN

FAREWELL LETTER TO HIS MOTHER

Western Prison, German Section, Cell 411
April 4, 1945

Dear Mother: Today, together with Jörgen, Nils, and Ludwig, I was arraigned before a military tribunal. We were condemned to death. I know that you are a courageous woman, and that you will bear this, but, hear me, it is not enough to bear it, you must also understand it. I am an insignificant thing, and my person will soon be forgotten, but the thought, the life, the inspiration that filled me will live on. You will meet them everywhere—in the trees at springtime, in people who cross your path, in a loving little smile. You will encounter that something which perhaps had value in me, you will cherish it, and you will not forget me. And so I shall have a chance to grow, to become large and mature. I shall be living with all of you whose hearts I once filled. And you will all live on, knowing that I have preceded you, and not, as perhaps you thought at first, dropped out behind you. You know what my dearest wish has always been, and what I hoped to become. Follow me, my dear mother, on my path, and do not stop before the end, but linger with some of the matters belonging to the last space of time allotted to me, and you will find something that may be of value both to my sweetheart and to you, my mother.

I traveled a road that I have never regretted. I have never evaded the dictate of my heart, and now things seem to fall into place. I am not old, I should not be dying, yet it seems so natural to me, so simple. It is only the abrupt manner of it that frightens us at first. The time is short, I cannot properly explain it, but my soul is perfectly at rest. . . .

When I come right down to it, how strange it is to be sitting here and writing this testament. Every word must stand, it can never be amended, erased, or changed. I have so many thoughts. Jörgen is sitting here before me writing his two-year-old daughter a letter for her confirmation. A document for life. He and I have lived together, and now we die together, two comrades. . . .

I see the course that things are taking in our country, and I know that Grandfather will prove to have been right, but remember—and all of you must remember this—that your dream must not be to return to the time before the war, but that all of you, young and old, should create conditions that are not arbitrary but that will bring to realization a genuinely human ideal, something that every person will see and feel to be an ideal for all of us. That is the great gift for which our country thirsts—something for which every humble peasant boy can yearn, and which he can joyously feel himself to have a part in and to be working for.

Finally, there is the girl whom I call mine. Make her realize that the stars still shine and that I have been only a milestone on her road. Help her on: she can still become very happy.

In haste—your eldest child and only son,

Kim

The press bureau of the chief of the SS and the police force in Denmark on Sunday, April 8, 1945, issued the following announcement:

> Condemned to death: Seaman Kim Malthe-Bruun, born July 8, 1923, in Saskatchewan, Canada, resident in Copenhagen, because, as a member of an illegal organization, he possessed himself of a revenue service boat and took it to Sweden. In addition he procured arms for his organization and took part in transporting arms. The death sentence was carried out by a firing squad.

A distinguished Berlin minister spent the final days of his life in prison because he dared to defy the Nazis by speaking out publicly against their policies. He died in 1943, as the Nazis were sending him to Dachau Concentration Camp on the grounds of "jeopardy to public order." This selection is from *Dying We Live: The Final Messages and Records of the Resistance.*

Bernhard Lichtenberg, Prelate

B ernhard Lichtenberg, born December 3, 1875, at Ohlau in Silesia, had been dean of the Cathedral of St. Hedwig in Berlin since 1938. When the great trial of his life came to him, he was well advanced in years, a venerable priest whose body, consumed by long years of self-sacrificing pastoral service, continued to function only under compulsion of a fiery will. In him were combined the tenderness of the ardent worshipper and the hardihood of a crusader battling for injured justice. He was of those who hunger and thirst after righteousness. Thus a conflict with National Socialism was inevitable.

Even before the brown-shirted cohorts seized power, Father Lichtenberg was an object of hatred to them as a pacifist. And when in Germany terror was made a form of government, he could not and would not remain silent, because for a priest silence meant complicity. In October of 1941, the Party disseminated inflammatory pamphlets directed against the Jews; in answer to these, he had the following announcement read from the pulpits of all the churches of the diocese.

> ANNOUNCEMENT. An inflammatory pamphlet anonymously attacking the Jews is being disseminated among the houses of Berlin. It declares that any German who, because of allegedly false sentimentality, aids the Jews in any way, be it only through a friendly gesture, is guilty of betraying his people. Do not allow yourselves to be confused by this un-Christian attitude, but act according to the strict commandment of Jesus Christ: "Thou shalt love thy neighbor as thyself."

No one ever saw him raise his hand in the Hitler salute. When he was asked how he felt toward the Führer, he replied to the Gestapo commissioner: "I have only one Führer, Jesus Christ."

He was denounced for his public prayers on behalf of concentration camp prisoners and of Jews. On October 23, 1941, he was arrested, tried, and condemned to two years in prison. "I knew of the many priests who had been arrested," he admitted at the trial, "and even then surmised what I know today, because I have now been having a taste of it these last seven months and have been made to feel it in my own body how hard the fate of imprisonment is even for a priest, and how greatly, in such distress, even he stands in need of strength and consolation from God." . . .

The deprivation of freedom was synonymous with a death sentence. Dean Lichtenberg died November 5, 1943, in Hof, on the way to Dachau, where the Gestapo was sending him after the expiration of his term of imprisonment at Tegel, on the ground of "jeopardy to public order."

Could the Holocaust have been prevented? Quite possibly yes, but no one really tried. That is the chilling message of this harsh indictment of world indifference. Despite the seeming concern and good intentions of many people in western countries, little action was taken by their governments either to interfere with the Nazi program, or to provide refuge for fleeing Jews.

The selection is by Judah Pilch, from *The Jewish Catastrophe in Europe.*

The World Was Silent

JUDAH PILCH

The story of the Holocaust will not be complete unless some reference is made to the two basic questions which are uppermost in the minds of all students of the Tragedy. Why was the civilized world silent, and why did the Churches not raise their voices on behalf of the Jews? These are difficult questions to which there are no ready-made answers. Yet it is important to establish the truth that the civilized world and the Churches knew of the tragedy but did not bring pressure to bear on the Nazi leaders to halt Jewish persecution.

THE INACTION OF THE GOVERNMENTS

In the years 1933–39, when the German government was still mindful of the reaction of the rest of the world, and during the years of the Holocaust (1939–1945), when the slaughter was under way, the mild protests of some statesmen, intellectuals, and clergy notwithstanding, the enlightened world remained, on the whole, silent. These are the facts: More than 2,000,000 Germans were directly connected with the Nazi machinery of destruction, and many more millions profited from the pillage and loot. The masses of the German and Austrian populations *knew* of the anti-Jewish measures. Many were also aware of the ghettos and concentration camps. For a number of years they heard Hitler and his associates employ the terms *Ausrottung* (annihilation) and *Vernichtung* (destruction) when they talked about the Jews. Yet the vast majority of the Germans were silent. It is apparent that the collective conscience of these people changed radically in the 1930s. Nearly every person of German ancestry everywhere in the world became an apologist for the new Hitler policies, and the anti-Semites among them became Nazi collaborators. Within the Reich they were willing to conform to all Nazi plans. The Nazi leadership, in unleashing a propaganda campaign laden with racialism and anti-Semitism, succeeded in fashioning a dehumanized "new Nazi man," who was ready to torture the Jew and wipe him off the face of the earth. It is true that very small segments of the German community did oppose Nazi theory and practice. Certain Church leaders were opposed to Hitlerian ideas and deplored the Nazi acts in public. Here and there, some pastors made concerted efforts to get Jews out of the country. Scattered groups from among the professionals, working classes and former aristocrats resisted Nazi brutality, but by and large the Germans as a people did not protest. For 10 years they heard the brownshirted fellow Germans singing: *"Wenn das Judenblut vom Messer spritzt, dann geht's noch mal so gut"* (When Jewish blood drips from the knife, then things are twice as good), but they did not condemn this bloody slogan of their compatriots. As Dr. Karl Jaspers, the German philosopher, put it at the meeting of the World Jewish Congress held in Brussels in August 1966: "When our Jewish friends were taken away, we did not go down into the street, we did not cry out until we, too, were exterminated. We preferred to remain alive, alleging—truthfully but weakly—that our death would not have made any difference."

As for the Poles, they, too, were indifferent to Jewish sufferings in the ghettos, and they were unmoved in the hour of Jewish deportations to the extermination centers. "They did not even express ordinary human compassion at the spectacle of our ordeal—let alone some manifestations of Christian charity.... While we bled and died, their attitude was at best indifference, and all too often it was 'friendly neutrality' toward the Germans ('let the Germans do this dirty job for us'). And there were far too many cases of willing, active, enthusiastic Polish assistance to the Nazi murderers. There was a handful of noble Poles, of course, but nobody listened to them. Their voices never carried above the continual screams of hatred. Heroically, they managed to save individuals, but they could not bring about the slightest mitigation of Nazi ferocity."

The extent of Polish animosity to the Jew may best be illustrated by referring to the Kielce pogrom. After millions of Polish Jews had perished during the Nazi occupation, the Polish masses were still animated by hatred of the Jews. The Kielce pogrom of July 4, 1946, took the lives of 42 Jews in a massacre planned and perpetrated by bigots. This was done at a time when only remnants of Polish Jewry remained alive and sought to build their lives anew in their native country.

There were certainly acts of heroism on the part of individual Poles as well as some groups. Some of the leftist groups offered assistance to Jewish escapees. Some kindhearted and courageous individuals risked their lives to rescue Jews. However, the overwhelming majority of the Polish population manifested an apathy to the Jewish tragedy and, as already mentioned, substantial numbers of them collaborated with the Nazis in the persecution of the Jews.

It is apparently no accident that the Nazis chose Poland as the slaughterhouse of the Jews of Europe. Poland was the most "convenient" region for concentration camps because the centuries-old climate of anti-Semitism in that country was conducive to acts of terror against the Jews.

In the Ukraine, to the east of Poland, the attitude toward the Jewish Catastrophe seems to have been much the same. In the territory of the U.S.S.R. the extermination of the Jews by the Nazis did not take long. It was a sudden blow at the beginning of the occupation which caught the Jews in a state of total bewilderment. The native populations of the overrun regions—Letts, Lithuanians, Byelorussians, and especially Ukrainians—regarded the liquidation of the Jews calmly, and some with satisfaction. It is a matter of record that the Ukrainian collaboration with the German units in charge of the extermination program prompted the famous Russian poet, Yevgeny Yevtushenko, to write his "Babi Yar," a poem in which he deplored the participation of the civilian population in the mass killing of 40,000 Jews in the ravine of Babi Yar in the outskirts of Kiev. Ukrainians and White Russians also worked for the Nazis in the death camps, especially in Treblinka.

The attitude to the Holocaust in the occupied countries of the West differed radically. Compassion for the Jews was general throughout western, northern and southeastern Europe. In Belgium deportations were prevented until the summer of 1942. The greater part of the population was opposed to persecution of Jews. Some of the clergy offered refuge to Jewish children. Other citizens helped their Jewish friends. In France some Frenchmen in the nonoccupied part helped Jews to hide or to flee the country. The population of Denmark inscribed in its history a glorious page of heroism and self-sacrifice by a well-organized operation in transporting almost 7,000 Jews to Sweden. Other Scandinavian countries (Sweden in particular) made heroic efforts to rescue the harassed Jews. In Italy, too, efforts were made to save the Jews from Nazi tyranny. Jews found a haven in Hungary until the occupation of the country by the Germans. In Bulgaria, the population as well as the clergy protested against deportation of Jews. In Greece clergymen in high office and many of the officials not only saved individual Jews but also voiced official protests against anti-Jewish measures. But sporadic acts of humanity and of compassion could not prevent the Holocaust.

Notwithstanding the good intentions of people from all walks of life who were shocked by the Nazi tyranny and tried to relieve the plight of the Jews, there was even in the West no organized and systematic rescue work, when rescue was still possible, and no mass action against Nazi brutalities. The civilized world remained officially content to consider the anti-Nazi measures of 1933–1939 as Germany's internal affair. Although the Racial Laws of September 1935 and the *Kristallnacht* of November 9, 1938, left no doubt as to the Nazi intentions, for, as a matter of fact, the Nazis themselves made no attempt to conceal them, the free world was still "minding its own business." James G. MacDonald, the American High Commissioner for Refugees, who had been appointed by the League of Nations to find havens for the multitudes of refugees streaming out of Germany, resigned from his post two years later because of his inability to find such asylum. In his letter of resignation he called the world's attention to the need either for bringing pressure to bear upon Germany to stop creating refugees, or else for opening the doors of new countries to them. His dramatic gesture proved fruitless.

It is true that President Roosevelt convened a conference, in July 1938, in Evian, at which the need for finding homes for the uprooted was discussed, but most participating countries were unable to find ways of admitting even part of the helpless refugees. America herself was not prepared to change the national quota system. The French insisted that they could not receive any more Jews. The Swiss complained against "the mass crossing of the borders by Jewish refugees." Britain and Australia admitted some refugees but were reluctant to do more. Admission of Jewish refugees to Palestine, the only country whose Jewish population was willing and ready to find room in their own community for unlimited numbers, was blocked by Britain, the Mandatory Power. The British White Paper of 1939 limited the number of Jewish immigrants to Palestine for the next five years to 15,000 per year.

A year and a half after the outbreak of World War II, reliable news of mass arrests, expulsions and massacres, concentration camps and gas chambers had already reached the governments of the civilized world, yet nothing was done. America was still unwilling to change its immigration laws. Britain was already engaged in the war and, anxious to please the Arabs, adhered to its White Paper of 1939 by refusing admission of Jewish refugees to Palestine. France and other western countries were struggling to keep alive, and the governments of the free world remained inactive. There was lip service but little action.

A concrete example of the free world's attitude to the Jewish refugee problem was the voyage of the ship *St. Louis* which sailed from Germany on May 13, 1939, with 930 refugees, all of whom had Cuban landing certificates. When they reached Havana, the Cuban authorities did not permit them to land. The American Government refused them admission although they held quota numbers which would have made it possible for them to enter the U.S. three months to three years after their arrival in Cuba. Only through the efforts of Jewish leaders were these refugees, still on the *St. Louis,* taking them back to Germany, finally admitted to Belgium, the Netherlands, Britain, and France.

The *Struma*, packed far beyond capacity with 769 Rumanian Jews, sank in the Bosporus on February 24, 1943—its fate another indication of the inaction of the civilized world. The *Struma*, which sailed from Rumania toward Palestine, was at sea for 74 days, but no country was willing to admit the helpless victims of Nazi persecution. The agonized plea of its refugees reached the ears of all civilized people during that time, but not their hearts. The British refused to allow them entrance to Palestine; Turkey did not permit them to disembark. Its 769 men, women and children perished in the depths of the sea, just a few miles from Istanbul.

In 1942, both the U.S. Congress and the British House of Commons adopted resolutions condemning Nazi atrocities, but no word was heard about measures to rescue at least some of the doomed people.

Dr. Chaim Weizmann in London urged the bombing of extermination camps, but the Foreign Office replied that "the air staff was compelled, in view of the very great difficulties involved, to refrain from carrying out the proposal. Similar requests to destroy extermination factories were submitted in Washington and received similar treatment. Early in 1944 the Jewish Agency submitted a scheme to the British authorities for the dropping of hundreds of Palestinian Jews by parachute into Hungary. . . . But after it was approved by all the military authorities concerned and arrangements had been initiated to carry it out, the Foreign and Colonial Offices interfered and, for political reasons, instructed the military authorities to abandon the scheme."

Time and again, the question was asked: Why had these two great powers, Britain and the United States, done so little to halt the process of extermination? The answers varied. Some assumed that the great western powers did not want to threaten the Germans with retaliation lest they be suspected of waging a "Jewish" war. Others maintained that from the vantage point of diplomacy a defense of the Jews would have hindered the plans of invasion. But no sound answer was given to the question about the stubborn British refusal to open the gates of Palestine to Jewish escapees and about the Mandatory Government's practice of imprisoning in detention camps in Cyprus and in Palestine those who reached the shores of the Jewish National Home without bona fide certificates of immigration.

As for the United States, not only did the Government exercise great caution in dealing with Hitler, but it refused to enlarge the quota for Polish nationals in 1939 when Germany overran Poland. Keeping the status quo, insofar as the immigration law was concerned, meant that the doors of America remained locked and that appreciable numbers of either Polish Jews or Gentiles could find no refuge in this great country. When the Quakers campaigned in Congress (1939) to bring 20,000 children (Jewish and non-Jewish) to the U.S., the Administration's inaction was largely responsible for its failure. But when, after the fall of France, England was threatened with possible invasion of the Nazis, the U.S. Government quickly issued visas for 10,000 English children. When Jewish leaders negotiated with Rumania and Hungary about the emigration of their Jewish subjects with the view to bringing a considerable number of them to the U.S., the American Government refused to change its policy. As late as August 1, 1942, at a time when about one and a half million European Jews were already dead, the State Department insisted on verifying the reports submitted by Rabbi Stephen S. Wise, then president of the American Jewish Congress to the effect that the Nazis were murdering Jews in Russia and in Poland. Checking the reports took more than three months. In the meantime more Jews perished. Finally, in November 1942, when the reports were confirmed, the U.S. Government joined the other Allied nations in a declaration entitled: "German Policy of Extermination of the Jewish Race," issued on December 17, 1942, which stated that the responsible perpetrators should not escape retribution. Although the framers of this declaration were in earnest and were no doubt eager to alleviate Jewish misery, the Nazis were hardly impressed with it. This manifestation of good will came too late. By the end of 1942, many more Jews had been liquidated by the Nazis. As Rabbi Wise put it in a letter to his friend, Rev. John H. Holmes, in 1943: "It appears to me that both authors, Eden [Foreign Minister of England] and Cordell Hull [Secretary of State], have been frozen into immobility." Nothing of any consequence was undertaken by these two great powers. There was a conference on refugees in Hamilton, Bermuda, on April 19, 1942. Yet neither Great Britain nor the U.S.A. was ready to admit the victims of Nazism. It was on June 12, 1944, almost five years after the launching of the extermination program, that the U.S. President Franklin Delano Roosevelt announced in a message to Congress "that America would bring to its shores 1,000 refugees, mostly women and children, who had escaped to Southern Italy."

And once again Rabbi Stephen S. Wise

> worked out a secret plan (in 1944) for smuggling out Jews in exchange for bribes to be deposited in Switzerland. Seventy thousand lives could have been saved. Roosevelt gave the plan his full support and Morgenthau backed it immediately. But the State Department now held matters up for months. The British Ministry of Economic Warfare was informed and wrote back saying that "the British Foreign Office is concerned with the difficulty of disposing of any considerable number of Jews should they be released from enemy territory!"
>
> . . . Ultimately, according to Stephen S. Wise, nothing was done owing to the shocking delay and sabotage . . . for five full months after the license had been approved by the President of the United States, the Secretary of State, and the Secretary of the Treasury.

Dr. Wise, one of the staunchest supporters of the Roosevelt administration, sums up the episode:

> Let history, therefore, record for all time that were it not for the State Department and Foreign Office bungling and callousness, thousands of lives might have been saved and the Jewish catastrophe partially averted.

Dr. Wise's statements were substantiated in a recently published book, *While Six Million Died*. The author, Arthur D. Morse, examined the inaction of the American Government and came to the conclusion that the upright men in the administration of the humanitarian President Roosevelt knew of Hitler's order for the "final solution," knew of the mass executions, but were overcautious in doing something about it. Mr. Morse indicts the Government's bureaucratic delays, refusal to try ransom and to revise immigration quotas. Thus, both America and England, through official procrastination, maintained their barriers against any serious rescue attempts.

Other great nations were also silent. The Russians were not concerned about the destruction of European Jewry. They signed a Soviet-Nazi pact during the short period of friendship between the Communists and the Nazis. The Russian press and radio ignored the existence of anti-Jewish measures in Greater Germany. As a matter of fact, Russian Jews remained unaware of what was in store for them when the German armies invaded Russia. During the German occupation of Russian territories, many Russians were employed by the Nazis to initiate pogroms and help in the process of extermination. It is also a known fact that during the Warsaw Ghetto uprising the Red Army failed to send help to the courageous Jewish fighters.

The people of Afro-Asia and Latin America displayed an attitude of indifference to the Jewish tragedy. Although some refugees were admitted to certain Latin American countries, the population as a whole registered through its government no official protest against Nazi barbarities. In the Arab lands the political as well as religious leadership were favorably impressed with Nazi actions against the Jews. It is a fact that Haj Amin al Husseini, the Mufti of Jerusalem, a high dignitary of the religion of Islam, was an ardent Hitler collaborator.

It is therefore no surprise that many young people who study this period in world history charge the free world with complicity in the murder of six million Jews and that some contemporary writers maintain that the conscience of the world was destroyed with the destruction of millions of innocent people.

THE SILENCE OF THE CHURCHES

An even more painful question is the silence of organized religion, Christianity, Islam, Buddhism, and other faiths. There is no doubt that the rescue work of Church officials who in the spirit of Christian charity opened their cloisters and monasteries to the harried Jews was an important factor in the survival of individual Jews. The courageous denunciation of Nazi barbarities by Church dignitaries of western Europe and especially the statement of Pope Pius XI that "in spirit we are Semites" had a considerable impact on many clergymen. The daring pronouncements against Nazi terror by Pastors Niemöller in Germany and Boegner in France rank high as inspiring acts of courage. By the same token the defiance of cardinals and bishops in France, Belgium, Galicia, and Netherlands are examples of true heroism—some paid with their lives for their compassion. There is no doubt that many of the survivors owe their lives to the humanitarian acts of both the clerics and compassionate laymen. But these righteous acts were isolated instances: they were the exception to the rule.

The fact is that no official representation was ever made by the heads of the Christian Churches (nor by the spokesmen of Islam and Buddhism) which could have expressed in the strongest possible terms the protest of all true believers. While the death factories operated at full blast, the papacy itself was silent. The silence of the Pope has been a subject of debate for 15 years. The playwright Rolf Hochhuth expressed the view in his play *The Deputy* that the Pope's failure to speak out against Nazi brutalities should be considered as telling evidence of his indifference to the plight of the Jews and thus a serious moral lapse. In "Sidelines on History," the appendix to his play, Hochhuth writes: ". . . It remains incomprehensible that His Holiness did not bestir himself to protest against Hitler, when it was clear that Germany had lost the war, while at the same time Auschwitz was just beginning its highest daily quota of killings." Other writers are not as ready to blacken the character of the Pope. Léon Poliakov, one of the outstanding researchers of the Holocaust, finds an explanation for the silence of the Pope. He writes:

> The immense church interests which were the Pope's responsibil-
> ity, the extensive means for blackmail which the Nazis enjoyed on
> a scale commensurate with the Universal Church, probably
> account for his failure to issue that solemn and public declaration
> which the persecuted looked forward to so ardently.

Guenther Lewy, on the other hand, explains the inaction of the Pope thus: "He did not view the plight of the Jews with a real sense of urgency and moral courage"; while Father Edward H. Flannery refutes the accusations against the Pope by saying that, "at the insistence of the Vatican, protests against the deportations *were* made to several governments with Catholic majorities, such as Slovakia, Poland, Italy and Hungary." But no matter what the reasons for the Vatican's silence, and no matter whether Hochhuth's conclusions are right or wrong—all agree that the Pope *was* silent. For the same writers who try to justify his silence are, nonetheless, disturbed about it. Poliakov states: "It is painful to have to say that during the war, while the death factories ran full blast, the Papacy kept silent." Flannery notes: "Pius XII made only indirect allusions to the anti-Semitic campaign in his public pronouncements but encouraged the use of his nunciatures and chanceries throughout Europe to protect and save Jews."

We thus see that no attempt was made to mobilize the resources of the world religious institutions for the defense of Nazi victims. The religious leaders were no doubt concerned but apparently did not want to antagonize the Nazis lest they take vengeance on Church functionaries and properties. The Catholic Church did not even deem it advisable to use its power to threaten with excommunication those Catholics who participated in the Nazi treatment of Jews and other "undesirables." In the midst of the enormity of the Nazi atrocities the "true believers" conducted their affairs by the discreet rule of "business as usual."

THE SILENCE OF THE INTELLECTUAL COMMUNITY
As for the intellectual community, save for a number of sporadic denunciations by some writers, scientists, and academicians, the majority did not raise their voices in protest against Nazi genocide. The academic com-

munities did not react en masse in a collective *J'accuse*. The pen clubs of the world did not sow the seed of revolt in the 1930s when outside of Germany it was still possible to arouse the people against Nazi theory and practice. They did not issue proclamations calling upon millions of readers to stand up and be heard. There were few anti-Nazi rallies conducted by the intellectuals on the campuses, in public forums, and there was little utilization of the mass media for the purpose of informing the public of the Hitlerite menace. The reactions of the liberals and progressives in the labor movement and in socio-cultural organizations were those of sympathy for and solidarity with the suffering Jews, but these feelings were not translated in terms of active and positive actions on their behalf. Had the multitudes of free men in the free world reacted courageously and vigorously, many of the Nazi acts of terror might have been averted.

DID JEWRY DO EVERYTHING POSSIBLE?

There is also the very disturbing fact of the lack of mass action by the Jewish communities in the countries not overrun by the Nazis, especially in America. It has been pointed out by students of the Holocaust period that the masses of the Jewish people could not believe the news which reached them from the ghettos of Europe and the death camps and that the true facts, when they became known, had a paralyzing effect upon most of them. Furthermore, the loyalty of Jews as citizens of the free countries made them sensitive to the plea not to hamper the war effort by any "exaggerated" demands. Thus, rescue activities were confined to the philanthropic agencies and to the Palestinian Jews through the Jewish Agency. In America, the anti-Nazi boycott conducted by the Joint Boycott Council, which resulted in a decline of Germany's place in the world economy, and the anti-Nazi campaign carried out by the various organizations were efforts to unmask the true face of the Nazis and to combat mounting anti-Jewish feeling on the American continent. But the *masses* of Jews in the U.S. and in other free lands did not make *extraordinary* efforts to impress on their governments that official inaction doomed their brethren to certain death. Those American Jews who were ready to take overall collective actions of protest and rescue found themselves in a very awkward position because the State Department argued that any independent rescue action would hamper the Allied war effort. The facts are that during the period 1933–45 there were no "sit-ins" nor mass demonstrations in the dense Jewish population centers. There were no marches of Jewish masses to Washington, Ottawa, London, Johannesburg, Buenos Aires, and Rio de Janeiro. No public fast days were instituted to express solidarity with the victims. Most of the protests that took place were a byproduct of the feverish activities of a number of restless Jewish lay leaders and professional workers. The average Jew, however, although intensely hurt, did not do the impossible. This pitiful inertia of world Jewry was prophetically foreshadowed in a verse by Bialik, written in the days of Herzl's call to action (by joining the Zionist movement): *"we-lo na we-low za we-lo harad ha-am"* (and the people did not stir and were not agitated). The majority of the Jewish people during the period of the great catastrophe did not tremble sufficiently to inject a chill into the hearts of their Christian neighbors. There are now young Jews and Jewesses who fight for civil rights for the Negro, a cause that is cherished by every person of conscience as well as by the intelligent Jew who is committed to the Jewish concept of liberty. But in the years of the Holocaust there were no demonstrations by Jewish youth in the cause of their own kin trapped in the Nazi web of destruction. They did not parade; they did not go on hunger strikes. Young Jews were not ready to destroy their citizenship papers and denounce the Roosevelt administration, especially the State Department, for its apathy to the Jewish agony. Recipients of honors did not return their medals in protest. Leaders of Jewish religious schools did not assemble their pupils in the public squares to protest the persecution of their coreligionists, especially the fate of the children of their own age who were so cruelly done away with. Jews did not pluck up the courage to follow the deed of their ancestor Mordecai by assembling in the streets and "shouting bitterly" because of the threat of the Haman of their day. None proclaimed their readiness to follow the example of their Palestinian brethren who dared to parachute into Nazi-occupied territory for specific rescue missions.

Nelly Sachs, the recipient of the Nobel Award in Literature in 1966 in whose poetry we find a very intense reaction to the Tragedy, echoes its realities in one of her poems. The last stanza of this poem from *The Chorus of the Orphans* reads as follows:

> We Orphans we lament to the world:
> World, why have you taken our soft mothers from us.
> And the fathers who say: My child you are like me!
> We Orphans are like no one in this world any more.
> Oh world
> We accuse you!

The next two readings are from major newspapers, one published in New York *(The New York Times)*, the other in London *(The Times)*, both carrying articles from the same year, 1943, just months apart, and both making very clear and very public exactly what the Nazis were doing.

The claim is often made that people could not have known what was being done to the Jews. These newspaper accounts prove otherwise. In the face of these and similar articles, the excuse that, "We didn't know," loses much of its veracity.

Nazi Brutality to Jews

TIMES OF LONDON, JUNE 1, 1943

From many parts of Europe comes evidence that the German leaders are driving forward their campaign against Jews with even greater ferocity, and more widely, than before. From Poland—where repression of all kinds is greater than anywhere else—the anti-Jewish measures are spreading to the Balkans.

In Rumania the Commissioner for Jewish Affairs, Leka, carrying out Marshal Antonescu's orders, has levied an additional tax of 4,000,000 lei on the Jewish community. Half of this fabulous sum, equal to about a fifth of the normal annual revenue for the whole country, has to be paid by the middle of this month. All Jews unable to subscribe their quota will be deported for forced labor in Transdniestria. Many have already been sent there, and almost 40,000 are already in Rumanian labor camps.

In Bulgaria the Jews have been driven from Sofia, and the authorities have held back exit permits from those applying to leave the country. Many have been told that they are to be deported to Poland.

In Hungary the Prime Minister, Kallay, has just declared that all Jews must ultimately be deported from the country, but—using guarded language and evidently referring to German demands for immediate action—he dared to add that Hungary could not deport large numbers until a fit area had been reserved for their settlement. In all these southeastern countries the threat most frequently used by the Germans is the threat of deportation to Poland.

MURDER IN THE GHETTOS

From Poland itself the reports, confirmed by independent intelligence, prove that in many towns the worst fears of a few months ago have been realized. German machine-guns and explosives are silent now in the Warsaw ghetto after a month of unparalleled murder. The Cracow ghetto has been emptied: 1,000 Jews were murdered in the streets and houses, and the others taken off to the Oswiecim concentration camp. A similar number have been killed at Lukow. From many other Polish towns— Radomsk, Krasnik, Sobolew, Radzymin, and others—come the same reports of murder and the deportation of thousands under conditions harder than life can bear for long—and the journeys are often very long.

In Russia the Red armies report that, when they advanced last winter into liberated villages, they found that the Jewish inhabitants had almost everywhere been murdered by the German soldiers. Russians were hanged and shot as well in large numbers, but for a Jew to escape was exceptional.

Allied peoples often are dumbfounded when Hitler continually raves against "the Jewish clique which began the war." Few people can follow the trends in his twisted mind. What is certain today is that the rage has found outlet for itself in a terrible form, not yet to be measured in scope. The ravings have to be taken as statements of a policy systematically applied.

2,000,000 Murders by Nazis Charged

NEW YORK TIMES, AUGUST 8, 1943

LONDON, Aug. 7—Polish Labor Fights, a publication issued here today, printed an account of a house maintained by the Germans at Treblinka, Poland, for the extermination of Jews. In this place alone, it is said the Germans have killed 2,000,000 persons.

The account of the executions opens with an announcement the Germans pinned up on the station where the victims arrive.

"You may be easy in your mind as to your future," the notice read. "You are going to the east to work and your wives will have care of your household. Before you leave you must have a bath and your clothing must be deloused. Your property will be restored to you in proper condition."

COMPLY WITH ORDER TO DISROBE

Men, women, and children comply with the order for disrobing and then, states Polish Labor Fights, comes the first scene in the last act of the Treblinka tragedy. The article continues:

"Children with women go first, urged on by whips of the Germans. Faster and faster they are driven and thicker and thicker fall the blows on heads paralyzed with terror and pain. The silence of the woods is shattered by the screams of women and the oaths of Germans.

"The victims now realize their doom is near. At the entrance of the death house the No. 1 chief himself drives them to cells, freely using a whip. The floor of the cell is slippery. Some fall and are unable to rise because of the pressure of those behind. Small children are flung over the heads of the women.

"When the cells are filled they are closed and sealed. Steam is forced through apertures and suffocation of the victims begins. At first cries can be heard but these gradually subside and after 15 minutes all is silent. The execution is over.

"When the trap is opened to let the bodies drop down they fall in a compact mass, stuck together by the heat and steam. Cold water is sprayed on them with a hose after which the gravediggers pile the corpses on a platform like the carcasses of slaughtered animals.

"Often a gravedigger is too weak to carry two bodies, as ordered, so he ties arms or legs together and runs to the burial ground, dragging them behind him.

MEN KILLED IN SAME WAY

"The execution of men is carried out in the same way. They are driven along the same path through the woods. On their way to death the reactions of the victims differ. Some blaspheme, but all eventually are silenced by blows.

"At times not all victims can be squeezed into the death cells at once, and those remaining are kept near the house of death. They can see and hear all that takes place, but are so numbed in their senses that there is no sign of the instinct of self-preservation.

"This is clear proof of the condition to which they have been reduced by ill treatment and starvation."

One small country, by contrast, put moral principle above all other considerations. This selection is from *The Jewish Catastrophe in Europe.*

The Righteous Danes

ABRAHAM FOXMAN

On the outskirts of Jerusalem stands a large building known as Yad Vashem. It is a national documentation center of the atrocities perpetrated against the Jews during World War II. It is the world's foremost research and recording center of the Holocaust. Near the museum there is a grove where trees have been planted to honor those Christians who at the risk, and sometimes the cost, of their lives helped to rescue Jews. These are the Righteous, whose actions were those of one who says: "*I am* my brother's keeper."

KING CHRISTIAN X OF DENMARK

The German army invaded Denmark in 1940. For two years the Germans did not take stringent actions against the Jews because of the Danes' persistent resistance against Nazi anti-Jewish measures. It is reported that King Christian X, in a conversation with a German official who used the phrase "Jewish problem," replied, "There is no Jewish problem in this country. There is only my people." It is also told that when the German officials reproached King Christian for his "negligence in resolving the Jewish problem," he answered, "Gentlemen, since we have never considered ourselves inferior to the Jews, we have no such problem here." On another occasion, King Christian announced, "If the Germans want to introduce the yellow star in Denmark, I and my whole family will wear it as a sign of the highest distinction." When in August 1943 a Nazi order was issued to deport all Jews, the Danish population mobilized all its resources to rescue the Jews. They succeeded in "smuggling" some 7,000 Jews to neutral, unoccupied Sweden. No other occupied country has achieved the distinction of rescuing the major part of its Jewish population.

Congressman Arthur W. Mitchell (1934–42) of Chicago was the first African-American Democrat elected to Congress. Born to former slaves, Mitchell once served as office boy for Booker T. Washington. When he was forced to leave a Pullman car because of his race, Congressman Mitchell took his case to the Supreme Court and won.

Congressman Mitchell expressed his concern over the Nazi persecution of Jewish people in this letter to President Franklin D. Roosevelt of October 12, 1938.

A Congressman Speaks for Minority Rights

ARTHUR W. MITCHELL

As a representative of a minority group in America, an underprivileged group which has been subjected to prejudice and mistreatment from time to time, we are interested in the attitude of majority groups throughout the world toward minority groups. At the present time we are greatly disturbed because of the intolerance of certain major groups toward the Jewish people residing in European countries and wish to have our voice heard in the interest of justice and fair play for all racial groups. We believe that the same spirit of intolerance which is working so tremendously against the safety and sacred rights of the Jewish people, if permitted to go unchallenged, will manifest itself sooner or later against all minority groups, perhaps in all parts of the world. [We] request you, the highest representative of our Government, to use every reasonable and peaceable means at your command in securing protection for the Jewish people in this hour of sad calamity.

This account of a murder that took place in 1964, in a quiet residential neighborhood of New York City, appears to have no bearing on the Holocaust. But as you read it, compare the behavior of the "38 witnesses" to that of millions of ordinary citizens in Germany in the 1930s. They, too, were witnesses.

The selection is from *The New York Times*, March 27, 1964.

Thirty-Eight Witnesses

MARTIN GANSBERG

For more than half an hour 38 respectable, law-abiding citizens in Queens watched a killer stalk and stab a woman in three separate attacks in Kew Gardens.

Twice the sound of their voices and the sudden glow of their bedroom lights interrupted him and frightened him off. Each time he returned, sought her out and stabbed her again. Not one person telephoned the police during the assault; one witness called after the woman was dead.

That was two weeks ago today. But Assistant Chief Inspector Frederick M. Lussen, in charge of the borough's detective force and a veteran of 25 years of homicide investigations, is still shocked.

He can give a matter-of-fact recitation of many murders. But the Kew Gardens slaying baffles him—not because it is a murder, but because the "good people" failed to call the police.

"As we have reconstructed the crime," he said, "the assailant had three chances to kill this woman during the 35-minute period. He returned twice to complete the job. If we had been called when he first attacked, the woman might not be dead now."

This is what the police say happened beginning at 3:20 A.M. in the staid, middle-class, tree-lined Austin Street area:

Twenty-eight-year-old Catherine Genovese, who was called Kitty by almost everyone in the neighborhood, was returning home from her job as a manager of a bar in Hollis. She parked her red Fiat in a lot adjacent to the Kew Gardens, Long Island, Railroad Station, facing Mowbray Place. Like many residents of the neighborhood, she had parked there day after day since her arrival from Connecticut a year ago, although the railroad frowns on the practice.

She turned off the lights of her car, locked the door and started to walk the 100 feet to the entrance of her apartment at 82-70 Austin Street, which is in a Tudor building, with stores on the first floor and apartments on the second.

The entrance to the apartment is in the rear of the building because the front is rented to retail stores. At night the quiet neighborhood is shrouded in the slumbering darkness that marks most residential areas.

Miss Genovese noticed a man at the far end of the lot, near a seven-story apartment house at 82-40 Austin Street. She halted, then, nervously, she headed up Austin Street toward Lefferts Boulevard, where there is a call box to the 102nd Police Precinct in nearby Richmond Hill.

She got as far as a street light in front of a bookstore before the man grabbed her. She screamed. Lights went on in the 10-story apartment house at 82-67 Austin Street, which faces the bookstore. Windows slid open and voices punctured the early morning stillness.

Miss Genovese screamed: "Oh, my God, he stabbed me! Please help me! Please help me!"

From one of the upper windows in the apartment house, a man called down: "Let that girl alone!"

The assailant looked at him, shrugged and walked down Austin Street toward a white sedan parked a short distance away. Miss Genovese struggled to her feet.

Lights went out. The killer returned to Miss Genovese, now trying to make her way around the side of the building by the parking lot to get to her apartment. The assailant stabbed her again.

"I'm dying!" she shrieked. "I'm dying!"

Windows were opened again, and lights went on in many apartments. The assailant got into his car and drove away. Miss Genovese staggered to her feet. A city bus, Q-10, the Lefferts Boulevard line to Kennedy International Airport, passed. It was 3:35 A.M.

The assailant returned. By then, Miss Genovese had crawled to the back of the building, where the freshly painted brown doors to the apartment house held out hope of safety. The killer tried the first door; she wasn't there. At the second door, 82-62 Austin Street, he saw her slumped on the floor at the foot of the stairs. He stabbed her a third time—fatally.

It was 3:50 by the time the police received their first call from a man who was a neighbor of Miss Genovese. In two minutes they were at the scene. The neighbor, a 70-year-old woman, and another woman were the only persons on the street. Nobody else came forward.

The man explained that he had called the police after much deliberation. He had phoned a friend in Nassau County for advice and then he had crossed the roof of the building to the apartment of the elderly woman to get her to make the call.

"I didn't want to get involved," he sheepishly told the police. . . .

Twentieth-Century Man

The evidence has mounted before us—cruelty, cowardice, callous indifference, and crazed thirst for blood, beat out courage, kindness, and willingness to sacrifice self for the good of others. Is man beast or angel?

The next selection, taken from the book Human Aggression by Anthony Storr, argues that aggression is a fundamental and necessary part of human nature, but one which can be either a positive or a negative force.

Man As Aggressor

ANTHONY STORR

That man is an aggressive creature will hardly be disputed. With the exception of certain rodents, no other vertebrate habitually destroys members of his own species. No other animal takes positive pleasure in the exercise of cruelty upon another of his own kind. We generally describe the most repulsive examples of man's cruelty as brutal or bestial, implying by these adjectives that such behavior is characteristic of less highly developed animals than ourselves. In truth, however, the extremes of "brutal" behavior are confined to man; and there is no parallel in nature to our savage treatment of each other. The somber fact is that we are the cruellest and most ruthless species that has ever walked the earth; and that, although we may recoil in horror when we read in newspaper or history book of the atrocities committed by man upon man, we know in our hearts that each one of us harbors within himself those same savage impulses which lead to murder, to torture and to war.

To write about human aggression is a difficult task because the term is used in so many different senses. Aggression is one of those words which everyone knows, but which is nevertheless hard to define. As psychologists and psychiatrists use it, it covers a very wide range of human behavior. The red-faced infant squalling for the bottle is being aggressive; and so is the judge who awards a 30-year sentence for robbery. The guard in a concentration camp who tortures his helpless victim is obviously acting aggressively. Less manifestly, but no less certainly, so is the neglected wife who threatens or attempts suicide in order to regain her husband's affection. When a word becomes so diffusely applied that it is used for both the competitive striving of a footballer and the bloody violence of a murderer, it ought either to be dropped or else more closely defined. Aggression is a portmanteau term which is fairly bursting at its seams. Yet, until we can more clearly designate and comprehend the various aspects of human behavior which are subsumed under this head, we cannot discard the concept.

One difficulty is that there is no clear dividing line between those forms of aggression which we all deplore and those which we must not disown if we are to survive. When a child rebels against authority it is being aggressive: but it is also manifesting a drive toward independence which is a necessary and valuable part of growing up. The desire for power has, in extreme form, disastrous aspects which we all acknowledge: but the drive to conquer difficulties, or to gain mastery over the external world underlies the greatest of human achievements. Some writers define aggression as "that response which follows frustration," or as "an act whose goal-response is injury to an organism (or organism surrogate)." In the author's view these definitions impose limits upon the concept of aggression which are not in accord with the underlying facts of human nature which the word is attempting to express. It is worth noticing, for instance, that the words we use to describe intellectual effort are aggressive words. We *attack* problems, or *get our teeth into* them. We *master* a subject when we have *struggled with* and *overcome* its difficulties. We *sharpen* our wits, hoping that our mind will develop *a keen edge* in order that we may better *dissect* a problem into its component parts. Although intellectual tasks are often frustrating, to argue that all intellectual effort is the result of frustration is to impose too negative a coloring upon the positive impulse to comprehend and master the external world.

The aggressive part of human nature is not only a necessary safeguard against predatory attack. It is also the basis of intellectual achievement, of the attainment of independence, and even of that proper pride which enables a man to hold his head high among his fellows.

The following selections, by two writers who experienced the Holocaust, reflect an amazing human capacity to be optimistic, and to believe in human goodness, in the face of considerable evidence to the contrary. The first is from Anne Frank's *The Diary of a Young Girl,* the second from *Man's Search for Meaning* by Viktor Frankl.

People Are Really Good at Heart

ANNE FRANK

"For in its innermost depths youth is lonelier than old age." I read this saying in some book and I've always remembered it, and found it to be true. Is it true then that grownups have a more difficult time here than we do? No. I know it isn't. Older people have formed their opinions about everything, and don't waver before they act. It's twice as hard for us young ones to hold our ground, and maintain our opinions, in a time when all ideals are being shattered and destroyed, when people are showing their worst side, and do not know whether to believe in truth and right and God.

Anyone who claims that the older ones have a more difficult time here certainly doesn't realize to what extent our problems weigh down on us, problems for which we are probably much too young, but which thrust themselves upon us continually, until, after a long time, we think we've found a solution, but the solution doesn't seem able to resist the facts which reduce it to nothing again. That's the difficulty in these times: ideals, dreams, and cherished hopes rise within us, only to meet the horrible truth and be shattered.

It's really a wonder that I haven't dropped all my ideals, because they seem so absurd and impossible to carry out. Yet I kept them, because in spite of everything I still believe that people are really good at heart. I simply can't build up my hopes on a foundation consisting of confusion, misery, and death. I see the world gradually being turned into a wilderness. I hear the ever approaching thunder, which will destroy us too. I can feel the sufferings of millions and yet, if I look up into the heavens, I think that it will all come right, that this cruelty too will end, and that peace and tranquility will return again.

The Decent and the Indecent

VIKTOR E. FRANKL

I t is apparent that the mere knowledge that a man was either a camp guard or a prisoner tells us almost nothing. Human kindness can be found in all groups, even those which as a whole it would be easy to condemn. The boundaries between groups overlapped and we must not try to simplify matters by saying that these men were angels and those were devils. Certainly, it was a considerable achievement for a guard or foreman to be kind to the prisoners in spite of all the camp's influences, and, on the other hand, the baseness of a prisoner who treated his own companions badly was exceptionally contemptible. Obviously the prisoners found the lack of character in such men especially upsetting, while they were profoundly moved by the smallest kindness received from any of the guards. I remember how one day a foreman secretly gave me a piece of bread which I knew he must have saved from his breakfast ration. It was far more than a small piece of bread which moved me to tears at that time. It was the human "something" which this man also gave to me—the word and look which accompanied the gift.

From all this we may learn that there are two races of men in this world, but only these two—the "race" of the decent man and the "race" of the indecent man. Both are found everywhere; they penetrate into all groups of society. No group consists entirely of decent or indecent people. In this sense, no group is of "pure race"—and therefore one occasionally found a decent fellow among the camp guards.

Behavior Under Stress

Optimism, faith, a tenacious holding on to life. These persisted in some people even as their world lay shattered about them. Behind the barbed wire, men, women, and children actually composed and sang songs of hope; they wrote poetry and painted pictures to express their deepest yearnings.

Music Out of Pain

PEAT BOG SOLDIERS

GERMAN CONCENTRATION CAMP SONG

Political prisoners, who composed this song while marching to and from their work in the peat bog, sang it with such enthusiasm, particularly in the last chorus, with its veiled meaning, that it was finally forbidden.

1. Far and wide as the eye can wander
   Heath and bog are everywhere,
   Not a bird sings out to cheer us
   Oaks are standing gaunt and bare.

   CHORUS:
   We are the peat bog soldiers,
   Marching with our spades—to the bog.

2. Up and down the guards are pacing,
   No one, no one can go through
   Flight would mean a sure death facing,
   Guns and barbed wire greet our view.

   CHORUS:
   We are . . .

3. But for us there is no complaining
   Winter will in time be past
   One day we shall cry rejoicing,
   Homeland, dear, you're mine at last!

   CHORUS:
   Then will the peat bog soldiers
   March no more with their spades—to the bog.

ANI MA'AMIN

This song was sung by Jews who were about to be cremated by the Nazis.

I believe with complete faith in the coming of the Messiah. And though he tarry, still shall I believe and await his coming.

JEWISH PARTISAN SONG

Throughout Europe, groups of partisans, Jews and non-Jews, formed to fight a guerrilla war and carry out acts of sabotage against the Nazis and their collaborators. Their natural bases were the forests and swamps and mountain caves.

Never say that there is only death for you
Though leaden skies may be concealing days of blue—
Because the hour we have hungered for is near;
Beneath our tread the earth shall tremble: We are here!

From land of palm-tree to the far-off land of snow
We shall be coming with our torment and our woe,
And everywhere our blood has sunk into the earth
Shall our bravery, our vigor blossom forth!

We'll have the morning sun to set our day aglow,
And all our yesterdays shall vanish with the foe,
And if the time is long before the sun appears,
Then let this song go like a signal through the years.

This song was written with our blood and not with lead;
It's not song that birds sing overhead,
It was a people, among toppling barricades,
That sang this song of ours with pistols and grenades.

So never say that there is only death for you.
Leaden skies may be concealing days of blue—
Yet the hour we have hungered for is near;
Beneath our tread the earth shall tremble: We are here!

Some 15,000 children under the age of 15 passed through Terezín between the years 1942 and 1944. About 150 of them survived. In all, more than 1,000,000 Jewish children were killed by the Nazis. In Terezín, children were housed in separate barracks, and at the request of Jewish leaders, a kind of school was actually organized for them. These and other poems, and numerous drawings, were created in that makeshift school.

The poems are reprinted from the book *I Never Saw Another Butterfly.*

Children's Writings

WE GOT USED TO ...

... We got used to standing in line at 7 o'clock in the morning, at 12 noon and again at seven o'clock in the evening. We stood in a long queue with a plate in our hand, into which they ladled a little warmed-up water with a salty or a coffee flavor. Or else they gave us a few potatoes. We got used to sleeping without a bed, to saluting every uniform, not to walk on the sidewalks and then again to walk on the sidewalks. We got used to undeserved slaps, blows and executions. We got accustomed to seeing people die in their own excrement, to seeing piled-up coffins full of corpses, to seeing the sick amidst dirt and filth and to seeing the helpless doctors. We got used to it that from time to time, one thousand unhappy souls would come here and that, from time to time, another thousand unhappy souls would go away. . . .

—*From the prose of 15-year-old Petr Fischl (born September 9, 1929), who perished in Auschwitz in 1944.*

I'D LIKE TO GO ALONE

> I'd like to go away alone
> Where there are other, nicer people,
> Somewhere into the far unknown,
> There, where no one kills another.
> Maybe more of us,

A thousand strong,
Will reach this goal
Before too long.

—*Alena Synkov*

IT ALL DEPENDS ON HOW YOU LOOK AT IT

I.
Terezín is full of beauty.
It's in your eyes now clear
And through the street the tramp
Of many marching feet I hear.

In the ghetto at Terezín,
It looks that way to me,
Is a square kilometer of earth
Cut off from the world that's free.

II.
Death, after all, claims everyone,
You find it everywhere.
It catches up with even those
Who wear their noses in the air.

The whole, wide world is ruled
With a certain justice, so
That helps perhaps to sweeten
The poor man's pain and woe.

—*Miroslav Košek*

HOMESICK

I've lived in the ghetto here more than a year,
In Terezín, in the black town now,
And when I remember my old home so dear,
I can love it more than I did, somehow.
Ah, home, home,
Why did they tear me away?

Here the weak die easy as a feather
And when they die, they die forever.

I'd like to go back home again,
It makes me think of sweet spring flowers.
Before, when I used to live at home,
It never seemed so dear and fair.

I remember now those golden days . . .
But maybe I'll be going there soon again.

People walk along the street,
You see at once on each you meet
That there's a ghetto here,
A place of evil and of fear.
There's little to eat and much to want,
Where bit by bit, it's horror to live.
But no one must give up!
The world turns and times change.

Yet we all hope the time will come
When we'll go home again.
Now I know how dear it is
And often I remember it.

—*Anonymous, March 9, 1943*

THE BUTTERFLY

The last, the very last,
So richly, brightly, dazzlingly yellow.
Perhaps if the sun's tear would sing
    against a white stone . . .

Such, such a yellow
Is carried lightly 'way up high.
It went away I'm sure because it wished to
    kiss the world goodbye.

For seven weeks I've lived in here,
Penned up inside this ghetto
But I have found my people here.
The dandelions call to me
And the white chestnut candles in the court.
Only I never saw another butterfly.

That butterfly was the last one.
Butterflies don't live in here,
    In the ghetto.

—Pavel Friedmann, June 4, 1942

THE GARDEN

A little garden,
Fragrant and full of roses.
The path is narrow
And a little boy walks along it.

A little boy, a sweet boy,
Like that growing blossom.
When the blossom comes to bloom,
The little boy will be no more.

—Franta Bass

Why didn't more victims fight back? Was revolt possible? Would any act of retaliation have been preferable to passive acceptance of death? These questions have been raised again and again by students of the Holocaust. The next four selections may not give you definitive answers to these questions, but they will provide you with additional insights into the whole problem of resistance.

Scholars and researchers have discovered that there was much more active resistance by Jews than was previously thought. Perhaps the reason so little was known about this subject is that most resistance efforts were fruitless. Nevertheless, they did occur. When we speak of "fighting back," remember that we are talking of civilian populations, unarmed, weakened, and demoralized, matching their strength against legions of highly trained soldiers, guns, and tanks. Two other factors militated against the use of force: one, the lack of dependable support from non-Jews outside the ghettos, and two, fears on the part of many, particularly older people, that any action against the Nazis would bring retaliation and make matters worse. The conflict seemed to boil down to these two views: to die "with honor," as most resistance leaders urged, or to try and find ways to survive, hoping for Nazi lenience.

The first reading, from *Encyclopedia Judaica*, presents a broad view of the subject, including comparisons with other prisoner situations.

The Behavior of the Victims

ENCYCLOPEDIA JUDAICA

After the life in the ghettos and camps, after having lost the power of resistance under the constant Nazi terror, and often having also lost entire or part of their families, nothing but blind obedience could have been expected of these former persons when they were shipped to gas chambers which were disguised as showers. All thoughtful observers agree that in the death camps the normality of death "caused death to lose its terror." The calm that reigned among death candidates impressed various witnesses, some of them seeing it as a characteristic of dignified death in view of the impossibility to live a dignified life. The special commandos in the death camps were forced to perform the macabre job of sometimes accompanying (in Auschwitz) the victims to the gas chambers and, after their death, disposing of the corpses, extracting gold teeth, cutting hair, etc. In a later period, people of this category (when in Auschwitz they were threatened with physical destruction) or of the working groups in other camps took active part in uprisings which occurred in Treblinka (August 2, 1943), Sobibor (October 14, 1943), and Chelmno (January 1945) at the cost of many Jewish lives as against the loss of only relatively few Nazi lives.

In the daily dilemma of the conflict between the instinctive will to remain alive at all cost and the faint hope of maintaining at least a certain amount of "God's image," the depth of human degradation for the condemned Jews was reached in the death camps. A look at comparable situations may be in order. In terms of numbers and ultimate fate, the Soviet prisoners of war came closest to the Jews, with two significant differences: they were young and mostly single and thus—among other things—spared the fate of having to witness the agony of their loved ones; and they were military men trained in the use of arms and indoctrinated with Soviet and Russian patriotism. Like the Jews, who were not protected by any international convention, these prisoners were also unprotected, since their government considered all of them as deserters and did not invoke the Geneva Convention on Prisoners of War. The remarks of a sympathetic observer, who spent some four months in three prisoners' camps in Soviet-occupied areas with a capacity of 90,000 prisoners, have a familiar ring: "It was intolerable to realize that before the eyes of the whole civilized world millions of innocent people died a slow death."

Here are a few Dantesque scenes of their behavior:

The exhausted comrades were considered by the less exhausted ones as living corpses, and some of the stronger prisoners watched the dying and upon their death stripped them naked, sometimes even before they gasped their last breath. Despite cruel punishment meted out to marauders by their own comrades, these crimes continued, since in the climate of total demoralization punishment did not work. Groups of marauders—each with their own sphere of influence—acted collectively and with exclusive claim to the "property" of their victims. Another phenomenon in these camps was cannibalism. Corpses were found in the morning with hearts, livers, and large pieces from their insides cut out. The cannibals, if caught, were delivered to the Germans for death by shooting. And still it went on.

Under the circumstances, Jewish masses could not and did not—as a rule—revolt. No significant acts of sabotage or other forms of resistance have been recorded for their part by prisoners of war (both those internationally protected by the Geneva Convention and remaining mostly in camps in their home countries and—*a fortiori*—unprotected Soviet prisoners of war) or the millions (on September 30, 1944—some seven and a half million) of European workers situated in the heart of Germany, many of them enjoying wide freedom of movement and other privileges or by non-Jewish prisoners of concentration camps (prior to 1945).

A problem that has been hotly debated between survivors and outsiders has been: who is competent to describe and evaluate authoritatively the behavior of the victims and their leaders. Many survivors held the view that "no one who has not had any personal experience of a German concentration camp can possibly have the remotest conception of concentration camp life." "Little does the outsider know of the hard fight for existence which raged among prisoners." Admittedly, they have the advantage of the immediate personal experience of a phenomenon not easily imaginable. But acceptance of this claim at its face value would mean that with the last survivor gone, research and evaluation of such behavior would also come to an end. Nor could the danger be ignored of generalization by survivors who sometimes on the basis of brief and local experience in a camp or in a ghetto, arrive at conclusions of broader applications. On the other hand, it is not beyond the capacities of a conscientious witness or student to acquire knowledge and understanding, and to arm himself with *Einfuehlungsvermoegen* which is the proper meaning of the talmudic saying, "Judge not thy neighbor until thou art come into his place," as formulated in modern terms by Viktor Frankl: "No man should judge unless he asks himself in absolute honesty whether in a similar situation he might not have done the same."

Any attempt to apply to the victims of the Holocaust or of comparable situations standards of behavior of a civilized society must fail. "Standards of normal society did not obtain in the ghettos and concentration camps. Theft, egotism, lack of consideration for others, disregarding all laws, all this was prohibited in pre-concentration camp days; inside the concentration camp, however, it was normal." In these conditions, "there was neither the time nor the desire to consider moral issues. Every man was controlled by one thought only: how to keep himself alive." The admitted purpose of the Nazis in regard to the Jewish victim—as long as he was alive—was to reduce the homo sapiens to the category of a primitive creature with steadily decreasing needs which were finally reduced to craving for food ("two hundred grams of bread ruled over life"—Solzhenitsyn; "general preoccupation with food"—Frankl; "I am hungry, I am cold; when I grow up I want to be a German, and then I shall no longer be hungry, and no longer be cold"—diary of a child in the Warsaw ghetto).

In a number of cities, Jews were ordered to move into walled-off neighborhoods so that they would be isolated and imprisoned in one area. They lived in vastly overcrowded, unsanitary conditions, never knowing what their fate would be. Many ghetto inhabitants were subsequently transferred to extermination camps.

Despite incredible odds, resistance groups did form in various ghettos, managing to smuggle in small quantities of arms, or to make their own crude weapons. Only in one ghetto, however, that of Warsaw, did the Jewish Combat Organization, as it was called, succeed in holding off the Nazis for any time. There, too, success was only for an instant; the Nazis set the ghetto ablaze. Some 75 survivors crawled through the sewers of Warsaw to safety.

In this selection, a composite of excerpts from diaries and memoirs published under the title *Martyrs and Fighters*, edited by Philip Friedman, we see again that some people resisted giving way to despair, and carried on active, useful lives. Nothing could rob them of their basic humanity.

The Warsaw Ghetto

At the beginning of September, 1940, the Central Entertainment Committee was established, and I was designated as the head of this body. The Central Entertainment Committee sought to raise the level of the performances and to lend its protective hand to all professional Jewish artists, such as actors, musicians, painters, dancers and to all who were professionally employed in this field. Special care was also devoted to the fostering of young talent. If anybody revealed extraordinary gifts at an early age, the Central Entertainment Committee agreed to public performances, as was the case with the 18-year-old Marysia Ajzensztadt, who later acquired such enormous popularity in the ghetto.

Then there was also the phenomenally gifted eight-year-old composer and pianist Yossimah Feldschuh.

In the short period from September 1940 to September 1941 (inclusive) we arranged 1,814 artistic spectacles, among them light symphony concerts. . . .

Besides the great symphony orchestra, which gave symphonic matinees once a week, (on Saturday or Sunday), there were also a few chamber music ensembles. . . .

There were also several choirs in the ghetto.

BENEK, ABRAM. 50 years old, 3 Krochmalna Street, apt. 27.
In re placement of the children in a children's home.

The applicant, a hatmaker by profession, became a widower at the start of the war. Lives in utter misery. He just sold his last piece of bedding and he is tearing out planks from the floor for fuel.

The study of starvation was started in February 1942. At that time hunger was the key to everyday life within the walls of the Warsaw Ghetto. Some of its manifestations were: crowds of beggars you often encountered in the streets, corpses covered with paper, statistics of mortality in the refugee centers and orphan homes and specific symptoms of starvation requiring hospitalization, with their ramifications: TB and typhoid fever.

A group of my fellow physicians, witnessing the manifestations of community life in the ghetto, grew increasingly aware that this tragic outcome of our gloomy epoch must be transformed into a scientific record. Ignoring all the obstacles, these physicians plunged into their work with great enthusiasm and devotion. External conditions were by no means favorable for their endeavor. . . .

March . . . From the highest ranks of the Roman Catholic hierarchy suddenly came the proposal to save the last three rabbis who still remained in the Warsaw Ghetto. The three rabbis now had to decide what to do, whether to accept or to reject. They had to make the decision quickly, and no time was to be lost, since the Nazis constantly kept asking the members of the Community Council whether there were still some rabbis in the ghetto.

So the last three Warsaw rabbis were sitting in a room and discussing the Roman Catholic offer. "Discussing" . . . in reality they were sitting silent, and did not utter a word.

Suddenly the silence was interrupted, and it was Rabbi Szapiro who broke it, uttering the following words:

"I am the youngest among you, and therefore my words are not binding on you. We already know that we cannot help them any longer, but by staying with them and by not abandoning them, we encourage them and strengthen their hopes, and this is the only encouragement we are able to give the last Jews. I simply do not have the strength to abandon these wretched people."

The end is well known. Rabbi Zemba and Rabbi Stockhamer went the way of annihilation. Only Rabbi David Szapiro was not burned. And he wears now the ghostly and tragic crown of the "last Warsaw rabbi," the last rabbi of a city of rabbis.

Wednesday, August 12, 1942. Today Korczak's orphanage is to be "evacuated." . . . Korczak himself may remain, physicians are needed. They are not marked for deportation.

But Korczak refuses to stay behind. He will not abandon "his" children, he will go with them.

And so a long line is formed in the front of the orphanage on Sliska Street. A long procession, children, small, tiny, rather precocious, emaciated, weak, shriveled and shrunk. They carry shabby packages, some have schoolbooks, notebooks under their arms. No one is crying.

Slowly they go down the steps, line up in rows, in perfect order and discipline, as usual. Their little eyes are turned towards the "doctor," they are strangely calm. The "doctor" is going with them. They are not alone, they are not abandoned.

Dr. Korczak busies himself with the children with a sober earnestness. He buttons the coat of one child, ties up a package of another, or straightens the cap of a third. Then he wipes off a tear which is rolling down the thin little face of a child . . .

Then the procession starts out. The children are marching quietly in orderly rows, calm and earnest, and at the head of them is Janusz Korczak. . . .

Shoah is a nine-and-a-half-hour film by Claude Lanzmann that remains an extraordinary oral history with contemporary footage—no archival footage—of a wide range of witnesses to the Holocaust. Among them are survivors as well as Polish villagers who worked their fields adjacent to the crematoria, guards at the concentration camps, and train engineers who took Jews on a one-way trip to the death camps. Lanzmann's nine-and-a-half-hours of testimony remains extremely significant evidence at a time when Holocaust deniers are contending that the Holocaust never happened.

Here, "Antek" and "Kajik" describe the Warsaw Ghetto uprising as they experienced it. Speaking years later, it is clear that these moments remain vivid and painful inside them.

"If You Could Lick My Heart, It Would Poison You."

ITZHAK "ANTEK" ZUCKERMANN AND
SIMHA "KAJIK" ROTTEM

I began drinking after the war. It was very difficult. Claude, you asked for my impression. If you could lick my heart, it would poison you.

At the request of Mordechaï Anielewicz, commander-in-chief of the Jewish Combat Organization, Antek had left the ghetto six days before the German attack. His mission: to ask Polish Resistance leaders to arm the Jews. They refused.

In fact, I left the ghetto six days before the uprising. I wanted to return on the 19th, the eve of Passover. I wrote to Mordechaï Anielewicz and to Zivia. Zivia was my wife. I got back a very polite letter, very formal, from Anielewicz, and a very aggressive letter from Zivia that said: "You haven't done a thing so far. Nothing." I decided to go back anyway. I had no idea what was going on in the ghetto. I couldn't imagine it. But Simha's companions knew of the German encirclement before I did.

SIMHA "KAJIK" ROTTEM

At Passover time we felt something was going to happen in the ghetto. We could feel the pressure. On Passover eve the Germans attacked. Not just the Germans, but the Ukrainians, too, along with the Lithuanians, the Polish police, and the Latvians, and this massive force entered the ghetto. We felt this was the end. On the morning the Germans went into the ghetto, the attack was concentrated on the central ghetto. We were a little away from it; we heard blasts, shots, the echo of the gunfire, and we knew the fighting was fierce in the central ghetto.

During the first three days of fighting, the Jews had the upper hand. The Germans retreated at once to the ghetto entrance, carrying dozens of wounded with them. From then on, their onslaught came entirely from the outside, through air attack and artillery. We couldn't resist the bombing, especially their method of setting fire to the ghetto. The whole ghetto was ablaze. All life vanished from the streets and houses. We hid in the cellars and bunkers. From there we made our sorties. We went out at night. The Germans were in the ghetto mostly by day, leaving at night. They were afraid to enter the ghetto at night.

The bunkers were prepared by the residents, not by the fighters. When we could no longer stay in the streets, we fell back on the bunkers. All the bunkers were alike inside. The most striking thing was the crowding, for there were a lot of us, and the heat. It was so hot you couldn't breathe. Not even a candle could burn in those bunkers. To breathe in that intense heat, you sometimes had to lie with your face to the ground. The fact that we fighters hadn't prepared bunkers proves we didn't expect to survive our fight against the Germans.

I don't think the human tongue can describe the horror we went through in the ghetto. In the streets, if you can call them that, for nothing was left of the streets, we had to step over heaps of corpses. There was no room to get around them. Besides fighting the Germans, we fought hunger, and thirst. We had no contact with the outside world; we were completely isolated, cut off from the world. We were in such a state that we could no longer understand the very meaning of why we went on fighting. We thought of attempting a breakout to the Aryan part of Warsaw, outside the ghetto.

Just before May 1, Sigmund and I were sent to try to contact Antek in Aryan Warsaw. We found a tunnel under Bonifratréska Street that led out into Aryan Warsaw. Early in the morning we suddenly emerged into a street in broad daylight. Imagine us on that sunny May 1, stunned to find ourselves in the street, among normal people. We'd come from another planet. People immediately jumped on us, because we certainly looked exhausted, skinny, in rags. Around the ghetto there were always suspicious Poles who grabbed Jews. By a miracle, we escaped them. In Aryan Warsaw, life went on as naturally and normally as before. The cafés operated normally, the restaurants, buses, streetcars, and movies were open. The ghetto was an isolated island amid normal life.

Our job was to contact Itzhak Zuckermann to try to mount a rescue operation, to try to save the few fighters who might still be alive in the ghetto. We managed to contact Zuckermann. We found two sewer workers. On the night of May 8–9 we decided to return to the ghetto with another buddy, Rijek, and the two sewer men. After the curfew we entered the sewers. We were entirely at the mercy of the two workmen, since only they knew the ghetto's underground layout. Halfway there they decided to turn back, they tried to drop us, and we had to threaten them with our guns. We went on through the sewers until one of the workmen told us we were under the ghetto. Rijek guarded them so they couldn't escape. I raised the manhole cover to go up into the ghetto.

At bunker Mila 18 [headquarters of the Jewish Combat Organization], I missed them by a day. I had returned the night of May 8–9. The Germans found the bunker on the morning of the eighth. Most of its survivors committed suicide, or succumbed to gas in the bunkers. I went to bunker Francziskanska 22. There was no answer when I yelled the password, so I had to go on through the ghetto. I suddenly heard a woman calling from the ruins. It was darkest night, no lights, you saw nothing. All the houses were in ruins, and I heard only one voice. I thought some evil spell had been cast on me, a woman's voice talking from the rubble. I circled the ruins. I didn't look at my watch, but I must have spent a half hour exploring, trying to find the woman whose voice guided me, but unfortunately I didn't find her.

Were there fires?

Strictly speaking, no, for the flames had died down, but there was still smoke, and that awful smell of charred flesh of people who had surely been burned alive. I continued on my way, going to other bunkers in search of fighting units, but it was the same everywhere. I'd give the password: "Jan."

That's a Polish first name, Jan?

Right. And I got no answer. I went from bunker to bunker, and after walking for hours in the ghetto, I went back toward the sewers.

Was he alone then?

Yes, I was alone all the time. Except for that woman's voice, and a man I met as I came out of the sewers, I was alone throughout my tour of the ghetto. I didn't meet a living soul. At one point I recall feeling a kind of peace, of serenity. I said to myself: "I'm the last Jew. I'll wait for morning, and for the Germans."

In this selection a survivor of the Holocaust, Abraham Foxman, shows why armed resistance, though heroic instances of it did occur, was ultimately impossible to carry out. Far from being totally passive, however, many Jews resisted in countless small ways, which, while largely ineffectual against the enemy, served to keep self-respect and hope alive in the victims. In considering the question of resistance, ask yourself this: if others at the time who possessed armies and weapons could not halt the madman's progress, what could a defenseless minority have done?

On Resistance

ABRAHAM FOXMAN

During the past 30 years, hundreds of books, periodicals and research papers have been published dealing with the Jewish catastrophe of 1939–1945. While the majority of these works focused upon the martyrdom of the European Jews, only recently have historians and researchers begun to examine the resistance aspect. Where earlier works had concentrated upon recording the fact of destruction, primarily in subjective terms, the more recent ones attempted to invoke objective value judgments. For example, Raul Hilberg, in *The Destruction of the European Jews*, submitted that the Jews actually aided the Germans in achieving their genocidal aims by "going like sheep to the slaughter"; Bruno Bettelheim, in *The Informed Heart*, concluded that the Jewish inmates of the concentration camps had lost their "will to live," thereby espousing a "death wish," and Hannah Arendt, in *Eichmann in Jerusalem*, said that the Jews were, to a great extent, responsible for their own death, claiming that they collaborated with the Germans.

Such judgments are a tortured analysis of historical fact and a misunderstanding of the conditions that existed in the ghettos and concentration camps of Europe. To the frequently asked question of whether there was Jewish resistance, the answer is yes!

Not only did Jews take part in every phase of the general resistance movements in the occupied countries, but there was a specific Jewish resistance which manifested itself in most surprising and unusual ways. This was so not only in countries such as Poland, the Baltic States,

254

Czechoslovakia, Hungary, and Rumania, where there were large, cohesive Jewish communities, but also in countries where Jews were a very small percentage of the population.

The word "resistance" usually connotates an organized, armed, collective action, carried out according to the rules of military strategy. But resistance is a concept which includes persons who resisted passively, who participated in uprisings in ghettos and concentration camps, who fought in partisan units in the forests, who participated in general underground movements. It also includes Jews who fought knowing that certain death awaited them, but who wanted to demonstrate the courage of the Jewish people and were willing to die for *K'vod Ha-am*, the honor of the nation. It includes still others who sacrificed their lives to rescue others, those who committed any act plainly against the laws of the German authorities or the goals of "the Final Solution."

Attempting to stay alive another day was resistance. Escaping from the ghetto or hiding in a bunker was resistance. So was giving birth to a child, praying in congregation, singing, studying the Bible or the Talmud, bringing flowers into the ghetto, keeping archives, writing humor under the shadow of death, rescuing Torah scrolls left lying in the streets.

One of the most brilliant aspects of Jewish life under these horrendous circumstances was in the area of spiritual resistance. Vilna, for example, which had for generations been a great Jewish cultural center called "The Jerusalem of Lithuania," became during the Holocaust "The Jerusalem of the Ghettos," a symbol of spiritual resistance against German authority. Aid for the needy was provided by organized social-aid groups, a hospital and infirmary were established, free food centers were provided, schools and youth clubs were set up, theaters and choirs gave performances—all in the shadow of death. Jewish cultural life remained vital and creative. This, too, was resistance.

While the Warsaw Ghetto uprising was a symbolic high point, it was not the only place where Jews took positions and fought their oppressors with fire-arms and bare hands. Organized battles and skirmishes took place in ghettos, concentration camps, and work camps—among them, Vilna, Bialystok, Krakow, Auschwitz, Treblinka, Chelmno.

The decision to participate in an underground movement and resist the Germans by force was not based solely on courage, although that was important. There were other factors.

One of the strongest drives in a human being is his will to survive. No man wants to believe that he is about to be killed. He will hang on to any straw of hope, even to the point of self-delusion. When the infamous Nuremberg Laws were passed, the German Jews minimized their importance, allowing themselves to believe that these laws were only temporary measures. When Hitler announced his plan to destroy the Jewish people, very few believed it to be more than propaganda. Transports of Jewish children were taken away from their parents, on the pretext that they were being sent to a "summer camp"; the children were even forced to write postcards home. When eyewitnesses told the parents that their children were no longer alive, the parents produced the postcards and refused to believe the truth.

The same desire to live manifested itself in the "normalization" of ghetto life—writing, singing, reading, and other amenities of civilized living. The archivist of the Vilna Ghetto, for example, noted that on the morrow of an *Aktion* which took 5,000 Jews to their doom, a line of 400 people stood outside the library doors. It was this stubborn faith in a brighter tomorrow that led many to their death.

The Jews maintained belief in the goodness of the human being and in the justice of mankind, and hoped that any day salvation would come. How can the world stand idly by, they asked themselves. How long can such events continue? Why risk losing redemption and freedom by taking up arms against the foe—the Allied Forces would surely raise their voices, destroy the ovens of Auschwitz, any day—after all, this was the 20th century and they lived in a Christian society. A poem found in the rubble of the destroyed Warsaw Ghetto, written by a 12-year-old boy named Motele, is a perfect example of naive hope:

> From tomorrow on, I shall be sad—
>   From Tomorrow on!
>   Today I will be gay.
> What is the use of sadness—tell me that?
> Because the evil winds begin to blow?
> Why should I grieve for tomorrow—
>   today?
> Tomorrow may be so good, so sunny.
> Tomorrow the sun may shine for us
>   again;
> We shall no longer need to be sad.
> From tomorrow on, I shall be sad—
>   From tomorrow on!
> Not today; No! today I will be glad.
> And every day, no matter how bitter it
>   be, I will say;
> From tomorrow on, I shall be sad—Not
>   today.

In the case of Orthodox Jewry, the concept of heroism was interwoven with the idea of spiritual courage, of sacrifice for the sake of religion, known as Kiddush Hashem, Sanctification of God's Name. It was resistance stemming from religious inspiration and contained a deeply rooted ancestral heritage epitomized by the saying "not by force but by the strength of spirit." Their attitude was that world evil should not be fought and cannot be defeated by physical force because the struggle between good and evil will be decided by Divine Providence. They believed the recital of a chapter of the Psalms would do more to affect the course of events than killing Germans.

The Orthodox Jews were also opposed to physical resistance from the *Halachic* (Law) point of view. Any act of open and active resistance was equivalent to suicide, which Judaism strongly opposes.

The Jewish underground and resistance movements, wherever they existed, were isolated from the outside world, and, in fact, were refused aid by national resistance movements which existed in most occupied countries. Most of the native population, where there was a long record of anti-Semitism, was openly hostile to the Jews. In many instances they volunteered to aid in "the Final Solution."

In several countries, the Nazi troops were met as liberators and not as conquerors. The Lithuanian population welcomed the German Army with flowers and cheers. In the streets of Vilna, the Nazi flag, the swastika, was flown next to the Lithuanian flag. Ukrainians, Letts, Estonians and others volunteered to help the Germans exterminate the Jews. Any active military resistance would have had to be done alone, without any support, moral or physical. Escape was in many cases futile, for the natives would only turn the escapee over to the Germans.

Thus, any attempt at resistance was an implicit act of suicide, the only object *K'vod Ha-Am*. The religious leaders considered such an act sinful. Still, there were Orthodox Jews who fought, resisted and actively participated in the Underground.

The Germans used the concept of collective responsibility to discourage the growth of resistance movements, as well as individual acts of resistance. For any such disorder, not only the individual would be punished by death, but the whole ghetto population.

Despite these obstacles, there were acts of resistance in every section of Nazi-occupied Europe. Unfortunately, however, the complete record of martyrdom and heroism will never be written. For most of the participants and witnesses did not survive.

Resistance in the Concentration Camps

ABRAHAM FOXMAN

To survive in a concentration camp for one day could be considered a form of resistance. Even had the Nazis not introduced direct methods of extermination, it would not have taken long for the inmates to die of starvation, exhaustion, or disease. But the Jews of the camps kept alive a spark of hope for ultimate survival. What other goal could there be for those doomed to mass extermination? The hope of survival wrought miracles, giving superhuman strength and endurance to the Jewish prisoners. It sustained them while they gritted their teeth and swallowed degradation. It nourished their will to live, the predominant factor in their ability to endure as long as they did. However, in addition to this "passive resistance," there were many instances of active Jewish courage and heroism.

REVOLT IN THE SOBIBOR DEATH CAMP

Under the leadership of Leon Feldhendler, a Jewish Red Army officer, and Alexander Pechersky, a partisan leader, a clandestine organization was established in the Sobibor death camp for the purpose of destroying the murder factory. The "staff" of the organization consisted of five men entrusted with special assignments. Thirty fighters were designated to kill all the guards within one hour during the planned revolt, and to gain control of the arms store. A variety of ruses were devised to lure the German guards into corners where they could be killed surreptitiously. The men would then collect the arms and transfer them immediately to the carpentry shop. Later, the workers of this shop, together with their work-gang leaders, would appear, as usual, at the regular roll call, form ranks, and march toward the gate. Those who spoke Russian would call out to the Ukrainians not to fire but rather to escape, as the

Germans had already lost the war. In the meantime, another group would rush to the arms store near the gate for additional arms to cover the fleeing inmates. Planks and stones would be thrown on the mined area to explode the mines in the ground before the gates.

The uprising, set for October 13, 1943, was for unknown reasons postponed to the next day, the 14th.

One of the survivors, Tuvia Blatt, described the events in testimony he gave to Yad Vashem in Jerusalem:

> "... It was 4 o'clock. There was no hint as to what was about to occur. With tension that is impossible to describe I peered through the door down the road leading to the First Section, where the conspirators were to appear. The hands of the clock had passed 16:00 hours. Had there been another postponement?—"They are coming!" I heard Waytzen whisper. I looked in the direction he indicated and saw "Kali-Mali" come around the corner with a jug in his hands. His real name was Shubayev, a Soviet Jew of about 35, a traffic engineer by profession. He was accompanied by the work group leader Benya, for it was forbidden for a prisoner to cross the area without an escort. A German was standing there and I saw a youngster named Phibs invite him into the store to try on a new leather coat. The leather coat was among the clothing that was being sorted. (It was the clothing of prisoners who had already been killed.) He suspected nothing and complied ... so it was the beginning. I left my job and went to the sorting barracks, just a minute before the German Wolf entered. In one of the compartments a number of prisoners were standing and, with assumed diligence, engaged in sorting the clothes. Next to them was the bait—a smooth, shining leather coat. . . . At the order of the work leader two of them handed the coat respectfully—so to speak— to the German, and helped him put his arms into the sleeves. At that moment the picture changed. The arms caught in the sleeves could not get out. In Kali's hand an axe glinted—and the Nazi fell. In a moment the body was hidden under a heap of sand. The trap was ready for a second victim.
>
> A moment later Phibs went out to call another German. My nervousness vanished immediately. I stood, quiet and restrained. Now the German, Beckmann, was invited into the store. He seemed to hesitate, but went over to the section where the valuables were stored. In spite of the inconvenient circumstances, they succeeded in liquidating him. After him, Staubel was killed. From the First Section came Drescher, a sanitary worker, and announced that they had killed the Deputy Commandant Neumann, the head of the camp guard named Greitschutz, and a Ukrainian named Klet.
>
> This was how it happened. SS Officer Neumann came to the Section mounted on a horse. At that moment one of the tailors came up to him, and asked him to come in and try on a new

uniform which had been made for him. (The workshops operated only for the Germans.) The tall officer tied his horse to a post and entered. As he entered he took off his belt and revolver and placed them on the table. Then he took off his tunic. The tailor saw to it that the officer would stand with his back to the Jew who was going to do the job, and the German was dead. Greitschutz, I was told, was killed in the shoemaker's shop where he had been invited to try on a pair of topboots; as he was putting them on, he was killed with a blow of an axe. At that moment Klet, the Ukrainian, came running in to call the officer to the telephone. . . . The Ukrainian did not get out. Gotzinger was killed in like fashion.

From the tower of the camp the peal of a bell was heard. The time had come for the roll call. The Jewish work-group leaders were leading the men, singing as they went to the First Section. On the surface everything was normal. Now I saw how many people were still unaware of what was happening. Those who did know no longer thought of supper, but began to form their ranks. But the others queued up to receive their food, as on every other day. Nevertheless the queue quickly melted away. The decisive moment was approaching. Further delay could result in discovery by the Germans who had remained alive. I was in the smithy. The foreman there was an energetic fellow called Shlomo Shmayzner, from Pulawy. He was examining the rifle just brought to him by Drescher from the Ukrainian barracks. A few moments earlier, the German overseer of barracks construction had been liquidated. He had been asked to come into the barracks on the pretext that he must give instructions on how to repair the bunks that had been broken. Sasha (Pechersky) and others readied the ranks for the exit. The men of the Ukrainian guard on the towers were still ignorant of what was happening. They thought, it seems, that these were the usual preparations at this hour for the roll call.

A number of prisoners rushed to the barbed-wire fence, trying to get away. I was in the group that ran to the main gate. The gate to the First Section was already behind us. We continued running. Then suddenly . . . shots. The German cook who had remained alive was firing. He stood with his back to the casino, retreating slowly, with the intention of getting away round the corner. I was in the front row where the bullets were falling. We tried to check ourselves, but were pushed from behind. I was pushed until I found myself inside the aisle between the barbed-wire fences intended for the Ukrainian guards. Behind us there were already two fences and a ditch full of water, and ahead there was only one wire fence and . . . mines. We stopped. Someone with a hoe in his hand tried to cut the barbed-wire fence with it. The wire was cut and we passed through. The moment I was passing through the wires, the whole fence collapsed and I under it. It is very likely that this saved my life, for while I was under the wires and the fleeing prisoners were treading on my feet I saw mines exploding. It had been said that we must put planks on the mined area to explode the mines, but the people did not do so. They could not wait, and chose the danger of sudden death, rather than to remain another minute in the place. All around was madness. There was the sound of shots, the explosion of mines, the rattle of machine-guns. As the first wave passed I tried to extricate myself from under the fence. Notwithstanding the barbed-wire I found it was quite easy. How? I got out of the coat I was wearing, leaving it on the wire, and got away. I ran through the mine line. I was free. I still had to get to the forest, which seemed to me to be so near. . . . In the field in front of me I saw bent forms, running away. I fell a number of times, thinking each time that I had been hit by a bullet. But I got up and continued running. Another 100 meters, another 50, 20 . . . then . . . I was in the forest."

From a recent study, *The War Record of Soviet Jewry*, we learn that the revolt in the Sobibor camp involved about 350 organized rebels in addition to the many inmates who assisted in the fighting. The end result of the revolt is given in the following account: "The rebels of Sobibor killed 10 SS men and wounded one; 38 Ukrainian guards were either killed or wounded in the fighting, while 40 others deserted rather than face the wrath of their Nazi masters. Almost 400 to 600 inmates broke out, but perhaps as many as half were killed or wounded in the mine-field. Pechersky led his 60 men and women eastward, toward the River Bug. . . . They broke up into six groups . . . and ran into Soviet partisans shortly afterward."

Elie Wiesel, eloquent spokesman for the victims of the Holocaust, suggests reasons for the victims' behavior in this excerpt from *Legend of Our Time*. At the same time, he deplores the very question "Why so little resistance?" as if somehow it is the victims who have been placed on trial.

Why So Little Resistance?

ELIE WIESEL

Reduced to a mere number, the man in the concentration camp at the same time lost his identity and his individual destiny. He came to realize that his presence in the camp was due solely to the fact that he was part of a forgotten and condemned collectivity. It is not written: I shall live or die, but: *someone*—today—will vanish, or will continue to suffer; and from the point of view of the collective, it makes no difference whether that someone is I or another. Only the number, only the quota counts. Thus, the one who had been spared, above all during the selections, could not repress his first spontaneous reflex of joy. A moment, a week, or an eternity later, this joy weighted with fear and anxiety will turn into guilt. *I am happy to have escaped death* becomes equivalent to admitting: *I am glad that someone else went in my place.* It was in order not to think about this that the prisoners so very quickly managed to forget their comrades or their relatives: those who had been selected. They forgot them quickly—trying to shut their eyes to the reproachful glances which still floated in the air around them.

Why did the Jews in the camps not choose a death with honor, knife in hand and hate on their lips? It is understandable that all of us should wonder why. Putting aside the technical and psychological reasons which made any attempt at revolt impossible (the Jews knew that they had been sacrificed, forgotten, crossed off by humanity), to answer we must consider the moral aspects of the question. The Jews, conscious of the curse weighing them down, came to believe that they were neither worthy nor capable of an act of honor. To die struggling would have meant a betrayal of those who had gone to their death submissive and silent. The only way was to follow in their footsteps, die their kind of death—only then could the living make their peace with those who had already gone.

I attended the Eichmann trial, I heard the prosecutor try to get the witnesses to talk by forcing them to expose themselves and to probe the innermost recesses of their being: Why didn't you resist? Why didn't you attack your assassins when you still outnumbered them?

Pale, embarrassed, ill at ease, the survivors all responded in the same way: "You cannot understand. Anyone who was not there cannot imagine it."

Well, I was there. And I still do not understand. I do not understand that child in the Warsaw Ghetto who wrote in his diary: "I'm hungry, I'm cold; when I grow up I want to be a German, and then I won't be hungry anymore, and I won't be cold anymore."

I still do not understand why I did not throw myself on the Kapo who was beating my father before my very eyes. In Galicia, Jews dug their own graves and lined up, without any trace of panic, at the edge of the trench to await the machine-gun barrage. I do not understand their calm. And that woman, that mother, in the bunker somewhere in Poland, I do not understand her either; her companions smothered her child for fear its cries might betray their presence; that woman, that mother, having lived this scene of biblical intensity, did not go mad. I do not understand her: why, and by what right, and in the name of what, did she not go mad?

I do not know why, but I forbid us to ask her the question. The world kept silent while the Jews were being massacred, while they were being reduced to the state of objects good for the fire; let the world at least have the decency to keep silent now as well. Its questions come a bit late; they should have been addressed to the executioner. Do they trouble us? Do they keep us from sleeping in peace? So much the better. We want to know, to understand, so we can turn the page: is that not true? So we can say to ourselves: the matter is closed and everything is back in order. Do not wait for the dead to come to our rescue. Their silence will survive them.

One explanation of Nazi behavior has been that Hitler and his followers were insane—that is, their actions could not possibly have been carried out by "normal" people. An interesting psychological study of Nazi war criminals, however, suggests that this was not the case, as summarized in this excerpt from an article by Molly Harrower in *Psychology Today* of July 1976.

Were Hitler's Henchmen Mad?

MOLLY HARROWER

It was easy to believe in 1945 that Adolf Hitler's henchmen were mad. It seemed impossible, for example, that Albert Speer, Hitler's confidant, Reich Minister for Armaments and War Production, and the man personally responsible for enslaving millions, could have been anything but a maniac. The lesson Hitler and the Nazis taught us seemed simple: keep insane people out of high office and the atrocities of the Third Reich will never happen again. Unfortunately, it wasn't that simple. The Nazis who went on trial at Nuremberg were as diverse a group of people as one might find in our own government today, or for that matter, in the leadership of the PTA.

In 1945, the Nazi war criminals took the Rorschach ink-blot test while they awaited trial. The Rorschach is a series of 10 cards with ink blots, some black and white, some with blobs of red, blue or yellow. The person being tested looks at each card and describes what the ink blot looks like to him. The ink blots are not intended to look like anything, so there is no right or wrong answer as there is, say, in an IQ test. The idea behind the Rorschach technique is that when a person describes what he sees, he reveals aspects of his personality, particularly his unconscious needs and desires.

In 1947, 10 Rorschach experts, including myself, received copies of the Nazi Rorschach answers and were asked to comment on them. Although all of us agreed to respond, not one of us followed through. I was vice chairman of the committee that initiated this project, so my own failure to participate was particularly puzzling to me. Over the years, I have come to believe that our reason for not commenting on the test results was that they did not show what we expected to see, and what the pressure of public opinion demanded that we see—that these men were demented creatures, as different from normal people as a scorpion is different from a puppy. What we saw was a wide range of personalities, from severely disturbed neurotics to the superbly well-adjusted. But only Douglas Kelley, the Nuremberg psychiatrist who interviewed the Nazis, said aloud in 1946 "that such personalities are not unique or insane [and] could be duplicated in any country of the world today." . . .

These results do not excuse the acts of the Nazis. Instead, they demonstrate that well-adjusted people may get caught up in a tangle of social forces that makes them goose-step their way toward such abominations as the calculated execution of six million Jews and the systematic elimination of the elderly and other unproductive people. It may be comforting to believe that the horrors of World War II were the work of a dozen or so insane men, but it is a dangerous belief, one that may give us a false sense of security.

It *can* happen here.

Maurice Ogden's allegorical poem illustrates the reluctance of people to get involved, as well as the importance of individual responsibility. Ogden traces what happens when a hangman, who becomes a metaphor for many forms of evil, comes to an imaginary town, builds a gallows-frame, and methodically destroys one after another of the townspeople while others do nothing to stop him. His message becomes clear: That those who stand by and watch evil bear some responsibility for that evil.

Should those people who stood by silently—in Germany and around the world—and watched Hitler and his collaborators annihilate millions of people, bear some of the guilt? Consider this question, and think also about those hangmen and bystanders of today, in so many places around the world.

The poem echoes the same progression of events as the German Protestant minister Dietrich Bonhoeffer cited when he spoke out against the Nazis, one of the few to do so, and was executed for his courage.

Hangman

MAURICE OGDEN

1.
Into our town the Hangman came,
Smelling of gold and blood and flame—
And he paced our bricks with a diffident air
And built his frame on the courthouse square.

The scaffold stood by the courthouse side,
Only as wide as the door was wide;
A frame as tall, or little more,
Than the capping sill of the courthouse door.

And we wondered, whenever we had the time,
Who the criminal, what the crime,
That Hangman judged with the yellow twist
Of knotted hemp in his busy fist.

And innocent though we were, with dread
We passed these eyes of buckshot lead;
Till one cried: "Hangman, who is he
For whom you raise the gallows-tree?"

Then a twinkle grew in the buckshot eye,
And he gave us a riddle instead of reply:
"He who serves me best," said he,
"Shall earn the rope on the gallows-tree."

And he stepped down, and laid his hand
On a man who came from another land—
And we breathed again, for another's grief
At the Hangman's hand was our relief.

And the gallows-frame on the courthouse lawn
By tomorrow's sun would be struck and gone.
So we gave him way, and no one spoke,
Out of respect for his hangman's cloak.

2.
The next day's sun looked mildly down
On roof and street in our quiet town
And, stark and black in the morning air,
The gallows-tree on the courthouse square.

And the Hangman stood at his usual stand
With the yellow hemp in his busy hand;
With his buckshot eye and his jaw like a pike
And his air so knowing and businesslike.

And we cried: "Hangman, have you not done,
Yesterday, with the alien one?"
Then we fell silent, and stood amazed:
"Oh, not for him was the gallows raised . . ."

He laughed a laugh as he looked at us:
". . . Did you think I'd gone to all this fuss
To hang one man? That's a thing I do
To stretch the rope when the rope is new."

Then one cried, "Murderer!" One cried, "Shame!"
And into our midst the Hangman came
To that man's place. "Do you hold," said he,
"With him that was meant for the gallows-tree?"

And he laid his hand on that one's arm,
And we shrank back in quick alarm,
And we gave him way, and no one spoke
Out of fear of his hangman's cloak.

That night we saw with dread surprise
The Hangman's scaffold had grown in size.
Fed by the blood beneath the chute
The gallows-tree had taken root;

Now as wide, or a little more,
Than the steps that led to the courthouse door,
As tall as the writing, or nearly as tall,
Halfway up on the courthouse wall.

3.
The third he took—we had all heard tell—
Was a usurer and infidel, And:
"What," said the Hangman, "have you to do
With the gallows-bound, and he a Jew?"

And we cried out: "Is this one he
Who has served you well and faithfully?"
The Hangman smiled: "It's a clever scheme
To try the strength of the gallows-beam."

The fourth man's dark, accusing song
Had scratched out comfort hard and long;
And "What concern," he gave us back,
"Have you for the doomed—the doomed and black?"

The fifth. The sixth. And we cried again:
"Hangman, Hangman, is this the man?"
"It's a trick," he said, "that we hangmen know
For easing the trap when the trap springs slow."

And so we ceased, and asked no more,
As the Hangman tallied his bloody score;
And sun by sun, and night by night,
The gallows grew to monstrous height.

The wings of the scaffold opened wide
Till they covered the square from side to side;
And the monster cross-beam, looking down,
Cast its shadow across the town.

4.
Then through the town the Hangman came
And called in the empty streets my name—
And I looked at the gallows soaring tall
And thought: "There is no one left at all

For hanging, and so he calls to me
To help pull down the gallows-tree."
And I went out with right good hope
To the Hangman's tree and the Hangman's rope.

He smiled at me as I came down
To the courthouse square through the silent town,
And supple and stretched in his busy hand
Was the yellow twist of the hempen strand.

And he whistled his tune as he tried the trap
And it sprang down with a ready snap—
And then with a smile of awful command
He laid his hand upon my hand.

"Your tricked me, Hangman!" I shouted then,
"That your scaffold was built for other men...
And I no henchman of yours," I cried,
"You lied to me, Hangman, foully lied!"

Then a twinkle grey in the buckshot eye:
"Lied to you? Tricked you?" he said, "Not I.
For I answered straight and I told you true:
The scaffold was raised for none but you.

"For who has served me more faithfully
Than you with your coward's hope?" said he,
"And where are the others that might have stood
Side by your side in the common good?"

"Dead," I whispered; and amiably
"Murdered," the Hangman corrected me;
"First the alien, then the Jew . . .
I did no more than you let me do."

Beneath the beam that blocked the sky,
None had stood so alone as I—
And the Hangman strapped me, and no voice there
Cried "Stay" for me in the empty square.

Why did certain people choose to resist Nazi barbarity, particularly people who appeared least likely to do so? That question comes to mind when you learn about Oskar Schindler, a Nazi businessman who saw in the war an opportunity for profit. While his motives are not easily determined, we do know that he chose actively to protect the lives of more than 1,000 Jews, under the guise of "needing healthy workers" for the success of his enamelware factory in Poland.

In this excerpt from his novel about these events, *Schindler's List*, Thomas Keneally reveals the moment when Schindler grew from a self-centered pleasure-seeker, gambler, and womanizer into a Righteous Gentile who could no longer stand by and watch the slaughter of innocent people. Director Steven Spielberg captured this scene faithfully in his film based on Keneally's book. The appearance of a toddler, "dressed in a small scarlet coat and cap" walking in the midst of an *Aktion*, or violent roundup of Jews, "speaks" to Schindler, and we are left to conclude that what he has been looking at for many months, he finally *sees*. He is at long last driven by conscience to act.

Incidentally, many of the *Schindlerjuden*, or Schindler's Jews, as those he saved came to be called, consider it blasphemous to question Schindler's motives. They only know they are alive today because of his actions.

Schindler's List

THOMAS KENEALLY

From the faces of his own workers, Oskar could read something of the ghetto's torment. For a person had no time to catch his breath there, no room to dig in, assert one's habits or set up family rituals. Many took refuge and a sort of comfort in suspicion of everyone—of the people in the same room as much as of the OD man in the street. But then, even the sanest were not sure whom to trust. "Each tenant," a young artist named Josef Bau wrote of a ghetto house, "has his own world of secrets and mysteries." Children suddenly stopped talking at a creaking in the stairwell. Adults woke from dreams of exile and dispossession to find themselves exiled and dispossessed in a crowded room in Podgórze—the events of their dreams, the very taste of fear in dreams, finding continuity in the fears of the day. Fierce rumors beset them in their room, on the street, on the factory floor. Spira had another list and it was either twice or three times as long as the last. All children would go to Tarnow to be shot, to Stutthof to be drowned, to Breslau to be indoctrinated, deracinated, operated upon. Do you have an elderly parent? They are taking everyone over 50 to the Wieliczka salt mines. To work? No. To seal them up in disused chambers.

All this hearsay, much of which reached Oskar, was based on a human instinct to prevent the evil by voicing it—to forestall the Fates by showing them that you could be as imaginative as they. But that June, all the worst of the dreams and whispers took concrete form, and the most unimaginable rumor became a fact.

South of the ghetto, beyond Rekawka Street, rose a hilly parkland. There was an intimacy, like that of medieval siege paintings, about the way you could look down over the ghetto's southern wall. As you rode along the brow of the hills, the ghetto's map was revealed, and you could see, as you passed them, what was happening in the streets below.

Schindler had noticed this advantage while riding here with Ingrid in the spring. Now, shocked by the sights of the Prokocim depot, he decided to go riding again. The morning after the rescue of Bankier, he rented horses from the stables in Park Bednarskiego. They were impeccably turned out, he and Ingrid, in long hacking jackets, riding breeches, and dazzling boots. Two *Sudeten* blonds high above the disturbed ant heap of the ghetto.

They rode up through the woods and had a short gallop over open meadows. From their saddles they could now see Wegierska Street, crowds of people around the hospital corner and, closer, a squad of SS working with dogs, entering houses, families pouring forth into the street, pulling on coats in spite of the heat, anticipating a long absence. Ingrid and Oskar reined in their horses in the shade of trees and considered this sight, beginning to notice refinements of the scene. OD men armed with truncheons worked with the SS. Some of these Jewish police seemed enthusiastic, for in a few minutes' view from the hill Oskar saw three reluctant women beaten across the shoulders. At first there was a naive anger in him. The SS were using Jews to flog Jews. It would become clear during the day, however, that some of the OD bludgeoned people to save them from worse things. And there was a new rule for the OD anyhow: if you failed to deliver a family into the street, your own family was forfeit.

Schindler noticed too that in Wegierska Street two lines were continually forming. One was stable, but the other, as it lengthened, was regularly marched away in segments around the corner into Józefińska

and out of sight. It was not hard to interpret this assembling and movement, since Schindler and Ingrid, fringed by pine trees and elevated above
the ghetto, were a distance of only two or three short blocks from the
Aktion.

As families were routed out of the apartments, they were separated forcibly into two lines without regard to family considerations.
Adolescent daughters with the proper papers went to the static line,
from which they called out to their middle-aged mothers in the other. A
night-shift worker, still sullen from disturbed sleep, was pointed to one
line, his wife and child to the other. In the middle of the street, the
young man argued with an OD policeman. The man was saying, Screw
the *Blauschein!* I want to go with Eva and the kid.

An armed SS man intervened. Beside the nondescript mass of
Ghettomenschen, such a being, in his freshly pressed summer uniform,
looked superbly fed and fresh. And from the hill you could see the oil on
the automatic pistol in his hand. The SS man hit the Jew on the ear and
was talking to him, loudly and harshly. Schindler, though he could not
hear, was sure it was a speech he'd encountered before, at Prokocim
Station. It doesn't make any difference to me. If you want to go with
your frigging Jewish whore, go! The man was led from one line to another. Schindler saw him edge along it to embrace his wife, and under
cover of this act of conjugal loyalty, another woman crept back indoors
and was not seen by the SS *Sonderkommando.*

Oskar and Ingrid turned their horses, crossed a deserted avenue,
and after a few meters, rode out onto a limestone platform facing directly down Krakusa. In its closer reaches, this street was not as hectic
as Wegierska. A line of women and children, not so long, was being led
away toward Piwna Street. A guard walked in front, another strolled
behind. There was an imbalance in the line: far more children than the
few women in it could themselves have borne. At the rear, dawdling,
was a toddler, boy or girl, dressed in a small scarlet coat and cap. The
reason it compelled Schindler's interest was that it made a statement,
the way the argumentative shift worker in Wegierska had. The statement had to do, of course, with a passion for red.

Schindler consulted Ingrid. It was definitely a little girl, said Ingrid.
Girls got obsessed by a color, especially a color like that.

As they watched, the *Waffen* SS man at the rear of the column
would occasionally put out his hand and correct the drift of this scarlet
node. He did not do it harshly—he could have been an elder brother.
Had he been asked by his officers to do something to allay the sentimen-
tal concern of watching civilians, he could not have done better. So the

moral anxiety of the two riders in Bednarskiego Park was, for a second, irrationally allayed. But it was brief comfort. For behind the departing column of women and children, to which the scarlet toddler placed a meandering period, SS teams with dogs worked north along either side of the street.

They rampaged through the fetid apartments; as a symptom of their rush, a suitcase flew from a second-story window and split open on the sidewalk. And, running before the dogs, the men and women and children who had hidden in attics or closets, inside drawerless dressers, the evaders of the first wave of search, jolted out onto the pavement, yelling and gasping in terror of the Doberman pinschers. Everything seemed speeded-up, difficult for the viewers on the hill to track. Those who had emerged were shot where they stood on the sidewalk, flying out over the gutters at the impact of the bullets, gushing blood into the drains. A mother and a boy, perhaps eight, perhaps a scrawny ten, had retreated under a windowsill on the western side of Krakusa Street. Schindler felt an intolerable fear for them, a terror in his own blood which loosened his thighs from the saddle and threatened to unhorse him. He looked at Ingrid and saw her hands knotted on the reins. He could hear her exclaiming and begging beside him.

His eyes slewed up Krakusa to the scarlet child. They were doing it within half a block of *her*; they hadn't waited for her column to turn out of sight into Józefińska. Schindler could not have explained at first how that compounded the murders on the sidewalk. Yet somehow it proved, in a way no one could ignore, their serious intent. While the scarlet child stopped in her column and turned to watch, they shot the woman in the neck, and one of them, when the boy slid down the wall whimpering, jammed a boot down on his head as if to hold it still and put the barrel against the back of the neck—the recommended SS stance—and fired.

Oskar looked again for the small red girl. She had stopped and turned and seen the boot descend. A gap had already widened between her and the next to last in the column. Again the SS guard corrected her drift fraternally, nudged her back into line. Here Schindler could not see why he did not bludgeon her with his rifle butt, since at the other end of Krakusa Street, mercy had been cancelled.

At last Schindler slipped from his horse, tripped, and found himself on his knees hugging the trunk of a pine tree. The urge to throw up his excellent breakfast was, he sensed, to be suppressed for he suspected it meant that all his cunning body was doing was making room to digest the horrors of Krakusa Street.

Their lack of shame, as men who had been born of women and had to write letters home (What did they put in them?), wasn't the worst aspect of what he'd seen. He *knew* they had no shame, since the guard at the base of the column had not felt any need to stop the red child from seeing things. But worst of all, if there was no shame, it meant there was official sanction. No one could find refuge anymore behind the idea of German culture, nor behind those pronouncements uttered by leaders to exempt anonymous men from stepping beyond their gardens, from looking out their office windows at the realities on the sidewalk. Oskar had seen in Krakusa Street a statement of his government's policy which could not be written off as a temporary aberration. The SS men were, Oskar believed, fulfilling there the orders of the leader, for otherwise their colleague at the rear of the column would not have let a child watch.

Later in the day, after he had absorbed a ration of brandy, Oskar understood the proposition in its clearest terms. They permitted witnesses, such witnesses as the red toddler, because they believed the witnesses all would perish too.

PART V

AFTERMATH

"After the war the weary world will return to its daily turmoil and struggle. Such is the law of life. Bread and circuses. Birkenau may drop out of the human vocabulary, and the terrible lesson of Auschwitz may fall on deaf ears. The human mind cannot conceive of extinction, but in this last terrible and miraculous moment I see life in all its four dimensions. I believe that the small, still voice of Israel will remain and continue to proclaim the law of truth and justice."

IRENE SCHWARTZ
The Root and the Bough

This excerpt from Richard Mayne's book *The Recovery of Europe* reveals the staggering impact of the war on the people of Europe: 60 million persons were uprooted from their homes. Numbers, of course, tell only part of the story; the real effects of the war, on individuals and on nations, can still be perceived in the world today.

The Uprooted

RICHARD MAYNE

Between 1939 and the end of 1945, at least 60 million Europeans—not counting servicemen and prisoners of war—had been uprooted from their homes. Twenty-seven million of them had left their own countries, or been driven out by force. Four and a half million had been deported by the Nazis for forced labor; many thousands more had been sent to Siberia by the Russians. When the war ended, two and a half million Poles and Czechs were transferred to the Soviet Union, and more than 12 million Germans fled or were expelled from Eastern Europe. At one period in 1945, 40,000 refugees a week were streaming into northwest Germany. All told, the shifts of population involved 55 ethnic groups from 27 countries. Some had been displaced more than once: one group—420,000 Karelians from between the Gulf of Finland and the White Sea—was shuttled to and fro no less than three times.

The homeless became known as DP's, "displaced persons," and they were cared for in special camps set up by the United Nations and Allied armies. By mid-1946, some 230,000 Jews were in DP camps. Some were survivors of concentration camps, others had been in hiding or with partisan groups, and still others had successfully posed as Aryans during the war. Most Jews could not, and would not, return to their former homes.

This next selection, excerpted from a collective journal written by a group of survivors and published originally in *Commentary* magazine of July and August 1946, describes the end of the war and the group's decision to settle in Palestine, in a kibbutz, a collective settlement. At that time, Palestine was not open to free immigration, and it was a dangerous undertaking to travel there. Ultimately, however, nearly two-thirds of the Jewish DP's settled in the new State of Israel, created in 1948. About 25 percent emigrated to the U.S., Canada, and other countries, and a small number remained in Europe.

Kibbutz Buchenwald

COMMENTARY

Those were dreary, endlessly monotonous days, the last days in Buchenwald. Gray, heavy hours went by. We lived in the barracks, slept on dirty narrow benches, and crept around the camp; in passing each other, we exchanged whispers about our fate. Would it soon be changed? We exchanged whispers in passing, whispers in all the languages of the world. For there were people from all lands, from all nations; there were French, Belgians, Dutch, Hungarians, Russians, Poles, Italians. And also, of course, Jews.

But during this last period there was no distinction of race in the concentration camp; all, even the Jews, were treated on the same level. All were hungry, all were oppressed, beaten, degraded. Therefore, there were no separate problems for people belonging to one nationality or another. The long, gray, hopeless days dragged on. Wraiths of human beings dragged themselves around the camp or sat against their barracks walls, staring with vacant eyes, and thinking of nothing. They were broken and apathetic.

But there was another world in the camp. This was the secret world of the underground. Here, too, there were people of all nations and all languages, including, of course, Jews. And there, too, there was no distinction of race or nationality. Their united interests held them together: the war against the Nazis, against evil and oppression, the will to live and free themselves. And they worked together, all, including the Jews, not as representatives of their nations, but as people.

Then came April 11, 1945. Liberation. An American commander took over the camp. Immediately, an international camp committee was set up. People now grouped themselves according to nationality, and there was a representative of each group on this committee. There were a few Jews on this committee, it is true, but not as Jews; they represented the countries of their birth. The entire committee was drawn from the former underground organization, and its Jewish members were men who had been leaders in the struggle for freedom.

Now, gradually, after the liberation, the inmates of Buchenwald began to live again. Once apathetic and hopeless, they now nearly went mad with joy. Freedom! Freedom! We lived to see it!

Their faces were ablaze. They began to talk about going home. To their own countries, to father, mother, wife, and child.

And the Jews? Well—the Jews . . .

The Jews suddenly faced themselves. Where now? Where to? They saw that they were different from all the other inmates of the camp. For them things were not so simple. To go back to Poland? To Hungary? To streets empty of Jews, towns empty of Jews, a world without Jews. To wander in those lands, lonely, homeless, always with the tragedy before one's eyes . . . and to meet again a former Gentile neighbor who would open his eyes wide and smile, remarking with double meaning, "What! Yankel! You're still alive!"

Perhaps for the thousandth time the Jewish committee in Buchenwald was holding a meeting on the question: Where to? A Polish Jew, a German, a Czech, a Hungarian—each faced the same burning problem. . . . The world, we had thought, would welcome our few survivors with open arms!

July 27th—A boy, Moshe, came to us today from Poland. He had been in Buchenwald until the liberation, and then had returned to Poland with a group of Buchenwald Jews. Poland, he told us, was ridden with anti-Semitism. He told of the loneliness and the fear of the handful of Jews remaining there. The majority of the Polish people, Moshe declared, have only one idea: to eliminate the Jews. In small towns, there are no Jews to be found; they have fled in terror to the cities. Moshe had once lived in the village of Koszenitz, and he had returned to Poland hoping to go home, but when he spoke to the Jews in Lodz, he realized that he would be risking his life in going alone to a small town like Koszenitz, and so he fled Poland. He wandered on the roads for several days, stole across borders, and managed somehow to get back to the region of Buchenwald. [One year later, on July 4, 1946, in the town of Kielce, Poland, a pogrom erupted. Forty-one Jews who had returned to their hometown were murdered. Like an epidemic, pogroms broke out all over Poland.]

Quickly enough, we saw that the world had other things on its mind than Jewish suffering. So where to?

Comrade Posnansky put forth an idea: into our own kibbutz. To build a group of Buchenwald's youth, and find a farm where we could prepare for Palestine. A wonderful idea. There would be no lack of candidates for the kibbutz, for energy was reawakening in the survivors and seeking an outlet.

From that idea sprang Kibbutz Buchenwald. . . .

September 3rd—We sailed from the French port of Toulon at 7:30 P.M. and a great crowd was assembled on the shore.

The *Matroah* is a military transport, normally carrying about 200 men; aboard her now are a thousand refugees, so the crowding can be imagined. The refugees are from four centers: Switzerland, Belgium, France, and Buchenwald.

There are old men and women with little children who were given refuge in Switzerland, and thus escaped the Hitler regime; there are prisoners who were saved by a succession of miracles; there are *halutzim* [pioneers] with work-roughened hands, and there are even women with painted mouths and lacquered fingernails.

September 8th—Sabbath, and the first day of Rosh Hashanah, and the day we first saw our homeland! We ate a hasty lunch, took our baggage in hand, and went on deck, impatiently awaiting the sight of Eretz Yisrael. Then we saw the distant shore. Many people had tears in their eyes. As the shore became clearer and English vessels passed near by, greeting us, loud cries of joy broke out. At 2:30 P.M. we came to Haifa port, singing "Hatikvah."

The next three readings deal with the fate of the Nazis at war's end, and with international efforts to prevent future catastrophes like the Holocaust.

The first selection, from *New Catholic Encyclopedia*, explains how the term "genocide" came into being, and discusses the Convention on Genocide adopted by the United Nations in 1948.

On the Genocide Convention

NEW CATHOLIC ENCYCLOPEDIA

When the victorious Allies brought the German leaders to trial after the war, international lawyers found it difficult to find a legal concept adequate for the crimes against minority groups. It was at this time that Professor Raphael Lemkin coined the hybrid word "genocide." It combines the Greek *genos* (race, nation, or tribe) with the Latin suffix *cide* (killing). The word was adopted in the Nuremberg trial, notably by the British prosecutor, Sir Hartley Shawcross, but this crime was included under the broader category of "crimes against humanity."

The Nazi leaders were convicted of crimes against humanity, but only with respect to acts committed during the war. Thus acts of genocide against their own people or peoples taken over before the war were not punished. This gap in international law has been filled by the development of the concept of genocide as a crime under both conventional and customary international law. On December 11, 1946, the UN General Assembly unanimously adopted a resolution affirming that "genocide is a crime under international law" and advising that international and unilateral measures be taken to suppress it. On December 9, 1948, the General Assembly adopted a Convention on Genocide. The Convention received sufficient adhesions to enter into force on January 12, 1951, but the U.S. has not ratified it partly because of a fear that foreign powers might seek to intervene in American racial difficulties.

The Convention defines genocide as any of the following acts: "(a) Killing members of the group; (b) Causing serious bodily or mental harm to members of the group; (c) Deliberately inflicting on the group conditions of life calculated to bring about its physical destruction in whole or in part; (d) Imposing measures intended to prevent births within the group; (e) Forcibly transferring children of the group to another group" (Article 2). The parties to the Convention "undertake to enact, in accordance with their respective Constitutions, the necessary legislation to give effect to the Convention and . . . to provide effective penalties" (Article 5). Following the Nuremberg precedent, genocide is treated as a crime for which individuals may be tried "by a competent tribunal of the state in the territory of which the act was committed, or by such international penal tribunal as may have jurisdiction with respect to those contracting parties which shall have accepted its jurisdiction" (Article 6).

No international penal tribunals have yet been established and the repression of genocide remains primarily a matter of unilateral action supported by world public opinion. To the extent that the UN develops a capacity to intervene on behalf of victims of policies of genocide, the Convention could be implemented on a truly international basis. Article 8 provides that "Any contracting Party may call upon the competent organs of the United Nations to take such action under the Charter of the United Nations as they consider appropriate for the prevention and suppression of acts of genocide or any of the other acts enumerated in Article III." The acts covered by Article 3 are: "genocide, conspiracy to commit genocide, direct and public incitement to commit genocide, complicity in genocide."

In 1945 and 1946, an International Military Tribunal met in Nuremberg, Germany, to try former Nazi leaders. The judges were representatives of the United States, Great Britain, France, and the Soviet Union. The following selections, from the book *The Nuremberg Trials* by Leo Kahn, first define the crimes over which the court had jurisdiction, then present a discussion of the arguments used by the Defense. Although the evidence against the defendants was overwhelming, the Defense fought hard, and used very interesting arguments, to try and win reduced sentences for the accused. This section concludes with a chart showing the sentences imposed by the International Military Tribunal on those tried.

The Nuremberg Trials passed judgment on many of the Nazis' top leaders, but others had escaped capture. Many fled to foreign countries where they took assumed names, and others remained in hiding in Germany. In the years since the end of World War II, and using the precedents established at Nuremberg, hundreds of ex-Nazis have been caught and tried in various countries. In 1962, Israeli undercover agents in Argentina captured Adolf Eichmann, a high-ranking officer who had been in charge of transporting prisoners to the camps. Eichmann was tried in Jerusalem, in a trial that drew worldwide attention, and was subsequently executed.

The Nuremberg Trials

LEO KAHN

T he following acts, or any of them, are crimes coming within the jurisdiction of the Tribunal for which there shall be individual responsibility:

(a) CRIMES AGAINST PEACE: namely, planning, preparation, initiation or waging of a war of aggression, or a war in violation of international treaties, agreements or assurances, or participation in a common plan or conspiracy for the accomplishment of any of the foregoing:

(b) WAR CRIMES: namely, violations of the laws or customs of war. Such violations shall include, but not be limited to, murder, ill-treatment or deportation to slave labor or for any other purpose of civilian population of or in occupied territory, murder or ill-treatment of prisoners of war or persons on the seas, killing of hostages, plunder of public or private property, wanton destruction of cities, towns, or villages, or devastation not justified by military necessity.

(c) CRIMES AGAINST HUMANITY: namely, murder, extermination, enslavement, deportation, and other inhumane acts committed against any civilian population, before or during the war; or persecutions on political, racial, or religious grounds in execution of or in connection with any crime within the jurisdiction of the Tribunal, whether or not in violation of the domestic law of the country where perpetrated.

Leaders, organizers, instigators, and accomplices participating in the formulation or execution of a common plan or conspiracy to commit any of the foregoing crimes are responsible for all acts performed by any persons in execution of such plan.

It took the prosecution teams almost four months to present their case, but when it was completed the defendants and their lawyers realized that they had to contend with a body of evidence much more extensive and concrete than they had thought possible when the trial started. A denial of the facts named in the indictment would clearly be futile, and so would any attempt to belittle their gravity. There was only limited scope for defensive strategy, but within those limits the Defense fought a tenacious struggle.

In the early stages of the trial, on November 19, 1945, all defense counsel adopted a joint motion challenging the validity of the International Military Tribunal charter inasmuch as it made individuals accountable for "crimes against peace": this, they argued, offended against the ancient principle that an act should not be treated as a crime, and nobody should be punished for it, unless it had been declared criminal by a law already in existence when the act was done—*nullum crimen sine lege, nulla poena sine lege* in its conventional Latin formulation. The problem, it will be remembered, had been a subject of discussion at the London Conference. It is a very difficult one, one which cannot be dealt with adequately in a few sentences. The tribunal rejected the Defense motion, not without some elaborate reasoning, but among lawyers the tribunal's ruling has caused more criticism than approval.

The Defense tried to make the most of an argument also best known in the form of a Latin tag: *tu quoque* ("you're another"), claiming that among the crimes charted there were at least some that had also been committed on the Allied side. Strictly speaking, the alleged or even proved similar guilt of somebody else can never be admissible as a valid legal defense, but its normal and psychological effect can be considerable; a fact which may well have saved the lives of Admiral Doenitz and

Raeder. Both had been charged with "waging unrestricted submarine warfare," and both were acquitted of this particular charge on the ground that Great Britain and the United States had admittedly done the same. It is true the Doenitz's counsel very skillfully drew a fine distinction between the legal point he was making in this context and the ordinary *tu quoque* argument, but it is doubtful whether the judges would have accepted his rather subtle legal reasoning if they had not welcomed this way of avoiding the reproach of "one law for the victor, another for the vanquished."

A more fundamental issue was the defense of "superior orders," for in most instances the defendants would rightly claim that they had issued their orders and decrees in obedience to the directives of Hitler as the Head of the Government and Supreme Commander of the Armed Forces. Under Article 8 of the IMT Charter this argument was available only as a plea in mitigation of punishment, and it cannot be said that the charter introduced a new principle in this respect. The position was as the tribunal defined it in the judgment: "The provisions of this article are in conformity with the law of all nations. That a soldier was ordered to kill or torture in violation of the international law of war has never been recognized as a defense to such acts of brutality. . . . The true test, which is found in varying degrees in the criminal law of most nations, is not the existence of the order, but whether moral choice was in fact possible."

This legal rule is unpopular with most military Establishments, but it really represents sound common sense. A man subject to military, or indeed any other similarly strict discipline does not thereby become an automaton without responsibility for criminal actions. On the other hand, he is neither supposed to query the legality of an order where its illegality is not blatantly illegal, nor is he required to be a hero. What he may or may not do depends on circumstances. He is entitled to take into account the risks of disobedience, but he must weight them against the gravity of the crime he is ordered to commit. There must be reasonable balance between the need for discipline and the duty to avoid crime. The higher the rank, the wider the scope for a "moral choice" is likely to be, and in the trial of the major war criminals there was actually not much scope for the defense of "superior orders"; but this was not so clearly recognized at the time.

Goering's attempt to create a united front among the defendants was frustrated as the evidence of the prosecution in all its strength became gradually known. Nobody wanted to be identified with the horrors of concentration camps, mass murder, and slave labor. Goering himself made a last determined effort to defend the Nazi regime and his own reputation during the nine days he was on the witness stand (from March 13 to 22, 1946). Since the prosecution had made accusations of a general, political kind, the judges thought it right that at least one of the accused should be allowed to reply in kind. They regarded Goering as the most suitable spokesman for the rest, and Goering was thus able to make lengthy speeches instead of giving brief replies to the question of counsel. Employing the tactics and manner which we have tried to describe he gained a triumph of prestige at first. He also did well, on the whole, under cross-examination by Jackson, who had been so sure of the righteousness of his cause that he made the fatal mistake of losing his temper when he met Goering's clever and arrogantly defiant resistance. But the cross-examination by Maxwell-Fyfe, which followed, was cool, patient, and matter-of-fact, and under this thoroughly professional questioning Goering's defense soon began to crumble. In the end he too, like the rest, was reduced to denying that he had been aware of facts which, in the light of the evidence, he must have known, and to assigning the ultimate responsibility for the worst crimes to the dead Führer, who "let Bormann and Himmler have their way." About Goering's guilt there remained no doubt, but at least he had relieved the growing tedium of the proceedings by his spirited duel with the prosecution, so that many people were not sorry when he managed to commit suicide before he could be delivered to the hangman.

The evidential material contained abundant proof, not only that the gravest possible crimes had been perpetrated in the systematic, centrally controlled manner alleged, but also that all the accused were, at least in a general way, implicated in this criminal system: so that at first the Prosecution relying on an extensive interpretation of "conspiracy," felt certain that the trial could have no other outcome than conviction and sentence of death in the case of each defendant. But the Bench soon made it clear that they would not regard a general involvement, whatever its moral or political significance, as sufficient for a criminal conviction; the Prosecution must show in every individual case that an accused was specifically and concretely implicated in the crime charged. A hard task, for it must be remembered that except in a few instances these defendants had neither initiated the crimes nor personally taken part in their physical execution: they were accused of having knowingly and willingly provided the necessary link between Hitler's intentions and their final realization. Knowledge and willingness, however, are states of mind, the existence of which is exceedingly difficult to prove "beyond reasonable doubt." A Nuremberg defendant would sometimes deny knowledge of an event even when shown his own signature on a document referring to that event; he had been too busy, he would claim, to read everything he was given to sign. Or he would plead in mitigation that behind the scenes he had remonstrated against a criminal order by Hitler, or tried to soften its impact, although in public he had made a show of eager obedience. Explanations of this kind were hardly ever convincing, and often patently absurd, yet just occasionally they had some substance; at any rate, they had to be listened to and meticulously examined, and this the tribunal did during a further seven weary months.

The table presents the judgment of the tribunal and the sentences passed. . . . With 19 convictions against only three acquittals the Prosecution could be well content. On the other hand, the fact that in a trial of this nature 10 out of 22 defendants escaped with their lives seems to demonstrate how carefully the legal point in their favor and all extenuating circumstances were taken into account.

Without attempting the impossible task of reviewing the whole of the evidence in detail the judgment could give no more than a mere indication of the reasoning behind particular findings; an unsatisfactory, if inevitable, feature of the trial. The death sentences were pronounced in those 12 cases where most people would expect it. Goering was obviously guilty on all counts, with practically nothing to be said in mitigation. "Goering was often, indeed almost always, the moving force, second only to his leader," said the judgment. Ribbentrop, not content with his part in bringing about the war, had also given zealous support to the wartime policies of oppression and genocide. Nobody has queried the unqualified guilt of Kaltenbrunner, second man in the SS "state within a state," or Bormann, in the last few years of the Third Reich probably the most powerful of Hitler's lieutenants, or Rosenberg, Frank, and Seyss-Inquart, Hitler's satraps in occupied territories. Frick had supplied the administrative tools for the incorporation and "Germanization" of conquered counties, and had also had administrative responsibility for the murder of several hundred thousand "useless eaters" under the so-called "euthanasia" program. Although Streicher's influence had been at its peak in Germany before the war, he had done enough to encourage genocide during the war to justify his conviction on Count Four. Sauckel had been in charge of a program which "involved deportation for slave labor of more than five million human beings." In respect of Keitel and Jodl it has sometimes been claimed that as professional soldiers they did not belong in the same category, even though they had gone too far in their obedience to superior orders. But would they really have deserved a more lenient sentence? Even from the few pieces of evidence which we have cited it is apparent that the *Wehrmacht* was deeply implicated in the crimes of aggression and terrorism. Among the German officers and other ranks in the field there had indeed been many who had felt disgraced by the barbarities which they had been ordered to assist or tolerate, and some had been brave enough to protest. But such sense of honor and moral courage had been sadly lacking at the top—where they should have been strongest.

Von Papen and Schacht had rendered great services to Nazism during the last phase of the Weimer Republic and the period known as the "consolidation of power," and even then they must have been aware of Hitler's general intentions. But the tribunal acquitted them, though not without some scathing remarks on the moral guilt of these two cunning and shifty gentlemen, on the ground that they had no longer been in positions of influence during the crucial time from 1937 onward. The Russian judge delivered a dissenting opinion in all three cases.

Lastly, a few comments on the prison sentences. Those of von Neurath (15 years) and Funk (life) have been criticized as comparatively harsh. Neurath's case was not so very different from that of Schacht and Papen, except that he was less adroit. Funk was not held to be one of the leading figures in the planning of aggressive war, though found guilty of taking part in the economic preparations, and the worst point against him in the context of atrocities was that as Reichsbank president he had accepted deposits of valuables which the SS had taken from their murdered victims. It should be noted that von Schirach was not convicted on account of his pernicious activities as leader of the Hitler Youth, but in connection with the deportation of Jews from Vienna. Speer had supported and used the slave labor program, but his responsibility was clearly not so heavy as Sauckel's. The two admirals, Doenitz and Raeder, were found guilty of having been "active in waging aggressive war" (Raeder also of taking part in the planning), and both had issued some of Hitler's criminal orders without protest, but they had been much less involved in war crimes than the army leaders, and they had not even been indicted for "crimes against humanity."

In our short exposition we have not been able to deal with the prosecution of the seven organizations or groups, of which four were declared criminal by the tribunal. Legally these prosecutions were something of an oddity, which practical effect only in the subsequent trials of war criminals. In future, membership in one of the criminal organizations could be an additional count in an indictment for other offenses, though it was not to be regarded as a separate offense. The evidence submitted on both sides has been an important historical source, but in all other respects the value of the proceedings against organizations is questionable.

The Sentences Imposed by the International Military Tribunal

Hermann Goering—death
Rudolf Hess—life imprisonment
Hans Frank—death
Wilhelm Frick—death
Julius Streicher—death
Walter Funk—life imprisonment
Fritz Sauckel—death
Alfred Jodl—death
Martin Bormann—death (in absentia)
Franz von Papen—acquittal
Joachim von Ribbentrop—death
Wilhelm Keitel—death
Ernst Kaltenbrunner—death
Alfred Rosenberg—death
Hjalmar Schacht—acquittal
Karl Doenitz—10 years imprisonment
Erich Raeder—life imprisonment
Baldur von Schirach—20 years imprisonment
Artur Seyss-Inquart—death
Albert Speer—20 years imprisonment
Constantin von Neurath—15 years imprisonment
Hans Fritzsche—acquittal

For survivors of the Holocaust, and for Jews elsewhere in the world, there were two matters of urgent priority: to provide a home for the displaced persons, and to make sure that Jews would never again be defenseless victims. The vehicle for accomplishing both these goals was to be an independent Jewish state, the State of Israel, situated in the ancient Jewish homeland. The dream of such a "national home" was not new by any means, and in fact the Jews had already built up a thriving community in Palestine. Nevertheless, it took the tragedy of the Holocaust, and the subsequent outpouring of sympathy on the part of people everywhere, to bring about the actual establishment of a recognized sovereign and independent state. This was in 1948.

The next reading is the complete text of Israel's "Proclamation of Independence," which sets forth the Jewish people's claims to an independent national existence, on its own soil.

State of Israel Proclamation of Independence

The Land of Israel was the birthplace of the Jewish people. Here their spiritual, religious, and national identity was formed. Here they achieved independence and created a culture of national and universal significance. Here they wrote and gave the Bible to the world.

Exiled from the Land of Israel the Jewish people remained faithful to it in all the countries of their dispersion, never ceasing to pray and hope for their return and the restoration of their national freedom.

Impelled by this historic association, Jews strove throughout the centuries to go back to the land of their fathers and regain their statehood. In recent decades they returned in their masses. They reclaimed the wilderness, revived their language, built cities and villages, and established a vigorous and ever-growing community, with its own economic and cultural life. They sought peace, yet were prepared to defend themselves. They brought the blessings of progress to all inhabitants of the country and looked forward to sovereign independence.

In the year 1897 the First Zionist Congress, inspired by Theodor Herzl's vision of the Jewish State, proclaimed the right of the Jewish people to national revival in their own country.

This right was acknowledged by the Balfour Declaration of November 2, 1917, and reaffirmed by the Mandate of the League of Nations, which gave explicit international recognition to the historic connection of the Jewish people with Palestine and their right to reconstitute their National Home.

The recent Holocaust, which engulfed millions of Jews in Europe, proved anew the need to solve the problem of the homelessness and lack of independence of the Jewish people by means of the reestablishment of the Jewish State, which would open the gates to all Jews and endow the Jewish people with equality of status among the family of nations.

The survivors of the disastrous slaughter in Europe, and also Jews from other lands, have not desisted from their efforts to reach Eretz-Yisrael, in face of difficulties, obstacles and perils; and have not ceased to urge their right to a life of dignity, freedom, and honest toil in their ancestral land.

In the Second World War the Jewish people in Palestine made their full contribution to the struggle of the freedom-loving nations against the Nazi evil. The sacrifices of their soldiers and their war effort gained them the right to rank with the nations which founded the United Nations.

On November 29, 1947, the General Assembly of the United Nations adopted a Resolution requiring the establishment of a Jewish State in Palestine. The General Assembly called upon the inhabitants of the country to take all the necessary steps on their part to put the plan into effect. This recognition by the United Nations of the right of the Jewish people to establish their independent State is unassailable.

It is the natural right of the Jewish people to lead, as do all other nations, an independent existence in its sovereign State.

ACCORDINGLY WE, the members of the National Council, representing the Jewish people in Palestine and the World Zionist Movement, are met together in solemn assembly today, the day of termination of the British Mandate for Palestine; and by virtue of the natural and historic right of the Jewish people and of the Resolution of the General Assembly of the United Nations.

WE HEREBY PROCLAIM the establishment of the Jewish State in Palestine, to be called Medinath Yisrael (The State of Israel).

WE HEREBY DECLARE that, as from the termination of the Mandate at midnight, the 14th-15th May, 1948, and pending the setting up of the duly elected bodies of the State in accordance with a Constitution, to be drawn up by the Constituent Assembly not later than the 1st October, 1948, the National Council shall act as the Provisional State Council, and that the National Administration shall constitute the Provisional Government of the Jewish State, which shall be known as Israel.

THE STATE OF ISRAEL will be open to the immigration of Jews from all countries of their dispersion; will promote the development of the country for the benefit of all its inhabitants; will be based on the principles of liberty, justice and peace as conceived by the Prophets of Israel; will uphold the full social and political equality of all its citizens, without distinction of religion, race, or sex; will guarantee freedom of religion, conscience, education and culture; will safeguard the Holy Places of all religions; and will loyally uphold the principles of the United Nations Charter.

THE STATE OF ISRAEL will be ready to cooperate with the organs and representatives of the United Nations in the implementation of the Resolution of the Assembly of November 29, 1947, and will take steps to bring about the Economic Union over the whole of Palestine.

We appeal to the United Nations to assist the Jewish people in the building of its State and to admit Israel into the family of nations.

In the midst of wanton aggression, we yet call upon the Arab inhabitants of the State of Israel to preserve the ways of peace and play their part in the development of the State, on the basis of full and equal citizenship and due representation in all its bodies and institutions—provisional and permanent.

We extend our hand in peace and neighborliness to all the neighboring states and their peoples, and invite them to cooperate with the independent Jewish nation for the common good of all. The State of Israel is prepared to make its contribution to the progress of the Middle East as a whole.

Our call goes out to the Jewish people all over the world to rally to our side in the task of immigration and development, and to stand by us in the great struggle for the fulfillment of the dream of generations for the redemption of Israel.

With trust in the Rock of Israel, we set our hand to this Declaration, at this Session of the Provisional State Council, on the soil of the Homeland, in the city of Tel-Aviv, on this Sabbath eve, the fifth of Iyar, 5708, the 14th of May, 1948.

At the end of the war, many Germans and Poles undoubtedly wished to see razed to the ground all vestiges of the infamous camps and crematoria. A number of camps were destroyed. At the insistence of the Allies, however, some camps were preserved, and designated as memorials or as places of historic interest. Many people felt, and still feel, that the people of Germany and Poland, where the camps were situated, should not be allowed to forget what took place in them. These memorials are also intended to teach the rest of the world the importance of remembering—however painful—in the hope that we will be alert to the danger of similar occurrences in our own time.

The next two selections describe the fate of two of the camps—Dachau in Germany, and Auschwitz in Poland. The first is excerpted from the publication *In Everlasting Remembrance*, published by the American Jewish Congress; the second is by William Helmreich, from an article in the book *Living After the Holocaust*.

Dachau: Munich Suburb

It was in Munich that Adolf Hitler made his first bid for power in the abortive beerhall putsch of 1923. It was in Munich that the Nazi Party's monster rallies were held—the boots in goose-step and the shouts of *"Sieg Heil."* When war came the city was all but destroyed by American B-17's. When war ended, the bombers were replaced by bulldozers and a new city arose, thanks in no small measure to American aid. But some reminders of the old Munich remain. The *Oktoberfest*—the month-long beer festival—still takes place every year. And the village of Dachau still stands, just 10 miles outside the city.

Dachau occupies a special niche in the hierarchy of Nazi concentration camps. It was here that the "medical" experiments were undertaken by German "doctors," among them a research project requested by the German Air Force to study the effects of immersing human beings in freezing water.

Today at Dachau the materials are gone and the concentration camp itself has vanished. In its place are two memorials. One is a set of stone blocks, placed one upon the other, with a Menorah carved on the uppermost stone. Engraved in German, Hebrew, and English is the inscription, "Remember the Victims."

The second memorial to the victims of Dachau is a Carmelite convent known as the Convent of Atonement. Here live 21 nuns who have taken a vow never to leave. The prioress of the convent was a member of the group led by a Jesuit priest, Alfred Delp, one of those executed by the Nazis for his part in the attempt to assassinate Hitler on July 20, 1944.

To enter the outer courtyard of the convent, one walks beneath an old watch tower, within the wall of the camp. The convent itself is new; each nun has her own cell.

Why did the Carmelites put a convent there? They gave this answer: The ground Dachau stood on can never be allowed to return to "normal" use. The convent is there to remind the visitor that when he leaves bright and busy Munich and arrives at Dachau, he is in another world.

A Visit to Auschwitz

WILLIAM HELMREICH

In the summer of 1972 I had the opportunity to travel through Poland. There I visited Auschwitz. As I got off the steps of the train I noticed that the supporting poles of the station were painted in alternating red and white stripes like pieces of peppermint candy. The litter baskets were shaped in the form of penguins with their mouths open. The atmosphere was a festive one as people waited for the buses to the camp. (As a matter of fact, one person on the train, a youth of about 20, informed me that the Auschwitz museum was a beautiful and fascinating place to visit.)

Upon arriving at the camp I was surprised to see that much of it had been preserved. The *"Arbeit Macht Frei"* sign was still there, as were the barracks (that had once housed the inmates) and several crematoria. Barbed wire surrounded the camp. Inside one of the buildings were exhibits behind glass walls showing human hair, articles of clothing, and various other items that had been in the camp storehouses when Auschwitz was liberated. Yet with the exception of one or two small exhibits (i.e., several prayer shawls suspended on what looked like clothes lines) there was little indication that Jews had been there, much less that they had died there in great numbers. . . .

I did not, however, find this nearly as disturbing as the general way in which the Holocaust was treated, an attitude of casualness and callousness that was impossible to miss. A hotel and two restaurants have been built on the premises of the camp. A souvenir stand sold pennants depicting the prison uniform on one side and a drawing of a guard looking out over a barbed wire enclosure on the other. Picture postcards and lapel pins were also available. Little children ran through the halls of a building laughing, shouting, and playing ball where ghastly medical experiments had once been performed. Inside another building were some teenage youths leaning out of a window and listening to popular music on a radio. In general people appeared to regard their visit to the camp as a family outing and a pleasurable experience. As I walked past one of the crematoria I stopped short. A woman of about 60 with a *babushka* on her head had clambered into the crematoria. She smiled broadly as a child of about 12 took her picture. At this point, I left the camp as quickly as possible.

In 1978, President Jimmy Carter established a National Holocaust Memorial Commission whose task it was to plan and bring to fruition the building of a museum in the nation's capital in memory of the victims of the Holocaust—a museum that would educate present and future generations. Such a structure would stand as a powerful reminder of America's beliefs in democracy and tolerance and a re-minder to people about what can happen when they do not act according to those beliefs.

In this article from the *New York Times*, April 23, 1993, several speakers at the dedication of the museum are quoted. Among them is Elie Wiesel, a member of the commission and a Holocaust survivor who has written several outstanding books on the subject. He refers to the "ethnic cleansing" in the former Yugoslavia and implies that the real meaning of this museum must be demonstrated in our stopping such bloodshed. His reference to the "excruciating sights of this old new war" remind us just how easy—*and* how difficult—it is to watch history being repeated.

Holocaust Museum Dedicated in Payment to Dead

DIANA JEAN SCHEMO

Washington, April 22—Nearly 50 years after the furnaces of Nazi Germany devoured their last victims, survivors and world leaders gathered beneath a bleak, disconsolate sky today to dedicate a museum chronicling man's descent into darkness and the indifference to evil that marked the era.

The United States Holocaust Memorial Museum was hailed not as the triumph of the human spirit over brutality or survival over genocide, but as a debt to the dead, a warning to future generations of the cost of detachment.

From the somber testimony of Elie Wiesel, who spoke of his

mother's murder at Auschwitz, to 68-year-old Marcie Krause, who wandered in the rain amid the 8,000 guests with a sign hanging from her neck bearing her maiden name and hometown in Poland in a futile search for family members, today's ceremony seemed dedicated to the enduring wounds of the survivors.

STARK, SOBER REMINDER

"The Holocaust reminds us forever that knowledge divorced from values can only serve to deepen the human nightmare, that a head without a heart is not humanity," President Clinton said. He hailed Allied soldiers, resistance fighters and private people who "manned the thin line of righteousness, who risked and lost their lives to save others."

The museum, built with private contributions on federally donated land, stands near the Mall, not far from the Washington Monument. Unlike the other national museums in the capital, it does not celebrate history or technology but stands as a stark, sober reminder of their perils.

"To forget would mean to kill the victims a second time," Mr. Wiesel said. "We could not prevent their first death; we must not allow them to be killed again."

The museum opens as Holocaust survivors enter their final years, many of them troubled by a recent survey indicating a majority of high school students know of the Holocaust only as a chapter of death and tragedy, not necessarily connected to Jews, Nazis, or Hitler.

Attending today's ceremonies were the leaders of a dozen foreign states that had some connection to the Holocaust, many of them splintered from the former East Bloc. Germany sent Vice Chancellor Klaus Kinkel, Premier Manfred Stolpe of Brandenburg, and several members of Parliament.

Most of the visiting leaders were applauded, though guests jeered the Croatian President, Franjo Tudjman. In a book that started his current political career, Mr. Tudjman wrote that estimates of six million Jewish dead were exaggerated, and said the "main characteristics" of Jews were "selfishness, craftiness, unreliability, miserliness, underhandedness, and secrecy."

"If he wants to apologize, this is his opportunity," said Israel Singer, Secretary General of the World Jewish Congress. "If he doesn't, he shouldn't be here and he should stay at home."

As the Croatian leader stepped to a seat near the podium, Mr. Wiesel, who had denounced Mr. Tudjman's presence, looked away from him.

The Croatian President, who has said that charges of anti-Semitism were based on mistranslations of his book, toured the museum for an hour today but refused questions afterward.

In addition to Mr. Tudjman, the presidents of Slovenia and Bosnia attended today's ceremony, where the specter of "ethnic cleansing" in their countries loomed over the memories of genocide. Slobodan Milosevic, the Serbian President, was not invited by museum officials, who said State Department officials had advised against it. Serbia has also been accused of supporting a terror campaign against Muslims in neighboring Bosnia.

But the omission of a representative for them angered many Serbs, who had been major victims of genocide by the Ustachi puppet regime allied with Nazi Germany. "This is a matter of historical record, irrespective of current political events or discredited attempts by some contemporary Balkan politicians to rewrite history and deny tragedy," Crown Prince Alexander of Yugoslavia wrote President Clinton.

Mr. Wiesel denounced the campaigns of ethnic cleansing in the former Yugoslavia, which he said demanded an American response. "We cannot tolerate the excruciating sights of this old new war," Mr. Wiesel said, turning to Mr. Clinton. "Mr. President, this bloodshed must be stopped. It will not stop unless we stop it."

HORRORS, PAST AND PRESENT

Mr. Clinton also spoke of ethnic cleansing but did not address Mr. Wiesel's appeal. Instead, he spoke of brutality around the globe.

"We learn again and again that the world has yet to run its course of animosity and violence," Mr. Clinton said.

President Chaim Herzog of Israel, who recalled his horror upon discovering Bergen-Belsen and other concentration camps as a soldier in the British Army, said, "Nobody who saw those terrifying scenes will ever forget."

And the television journalist Ted Koppel, whose parents were refugees from the Holocaust, read Edward R. Murrow's famous 1945 broadcast from Buchenwald: "There surged around me an evil-smelling horde. Men and boys reached out to touch me; they were in rags and the remnants of uniform. Death had already marked many of them, but they were smiling with their eyes."

Some wept as they heard Elie Wiesel describe a Jewish woman somewhere in the Carpathian mountains, who read a short newspaper article about the Warsaw Ghetto uprising. "She wondered aloud: 'Why are our

Jews in Warsaw behaving like this? Why are they fighting? Couldn't they have waited quietly until the end of the war?'

"Treblinka, Ponar, Belzec, Chelmno, Birkenau; she had never heard of these places. One year later, together with her entire family, she was in a cattle-car traveling to the black hole of history named Auschwitz." At the end of his speech, the writer said, "She was my mother."

Peter Sichrovsky, who wrote the book, *Born Guilty,* from which this next excerpt is taken, was born in 1947 to Jewish emigrants who left Austria before the war and returned to Vienna following it. Thus, he points out, he grew up surrounded by children whose parents "only yesterday had wanted to murder my parents." In his interviews with children of high-ranking Nazi officials as well as bureaucrats—policemen, mayors, rail employees, teachers—he learned that these children were in many cases unable to talk about things they had never been told. They had "shoved things under the rug until the pile of dirt grew so big that one trips over it."

Not all children of Nazis responded in the same way to their situation: Some tried to confront the past in order to go on with their lives; others were afflicted by guilt assigned to them as the offspring of Nazis; and still others, like Stefan, are angry, believing *they* are the victims of both their parents' silence or abuse and of the world's scorn. They are bitter because no one seems to recognize their suffering. As you read Stefan's words, think about what effects his anger might have on the attitudes towards Jews of future generations in Germany. And also consider whether or not these children are unfairly paying for the sins of their fathers.

Stefan, the Sufferer

PETER SICHROVSKY

I'm in the same boat as you. I was the Jew in my family. Father, Mother, Grandmother—all of them conspired to perpetuate the terror in the family. And I was their target. No, they weren't out to kill me, because that would have been too easy. They just wanted to make me suffer, like tearing the wings off a fly and watching it writhe in agony, trying to escape.

I tried to shrug it off, not to let it get me, pretend that it didn't bother me. When something threatened to bother me I wouldn't let my feelings get the upper hand. My parents had a sixth sense for it. They only had to suspect that they had touched a raw nerve and they moved in. They smelled every wound and delighted in finding my weak spot. When I was little I thought the only way I could survive was to hide from them, because all they had to do was see a wound and they'd pour salt into it. If I came home with scraped knees they beat me because I'd dirtied my pants. And if I cried they hit me because I didn't behave like a man. And if I tried to get help they laughed at me. They wore out their shoe leather stepping on me.

There's all that talk about you Jews being the victims of the war. But for those of you who survived, the suffering ended with Hitler's death. But for us, the children of the Nazis, it didn't end. When their world collapsed in ruins and ashes, the heroes of the Third Reich staked out another battleground—the family.

With their invaluable help I developed an inferiority complex of unimaginable dimensions. As a child I was a real idiot, afraid of everything that came my way. In school the other kids beat me up, and it didn't occur to me that I could defend myself. And that's still so. Confronted with authority, I become insecure and tense.

Well, when my first affair broke up I was still stupid enough to confide in my mother, hoping for tenderness and understanding. But all my mother had to say was that I probably had myself to blame. They always did everything in their power to belittle me, regardless of what I asked of them.

Tenderness didn't exist. I can't remember ever being held on my mother's lap or being hugged by her or having my father show any affection. And, of course, no kisses ever.

Later I developed such a confused view of women. In my imagination there existed only two kinds—goddesses and whores. Ninety-nine percent were whores, and the rare goddesses were nowhere to be found. I thought that if I gave them whatever their hearts desired they'd love me. And I did give them whatever I could. I spoiled them, showered them with presents, anticipated all their wishes, but they cheated on me. When I was 18 I wanted to take my girlfriend—my first one—to Italy, and I saved up for the trip for half a year. I gave her the money for the fare, and that's the last I saw of her. And that was only the beginning.

And then the business of religion. At 14 I became very religious, going to church regularly, not eating meat on Fridays, and praying all the time. But I soon gave it up when I found that didn't help either. Then I became interested in Buddhism, such a gentle religion, everything is love and touching. It appealed to me. I guess I could have converted, but I was afraid. My parents had robbed me of my willpower. Everything was taboo. I took all they dished out, and it certainly never occurred to me to question them, let alone assert myself.

When I was around 20 I began to feel that nothing was going right, and I started to lose a lot of weight. My whole life was turning into one big setback. I once confided in my father that I wasn't doing so well in the woman department, and all the advice he had to offer was to try a brothel. That's the kind of support I got from him. I think that the only time I was strong was when I was little. But the older I got the weaker I became. Other people as they grow older mature and gradually become independent and able to cope, but I became more insecure and fearful. More and more I looked for protection and security. But who's there now to protect me? Today I'm as endangered as the Jews. That's what I have in common with you. And that's also the reason I find you so sympathetic. I'm sure that in the old days my father brutalized Jews, but after the war there weren't any left. There was only me.

He was proud of what he'd done. He showed them, he used to say. They trembled before him. At first he was in the SA, but he changed over in time. He despised everybody—Jews, Gypsies, homosexuals, Communists—and he still does, except he's too much of a coward to say so out loud. Only behind closed doors, in the safety of his own four walls, does he still dare to play the hero. And after the war I became his chosen victim. I'm not responsible for what my father did. I wasn't born then and have nothing to do with it. And I don't feel responsible for it. And I think that words like "complicity" and "shared responsibility" or "continuing to mourn" are inappropriate. I can't apologize for what my father did. It's he who did it, not I. I have as little to do with what he did as with him. I am an entirely different person, perhaps even his exact opposite. I think of myself as being in the other camp, someone who is suffering under him just as all those others during the Third Reich. Today his brutality and aggressiveness threaten *me*, not those others against whom he keeps on ranting, but that's only talk.

But I've been mistreated by him all my life! Why am I now supposed to feel any special compassion for the victims of National Socialism? For them it's over, and those who survived got lots of assistance. But nobody takes us, the descendants of the Nazis, seriously. On the contrary! Some people even claim that we're just like our fathers. How often did I have to listen to a teacher who saw me fight tell me that that's just what he'd expect of me. Always those allusion to my father.

For a time he was the local SS chief, and the Socialists here really hate him. He sent quite a few of them to prison. None of the Jews returned after the war. Maybe none of them survived, I don't know.

I'm sure I wouldn't have joined the SS if I'd been around then. I would probably have been one of the first to be arrested. I'm not the activist type, not like some of those tough, crude friends of Father's. They can drink beer by the gallon and not get drunk. I get sick after only a glass or two. They can probably sleep with any woman, whether they love her or not. They stuff themselves, guzzle and whore their way through life, and anyone who gets in their way is shoved aside, squashed like a pesky fly.

With a father like that I was doomed to fail. There's no escape. I'd trade him for anybody. And my mother isn't any better. She took up where he left off. Of course I made even greater demands on her as regards affection. But she was always one of those upright German women, big and fat, with hands like a butcher. When I was little she'd take my hand as we crossed the street, and when she let go my hand would be white, drained of all blood.

My mother was illegitimate. Her mother worked in her father's grocery. I think my mother never knew who her father was. My grandmother is still alive, a nasty old woman, always in a bad mood, with a beard like a Gypsy.

Grandmother also is still an enthusiastic Nazi. Her favorite saying is that under the next Hitler it won't end like the last time. The next one won't let others bring him down. She's convinced that there'll be another Hitler. And when I try to argue with her or talk of the horrors of the Nazis, she screams at me that I don't know anything about what really happened, that I'd been listening to the propaganda of all the Jews and Communists who are in power today. Once I told her that I was like the Jews, persecuted by the criminals in our society, like the kind she is, and she threw a slipper at me. She can't walk so well anymore.

I visit my folks only rarely, at most once a month. Nothing has changed there, always the same speeches and attitudes, the same thing year in, year out. Father abuses the Russians; Mother, the woman who sells vegetables; and neither of them ever asks me anything, except maybe the usual meaningless question about how I'm doing at school. But before I can even answer they're already talking about something else.

Father is retired. After the war he worked for a construction firm as a purchasing agent. His boss was the same sort of Nazi as he. When the two of them got together they talked only about the war and arrests. They both were in the SS and used to arrest people in their apartments, and they're still proud of it. They'd laugh when they told how grown men cried and begged them to let them take some things with them. They were always so proud of their crimes. And these stories didn't upset Mother either. She'd sit there and knit and smile. If I got up and left the room she'd call after me to look at Father, what a hero he was, not a sad sap like me.

Father also shot some people. He said they wanted to run away to avoid military service. He described in detail how he did it. Today he hates the conscientious objectors, but also the officers. The first are nothing but malingerers, and the others sit around in their club and let others do the fighting.

My father's boss, who served with him in the war, also has a son. I often used to talk with him about our situation. We're the victims of the Nazis who're still alive, the victims of the survivors. Nobody really understands this. Hitler may have died, but most of his henchmen survived and looked for fresh victims. I now feel drawn to the Gypsies, homosexuals, and Jews. I really feel that I'm one of them. Except for our two cats nobody at home ever showed me any affection. And my father also mistreated the cats. He kicked them and tried to grab them by the tail. Nobody was safe from his brutality.

I can find no allies. I'm also disappointed in the Jews. They wouldn't admit me into their student group, and I have the feeling that they don't want to have anything to do with me. Well, yes, when I think of Israel I can see why. They're no longer the victims. Now the Jews have joined the ranks of the aggressors. Especially the students here are unbelievably supercilious. Solidarity means nothing to them, and they don't see the suffering of others. They can only see themselves and the Holocaust. But that's over and done with. Today others are suffering. The Jews now are better off then anybody else. They're being pampered, just like the blacks.

Only we, the children of the Nazis, are ignored and overlooked. We're the true heirs of the Nazi ideology, the product of the union of the Devil and the tortured creatures of fascism. I no longer feel pity for anybody. All those groups that have sprung up at the university, for South Africa, for Chile, for Soviet Jews. The hell with 'em. They pick their victims as far away as possible so that they don't have to come into contact with them. They demonstrate on behalf of some trees and against rockets only because they're afraid they might be killed. It's all selfishness or pretended compassion to make themselves important. But nobody sees the real victims, the disadvantaged right here at home.

Sensibility and feeling are not in demand in this country. I'm not the victor type and I won't get very far here. Nobody except my new girlfriend knows anything about devotion and sacrifice. I'm a cripple among athletes who talk of nothing but setting records. But they don't even see me, sitting among them in a wheelchair. This world is not my world.

PART VI

COULD IT HAPPEN AGAIN?

"Political analysts talk of nuclear holocaust. Racism, fascism, totalitarianism, dictatorship, complicity, passivity: words heavy with past significance which explains their impact on your comrades. By criticizing regimes, they indict yesterday's corruption. That is why it is important to put society on trial, this society which was and still is ours. By scorning its defenders, you place yourself on the side of the victims."

ELIE WIESEL
"To a Young Jew of Today"

Parallels in Literature and Life

In this final section, we ask the reader to consider whether events similar to the Holocaust have occurred or could ever occur again. Specifically, could another innocent people be singled out for mass destruction while the rest of the world closes its eyes to what it would rather not see? Could another crazed fanatic seek—and achieve—total domination over millions of compliant subjects?

While there has been nothing in history to equal the dimensions of the Holocaust, movements like Nazism and attempts to wipe out entire groups of people have taken place—may even be taking place now.

In 1932, just as Hitler was beginning his rise to power, Aldous Huxley wrote a book of science fiction called *Brave New World,* that turned out to be amazingly prophetic. Note the parallels between the controlled society that Huxley created from his imagination, and the real policies and programs of the Third Reich.

Utopia:
The Controlled Society

ALDOUS HUXLEY

The room into which the three were ushered was the Controller's study.

"His fordship will be down in a moment." The Gamma butler left them to themselves.

Helmholtz laughed aloud.

"It's more like a caffeine-solution party than a trial," he said, and let himself fall into the most luxurious of the pneumatic arm-chairs. "Cheer up, Bernard," he added, catching sight of his friend's green unhappy face. But Bernard would not be cheered; without answering, without even looking at Helmholtz, he went and sat down on the most uncomfortable chair in the room, careful chosen in the obscure hope of somehow deprecating the wrath of the higher powers.

The Savage meanwhile wandered restlessly round the room, peering with a vague superficial inquisitiveness at the books in the shelves, at the sound-track rolls and reading machine bobbins in their numbered pigeon-holes. On the table under the window lay a massive volume bound in limp black leather-surrogate, and stamped with large golden T's. He picked it up and opened it. MY LIFE AND WORK, BY OUR FORD. The book had been published at Detroit by the Society for the Propagation of Fordian Knowledge. Idly he turned the pages, read a sentence here, a paragraph there, and had just come to the conclusion that the book didn't interest him, when the door opened, and the Resident World Controller for Western Europe walked briskly into the room.

Mustapha Mond shook hands with all three of them; but it was to the Savage that he addressed himself. "So you don't much like civilization, Mr. Savage," he said.

The Savage looked at him. He had been prepared to lie, to bluster, to remain sullenly unresponsive; but, reassured by the good-humored intelligence of the Controller's face, he decided to tell the truth, straightforwardly. "No." He shook his head.

Bernard started and looked horrified. What would the Controller think? To be labelled as the friend of a man who said that he didn't like civilization—said it openly and, of all people, to the Controller—it was terrible. "But, John," he began. A look from Mustapha Mond reduced him to an abject silence.

"Of course," the Savage went on to admit, "there are some very nice things. All that music in the air, for instance . . ."

"Sometimes a thousand twangling instruments will hum about my ears and sometimes voices."

The Savage's face lit up with a sudden pleasure. "Haven't you read it too?" he asked. "I thought nobody knew about that book here, in England."

"Almost nobody. I'm one of the very few. It's prohibited, you see. But as I make the laws here, I can also break them. With impunity, Mr. Marx," he added, turning to Bernard. "Which I'm afraid you *can't* do."

Bernard sank into a yet more hopeless misery.

"But why is it prohibited?" asked the Savage. In the excitement of meeting a man who had read Shakespeare he had momentarily forgotten everything else.

The Controller shrugged his shoulders. "Because it's old; that's the chief reason. We haven't any use for old things here."

"Even when they're beautiful?"

"Particularly when they're beautiful. Beauty's attractive, and we don't want people to be attracted by old things. We want them to like the new ones."

"But the new ones are so stupid and horrible. Those plays, where there's nothing but helicopters about and you *feel* the people kissing." He made a grimace. "Goats and monkeys!" Only in Othello's words could he find an adequate vehicle for his contempt and hatred.

"Nice tame animals, anyhow," the Controller murmured parenthetically.

"Why don't you let them see *Othello* instead?"

"I've told you; it's old. Besides, they couldn't understand it."

Yes, that was true. He remembered how Helmholtz had laughed at *Romeo and Juliet*. "Well then," he said, after a pause, "something new that's like *Othello*, and that they could understand."

"That's what we've all been wanting to write," said Helmholtz, breaking a long silence.

"And it's what you never will write," said the Controller. "Because, if it were really like *Othello* nobody could understand it, however new it might be. And if it were new, it couldn't possibly be like *Othello*."

"Why not?"

"Yes, why not?" Helmholtz repeated. He too was forgetting the unpleasant realities of the situation. Green with anxiety and apprehension, only Bernard remembered them; the others ignored him. "Why not?"

"Because our world is not the same as Othello's world. You can't make flivvers without steel—and you can't make tragedies without social instability. The world's stable now. People are happy; they get what they want, and they never want what they can't get. They're well off; they're safe; they're never ill; they're not afraid of death; they're blissfully ignorant of passion and old age; they're plagued with no mothers or fathers; they've got no wives, or children, or lovers to feel strongly about; they're so conditioned that they practically can't help behaving as they ought to behave. And if anything should go wrong, there's *soma*. Which you go and chuck out of the window in the name of liberty, Mr. Savage. *Liberty!*" He laughed. "Expecting Deltas to know what liberty is! And now expecting them to understand *Othello!* My good boy!"

The Savage was silent for a little. "All the same," he insisted obstinately, *Othello's* good, *Othello's* better than those feelies."

"Of course it is," the Controller agreed. "But that's the price we have to pay for stability. You've got to choose between happiness and what people used to call high art. We've sacrificed the high art. We have the feelies and the scent organ instead."

"But they don't mean anything."

"They mean themselves; they mean a lot of agreeable sensations to the audience."

"But they're . . . they're told by an idiot."

The Controller laughed. "You're not being very polite to your friend, Mr. Watson. One of our most distinguished Emotional Engineers . . . "

"But he's right," said Helmholtz gloomily. "Because it *is* idiotic. Writing when there's nothing to say . . ."

"Precisely. But that requires the most enormous ingenuity. You're making flivvers out of the absolute minimum of steel—works of art out of practically nothing but pure sensation."

The Savage shook his head. "It all seems to me quite horrible."

"Of course it does. Actual happiness always looks pretty squalid in comparison with the over-compensations for misery. And, of course, stability isn't nearly so spectacular as instability. And being contented has none of the glamour of a good fight against misfortune, none of the picturesqueness of a struggle with temptation, or a fatal overthrow by passion or doubt. Happiness is never grand."

"I suppose not," said the Savage after a silence. "But need it be quite so bad as those twins?" He passed his hand over his eyes as though he were trying to wipe away the remembered image of those long rows of identical midgets at the assembling tables, those queued-up twin-herds at the entrance to the Brentford monorail station, those human maggots swarming round Linda's bed of death, the endlessly repeated face of his assailants. He looked at his bandaged left hand and shuddered. "Horrible!"

"But how useful! I see you don't like our Bokanovsky Groups; but, I assure you, they're the foundation on which everything else is built. They're the gyroscope that stabilizes the rocket plane of state on its unswerving course." The deep voice thrillingly vibrated; the gesticulating hand implied all space and the onrush of the irresistible machine. Mustapha Mond's oratory was almost up to synthetic standards.

"I was wondering," said the Savage, "why you had them at all—seeing that you can get whatever you want out of those bottles. Why don't you make everybody an Alpha Double Plus while you're about it?"

Mustapha Mond laughed. "Because we have no wish to have our throats cut," he answered. "We believe in happiness and stability. A society of Alphas couldn't fail to be unstable and miserable. Imagine a factory staffed by Alphas—that is to say by separate and unrelated individuals of good heredity and conditioned so as to be capable (within limits) of making a free choice and assuming responsibilities. Imagine it!" he repeated.

The Savage tried to imagine it, not very successfully.

"It's an absurdity. An Alpha-decanted, Alpha-conditioned man would go mad if he had to do Epsilon Semi-Moron work—go mad, or start smashing things up. Alphas can be completely socialized—but only on condition that you make them do Alpha work. Only an Epsilon can be expected to make Epsilon sacrifices, for the good reason that for him they aren't sacrifices; they're the line of least resistance. His conditioning has laid down rails along which he's got to run. He can't help himself; he's foredoomed. Even after decanting, he's still inside a bottle—an invisible bottle of infantile and embryonic fixations. Each one of us, of course," the Controller meditatively continued, "goes through life inside a bottle. But if we happen to be Alphas, our bottles are, relatively speaking, enormous. We should suffer acutely if we were

314

confined in a narrower space. You cannot pour upper-caste champagne-surrogate into lower-caste bottles. It's obvious theoretically. But it has also been proved in actual practice. The result of the Cyprus experiment was convincing."

"What was that?" asked the Savage.

Mustapha Mond smiled. "Well, you can call it an experiment in rebottling if you like. It began in A.F. 473. The Controllers had the island of Cyprus cleared of all its existing inhabitants and re-colonized with a specially prepared batch of 22,000 Alphas. All agricultural and industrial equipment was handed over to them and they were left to manage their own affairs. The result exactly fulfilled all the theoretical predictions. The land wasn't properly worked; there were strikes in all the factories; the laws were set at naught, orders disobeyed; all the people detailed for a spell of low-grade work were perpetually intriguing for high-grade jobs, and all the people with high-grade jobs were counter-intriguing at all costs to stay where they were. Within six years they were having a first-class civil war. When 19 out of the 22,000 had been killed, the survivors unanimously petitioned the World Controllers to resume the government of the island. Which they did. And that was the end of the only society of Alphas that the world has ever seen."

The Savage sighed, profoundly.

"The optimum population," said Mustapha Mond, "is modelled on the iceberg—eight-ninths below the water line, one-ninth above."

"And they're happy below the water line?"

"Happier than above it. Happier than your friend here, for example." He pointed.

"In spite of that awful work?"

"Awful? *They* don't find it so. On the contrary, they like it. It's light, it's childishly simple. No strain on the mind or the muscles. Seven and a half hours of mild, unexhausting labor, and then the *soma* ration and games and unrestricted copulation and the feelies. What more can they ask for? True," he added, "they might ask for shorter hours. And of course we could give them shorter hours. Technically, it would be perfectly simple to reduce all lower-caste working hours to three or four a day. But would they be any the happier for that? No, they wouldn't. The experiment was tried, more than a century and a half ago. The whole of Ireland was put on the four-hour day. What was the result? Unrest and a large increase in the consumption of *soma*; that was all. Those three and a half hours of extra leisure were so far from being a source of happiness, that people felt constrained to take a holiday from them. The Inventions Office is stuffed with plans for labor-saving processes. Thousands of them." Mustapha Mond made a lavish gesture. "And why don't we put them into execution? For the sake of the laborers; it would be sheer cruelty to afflict them with excessive leisure. It's the same with agriculture. We could synthesize every morsel of food, if we wanted to. But we don't. We prefer to keep a third of the population on the land. For their own sakes—because it takes *longer* to get food out of the land than out of a factory. Besides, we have our stability to think of. We don't want to change. Every change is a menace to stability. That's another reason why we're so chary of applying new inventions. Every discovery in pure science is potentially subversive; even science must sometimes be treated as a possible enemy. Yes, even science."

Science? The Savage frowned. He knew the word. But what it exactly signified he could not say. Shakespeare and the old men of the pueblo had never mentioned science, and from Linda he had only gathered the vaguest hints: science was something you made helicopters with, something that caused you to laugh at the Corn Dances, something that prevented you from being wrinkled and losing your teeth. He made a desperate effort to take the Controller's meaning.

"Yes," Mustapha Mond was saying, "that's another item in the cost of stability. It isn't only art that's incompatible with happiness; it's also science. Science is dangerous; we have to keep it most carefully chained and muzzled."

"What?" said Helmholtz, in astonishment. "But we're always saying that science is everything. It's a hypnoaedic platitude."

"Three times a week between 13 and 17," put in Bernard.

"And all the science propaganda we do at the College . . ."

"Yes; but what sort of science?" asked Mustapha Mond sarcastically. "You've had no scientific training, so you can't judge. I was a pretty good physicist in my time. Too good—good enough to realize that all our science is just a cookery book, with an orthodox theory of cooking that nobody's allowed to question, and a list of recipes that mustn't be added to except by special permission from the head cook. I'm the head cook now. But I was an inquisitive young scullion once. I started doing a bit of cooking on my own. Unorthodox cooking, illicit cooking. A bit of real science, in fact." He was silent.

"What happened?" asked Helmholtz Watson.

The Controller sighed. "Very nearly what's going to happen to you young men. I was on the point of being sent to an island."

Another image of totalitarian society was created by George Orwell in his novel *1984*, published after World War II and no doubt influenced by it. This society was the opposite of the world of perfect contentment depicted in Huxley's book. In Orwell's world, man is controlled so as to heighten his worst characteristics.

The All-Powerful State

GEORGE ORWELL

"How does one man assert his power over another, Winston?" Winston thought. "By making him suffer," he said.

"Exactly. By making him suffer. Obedience is not enough. Unless he is suffering, how can you be sure that he is obeying your will and not his own? Power is in inflicting pain and humiliation. Power is in tearing human minds to pieces and putting them together again in new shapes of your own choosing. Do you begin to see, then, what kind of world we are creating? It is the exact opposite of the stupid hedonistic Utopias that the old reformers imagined. A world of fear and treachery and torment, a world of trampling and being trampled upon, a world which will grow not less but *more* merciless as it refines itself. Progress in our world will be progress toward more pain. The old civilizations claimed that they were founded on love and justice. Ours is founded upon hatred. In our world there will be no emotions except fear, rage, triumph, and self-abasement. Everything else we shall destroy—everything. Already we are breaking down the habits of thought which have survived from before the Revolution. We have cut the links between child and parent, and between man and man, and between man and woman. No one dares trust a wife or a child or a friend any longer. But in the future there will be no wives and no friends. Children will be taken from their mothers at birth, as one takes eggs from a hen. The sex instinct will be eradicated. Procreation will be an annual formality like the renewal of a ration card. We shall abolish the orgasm. Our neurologists are at work upon it now. There will be no loyalty, except loyalty toward the Party. There will be no love, except the love of Big Brother. There will be no laughter, except the laugh of triumph over a defeated enemy. There will be no art, no literature, no science. When we are omnipotent we shall have no more need of science. When we are omnipotent we shall have no more need of science. There will be no distinction between beauty and ugliness. There will be no curiosity, no employment of the process of life. All competing pleasures will be destroyed. But always—do not forget this, Winston—always there will be the intoxication of power, constantly increasing and constantly growing subtler. Always, at every moment, there will be the thrill of victory, the sensation of trampling on an enemy who is helpless. If you want a picture of the future, imagine a boot stamping on a human face—forever."

He paused as though he expected Winston to speak. Winston had tried to shrink back into the surface of the bed again. He could not say anything. His heart seemed to be frozen. O'Brien went on:

"And remember that it is forever. The face will always be there to be stamped upon. The heretic, the enemy of society, will always be there, so that he can be defeated and humiliated over again. Everything that you have undergone since you have been in our hands—all that will continue, and worse. The espionage, the betrayals, the arrests, the tortures, the executions, the disappearances will never cease. It will be a world of terror as much as a world of triumph. The more the Party is powerful, the less it will be tolerant; the weaker the opposition, the tighter the despotism. Goldstein and his heresies will live forever. Every day, at every moment, they will be defeated, discredited, ridiculed, spat upon—and yet they will always survive. This drama that I have played out with you during seven years will be played out over and over again, generation after generation, always in subtler forms. Always we shall have the heretic here at our mercy, screaming with pain, broken up, contemptible—and in the end utterly penitent, saved from himself, crawling to our feet of his own accord. That is the world that we are preparing, Winston. A world of victory after victory, triumph after triumph after triumph: an endless pressing, pressing, pressing upon the nerve of power. You are beginning, I can see, to realize what that world will be like. But in the end you will do more than understand it. You will accept it, welcome it, become part of it."

As long as people can experience and suffer the pain of others, there may be hope. Yevgeny Yevtushenko, a Russian poet, a non-Jew, wrote this poem as an anguished protest—mourning an episode that took place in the past, and crying out against anti-Semitism.

Babi Yar is the name of a ravine near Kiev, in the Ukraine, where many thousands of Jews were massacred by the German army during World War II. After years of delay—35, to be exact—a monument was erected with the following inscription on it:

> Here in 1941–1943, the German Fascist invaders executed over 100,000 citizens of Kiev and prisoners of war.

As the Jews of Russia are persecuted in their lives, so the dead Jews of Kiev are denied their identity as martyrs. They were massacred not as "citizens of Kiev," but as Jews.

Babi Yar

YEVGENY YEVTUSHENKO

No monument stands over Babi Yar.
A drop sheer as a crude gravestone.
I am afraid.
       Today I am as old in years
as all the Jewish people.
Now I seem to be
         a Jew.
Here I plod through ancient Egypt.
Here I perish crucified, on the cross,
and to this day I bear the scars of nails.
I seem to be
     Dreyfus.
The Philistine
         is both informer and judge.
I am behind bars.
          Beset on every side.
Hounded,
      spat on,
          slandered.

Squealing, dainty ladies in flounced Brussels lace
stick their parasols into my face.
I seem to be then
                        a young boy in Byelostok.
Blood runs, spilling over the floors.
The bar-room rabble-rousers
give off a stench of vodka and onion.
A boot kicks me aside, helpless.
In vain I plead with these pogrom bullies.
While they jeer and shout,
                        "Beat the Yids. Save Russia!"
some grain-marketeer beats up my mother.
O my Russian people!
                        I know
                              you
are international to the core.
But those with unclean hands
have often made a jingle of your purest name.
I know the goodness of my land.
How vile these anti-Semites—
                        without a qualm
they pompously called themselves
"The Union of the Russian People"!
I seem to be
            Anne Frank
transparent
            as a branch in April.
And I love.
            And have no need of phrases.
My need
         is that we gaze into each other.
How little we can see
                  or smell!
We are denied the leaves,
                  we are denied the sky.
Yet we can do so much—
                  tenderly
embrace each other in a dark room.
They're coming here?
                  Be not afraid. Those are the booming
sounds of spring:
                  spring is coming here.

Come then to me.
                    Quick, give me your lips.
Are they smashing down the door?
                              No, it's the ice breaking . . .
The wild grasses rustle over Babi Yar.
The trees look ominous,
                    like judges.
Here all things scream silently,
                         and, baring my head,
slowly I feel myself
               turning gray.
And I myself
          am one massive, soundless scream
above the thousand thousand buried here.
I am
    each old man
                    here shot dead.
I am
    every child
              here shot dead.
Nothing in me
            shall ever forget!
The "Internationale," let it
                       thunder
when the last anti-Semite on earth
is buried forever.
In my blood there is no Jewish blood.
In their callous rage, all anti-Semites
must hate me now as a Jew.
For that reason
              I am a true Russian!

Claude McKay, one of eleven children of a Jamaican farmer, distinguished himself as a novelist, short-story writer, and poet. He became the first black man awarded the medal of the Institute of Arts and Sciences in Jamaica in 1912. In the 1920s he was a prominent figure in the Harlem Renaissance and in the American radical press. The bulk of his work, of course, was given over to the black experience. This poem, written out of that background, could speak for the anguish of an inmate in a concentration camp or a Jew in the Warsaw ghetto.

If We Must Die

CLAUDE McKAY

If we must die—let it not be like hogs
Hunted and penned in an inglorious spot,
While round us bark the mad and hungry dogs,
Making their mock at our accursed lot.
If we must die—oh, let us nobly die,
So that our precious blood may not be shed
In vain; then even the monsters we defy
Shall be constrained to honor us though dead!
Oh, Kinsmen! We must meet the common foe;
Though far outnumbered, let us show us brave,
And for their thousand blows deal one deathblow!
What though before us lies the open grave?
Like men we'll face the murderous, cowardly pack,
Pressed to the wall, dying, but fighting back!

The following two selections present views about human behavior that certainly can be applied to Nazi Germany, but that have relevance to our own society as well.

Arthur Koestler, in an excerpt from his book *Darkness at Noon*, argues that a humane society is impossible because political leaders will always sacrifice the individual to the needs and goals of the larger group.

Eric Hoffer, in an excerpt from the book *The True Believer*, describes how easily people become true believers, in any doctrine, and then block out everything that contradicts the truth they have accepted. This view clearly agrees with what we know about the behavior of the German people (and others) under Hitler.

Why There Has Never Been a Humane Society

ARTHUR KOESTLER

"There are only two conceptions of human ethics, and they are at opposite poles. One of them is Christian and humane, declares the individual to be sacrosanct, and asserts that the rules of arithmetic are not to be applied to human units. The other starts from the basic principle that a collective aim justifies all means, and not only allows, but demands, that the individual should in every way be subordinated and sacrificed to the community—which may dispose of it as an experimentation rabbit or a sacrificial lamb. The first conception could be called anti-vivisection morality, the second, vivisection morality. Humbugs and dilettantes have always tried to mix the two conceptions; in practice, it is impossible. Whoever is burdened with power and responsibility finds out on the first occasion that he has to choose; and he is fatally driven to the second alternative. Do you know, since the establishment of Christianity as a state religion, a single example of a state which really followed a Christian policy? You can't point out one. In times of need—and politics are chronically in a time of need—the rulers were always able to evoke 'exceptional circumstances,' which demanded exceptional measures of defense. Since the existence of nations and classes, they live in a permanent state of mutual self-defense, which forces them to defer to another time the putting into practice of humanism. . . ."

On Blind Faith

ERIC HOFFER

The readiness for self-sacrifice is contingent on an impervious ness to the realities of life. He who is free to draw conclusions from his individual experience and observation is not usually hospitable to the idea of martyrdom. For self-sacrifice is an unreasonable act. It cannot be the end-product of a process of probing and deliberating. All active mass movements strive, therefore, to interpose a fact-proof screen between the faithful and the realities of the world. They do this by claiming that the ultimate and absolute truth is already embodied in their doctrine and that there is no truth nor certitude outside it. The facts on which the true believer bases his conclusions must not be derived from his experience or observation but from holy writ. "So tenaciously should we cling to the world revealed by the Gospel, that were I to see all the Angels of Heaven coming down to me to tell me something different, not only would I not be tempted to doubt a single syllable, but I would shut my eyes and stop my ears, for they would not deserve to be either seen or heard." To rely on the evidence of the senses and of reason is heresy and treason. It is startling to realize how much unbelief is necessary to make belief possible. What we know as blind faith is sustained by innumerable unbeliefs. The fanatical Japanese in Brazil refused to believe for years the evidence of Japan's defeat. The fanatical Communist refuses to believe any unfavorable report or evidence about Russia, nor will he be disillusioned by seeing with his own eyes the cruel misery inside the Soviet promised land.

It is the true believer's ability to "shut his eyes and stop his ears" to facts that do not deserve to be either seen or heard which is the source of his unequaled fortitude and constancy. He cannot be frightened by danger nor disheartened by obstacles nor baffled by contradictions because he denies their existence. Strength of faith, as Bergson pointed out, manifests itself in moving mountains but in not seeing mountains to move. And it is the certitude of his infallible doctrine that renders the true believer impervious to the uncertainties, surprises and the unpleasant realities of the world around him.

Thus the effectiveness of a doctrine should not be judged by its profundity, sublimity or the validity of the truths it embodies, but

324

by how thoroughly it insulates the individual from his self and the world as it is. What Pascal said of an effective religion is true of any effective doctrine: It must be "contrary to nature, to common sense and to pleasure."

Jacob Stroyer, once a slave himself, wrote about the experiences of slavery in the United States in a series of volumes entitled *Sketches of My Life in the South*. This selection describes in moving terms the departure of a group of slaves who have been sold to new masters in Louisiana. Stroyer's depiction of this scene is a haunting parallel to the accounts of Jews who were rounded up and deported to concentration camps.

Sold to Louisiana

JACOB STROYER

... The victims were to take the cars from a station called Clarkson turnout, which was about four miles from master's place. The excitement was so great that the overseer and driver could not control the relatives and friends of those that were going away, as a large crowd of both old and young went down to the depot to see them off. Louisiana was considered by the slaves as a place of slaughter, so those who were going did not expect to see their friends again. While passing along, many of the Negroes left their master's fields and joined us as we marched to the cars; some were yelling and wringing their hands, while others were singing little hymns that they were accustomed to for the consolation of those that were going away, such as,

> *When we all meet in heaven,*
> *There is no parting there;*
> *When we all meet in heaven,*
> *There is parting no more.*

We arrived at the depot and had to wait for the cars to bring the others from the Sumterville Jail, but they soon came in sight, and when the noise of the cars died away we heard wailing and shrieks from those in the cars. While some were weeping, others were fiddling, picking banjo, and dancing as they used to do in their cabins on the plantations. Those who were so merry had very bad masters, and even though they stood a chance of being sold to one as bad or even worse yet they were glad to be rid of the one they knew.

While the cars were at the depot, a large crowd of white people gathered, and were laughing and talking about the prospect of Negro traffic; but when the cars began to start and the conductor cried out, "all who are going on this train must get aboard without delay," the colored people cried out with one voice as though the heavens and earth were coming together, and it was so pitiful, that those hardhearted white men who had been accustomed to driving slaves all their lives, shed tears like children. As the cars moved away we heard the weeping and wailing from the slaves, as far as human voice could be heard; and from that time to the present I have neither seen nor heard from my two sisters, nor any of those who left Clarkson depot, on that memorable day.

From fiction and philosophy to fact. Tragedies, smaller in scope, but similar in other respects to the Holocaust, have taken place in recent history. This article reprinted from *Newsweek* magazine, July 2, 1973, describes events, chillingly familiar, that happened in the early 1970s.

Slaughter of the Innocents

NEWSWEEK

In terms of sheer brutality, few events in post-World War II history can equal the massacre that took place last year in the beautiful central African republic of Burundi. At that time, members of the Bahutu tribe, which makes up 85 percent of the country's population, rose up against the towering Watusi overlords who have dominated them for centuries. The insurrection failed, and the "Tutsi" government of Col. Michel Micombero exacted a frightful vengeance—slaughtering up to 250,000 "Hutu" men, women and children. Some died from bullets or razor-sharp *panga* knives; others from long nails driven through their heads. Finally, the Tutsis' blood lust was sated and the killings came to an end. But last month, the Tutsis resumed the pogrom against their onetime vassals with a ferocity that smacks of outright genocide.

Once again, the murderous round of fighting was sparked by a Hutu rebellion, this one hatched in the refugee camps at Tabora and Kigoma in neighboring Tanzania. The Hutu strategy called for a three-pronged invasion—from Tanzania, Zaire and Rwanda—and the seizure of the Burundian capital of Bujumbura. In order to instill the spirit of bravery in their Hutu followers, the organizers of the venture—students just back from France and Belgium—asked Zaïrois witch doctors to administer potions that were supposed to render the recipients immune to harm from bullets. The signal for the attack was given and on May 12 some 4,000 ill-equipped Hutus marched across the border. But the magic potions apparently failed, and soon the outgunned Hutus were fleeing for their lives. It was then that the latest slaughter of innocent Hutus began.

Entrusted to carry out the bloodbath this time was the *"Jeunesse Révolutionnaire,"* an ill-disciplined paramilitary group of young men attached to Micombero's ruling party. Armed with machetes, spears and guns, they have been roaming the countryside, burning Hutu villages and murdering Hutus whenever they are found. Witnesses coming from Burundi report seeing open mass graves in Bujumbura and truckloads of bodies in the town of Gitega. Best estimates are that some 10,000 Hutus have been killed so far in the current outbreak—and the massacre is not yet over.

Not all of the Hutus have gone meekly to their death. Many thousands of them have fled to U.N.-administered refugee camps in neighboring countries, chiefly Tanzania. And in those squalid camps, the scenes of human misery are appalling. At the camp in Tabora last week, one 80-year-old Hutu woman stared blankly as doctors cleaned off the stump that once was her hand; before letting her cross the border, the Tutsis had hacked it off. And at Kigoma, 225 miles to the west, another exhausted Hutu woman arrived with two babies strapped to her back. When they were untied by the Portuguese nurse, it was discovered that one of the babies was dead, its spine crushed by a Tutsi spear. "The refugees tell me," says Rev. Ramón Vicens, a Catholic priest who heads a mission in Tanzania, "that women and girls had their bellies opened and breasts cut off. Pregnant women had their children cut out and left for dead by their sides."

The savage repression of the Hutus is in one way even worse than last year's. Then, the Tutsi government appeared to be selective in its campaign of murder, killing only the educated or influential Hutus. This year, the killing is indiscriminate, and officials in Rwanda—where the Hutus are in control—charge that Burundi has embarked on a program of calculated genocide. They insist that a secret Burundian document known as the "Simbananiye White Paper" specifically calls for the elimination of the "surplus" Hutu population in order to achieve numerical parity between the Tutsis (600,000) and the Hutu (3.6 million)—a parity that would require nothing short of an African holocaust. "Micombero," says one Hutu exile, "is a madman."

Madman or not, Micombero is once again shedding the blood of thousands of innocent people. And once again, the international community—including the major powers, the United Nations and the Organization of African States—appears to be helpless or even indifferent to the tragedy of the Hutus.

Another article from *Newsweek,* May 9, 1994, describes events chillingly similar to the last reading, "Slaughter of the Innocents;" except that some 20 years separate the two. Together, these two articles make perfectly clear that history can, and too often does, repeat itself.

Parallels to the Holocaust occur for similar reasons: age-old prejudices and economic hardships that re-fuel those prejudices. And, similarly, any action to stop the killing often comes slowly if at all. While the United Nations and countries around the world debate whether or not to take any action to stop the Rwandan genocide, thousands more are slaughtered. There are never simple answers to the violence, but after reading these two articles about Rwanda and recalling the inaction during the Holocaust, it is natural to wish for a change in the way the world responds to assaults on innocent people.

Mass Murder

NEWSWEEK

The piles of bodies recalled Jonestown. But this wasn't hundreds of dead. As many as 200,000 people have been murdered, mutilated and dumped like garbage in the streets of Kigali, the capital, and in the verdant countryside of Rwanda during weeks of savage tribal warfare. Wielding machetes, knives, clubs, and grenades, Hutu government forces and paramilitary extremists have hunted down and slaughtered Tutsi civilians and sympathizers in what one relief agency calls a campaign of "genocide." Refugee sites have become deathtraps. Rwandan troops shelled a sports stadium packed with 5,000 people seeking shelter in the southwest town of Cyangugu, then fired on them as they tried to escape. Hutu forces attacked a hospital in the southern village of Butare, killing about 170 patients.

The latest spasm of ethnic-based violence followed a suspicious plane crash on April 6 that killed the Hutu presidents of Rwanda and neighboring Burundi. The Tutsi-dominated rebels, while denying responsibility for the crash, have encircled Kigali and engaged government troops in a devastating standoff of mortar and artillery fire. Cut off from food and supplies of clean water, hundreds of thousands of Rwandans face starvation—and a cholera epidemic. Those who can are fleeing. In a

24-hour period, 250,000 or more people streamed southeast into Tanzania. UN forces, cut back to a token presence, could do little more than bear witness to the growing carnage—and build camps for the refugees.

The Armenians were the victims of genocide in 1915—almost 30 years before the term was coined. The Armenians, who have lived around Mount Ararat since before recorded history, share a common language, culture, and Church—they were the first nation to adopt Christianity. Although they had been conquered by many empires, they were especially oppressed—and many times massacred—under the Ottoman Empire (now Turkey) in the 19th century.

The motives of the leaders who ordered their death may be compared to those of the Nazi leaders who authorized the extermination of the Jews. Following the 1908 victory of the Young Turks, a faction arose among them who seized power in 1913, espousing the doctrine of Pan-Turanianism, a formula for justifying the domination of the Turks over the non-Turkic peoples (who were also non-Muslim and had only been tolerated by tradition). The Turkish government, soon after it entered World War I as Germany's ally, ordered the extermination of the Armenian minority. The government used the opportunity the war presented them with—lack of observation by and immunity to sanctions from the Allies—to conceal their crime, just as Hitler used World War II to conceal the "Final Solution." Like Hitler, the men who ordered the Armenians slain labeled their victims as enemies who were planning to attack them. After World War I, the ruling junta authorizing the genocide fled, but their successors were responsible for the massacre of Greek Christians in Smyrna in 1922.

The following passages are taken from *Accounting for Genocide: National Responses and Jewish Victimization During the Holocaust*, by Helen Fein.

The Armenians: An Example of Genocide

HELEN FEIN

T here was never any doubt as to who the victims were; no need to require their registration as Jews were registered in Germany in 1935. Their identity was known to tax collectors, public officials, and neighbors. The campaign began with measures to strip them of the means to resist and to segregate them sexually. Armenians were ordered to hand in their weapons, and they usually hastened to find weapons to hand in even if they had to buy them, for fear that charges of non-cooperation would be brought, used as evidence of disloyalty, and then employed to provoke violence against them. Armenian men in the army were segregated into special units ("labor battalions"), disarmed, and later slain. On the night of April 24, some 1,000 prominent Armenians were arrested in the capital and secretly murdered, leaving the others numbed by terror. The remaining males in each village were summoned by the town crier to report immediately, led out of town, and slain. Women, children, and a few infirm males previously exempted were then bidden by the crier to prepare themselves for deportation. They were driven into the desert by soldiers, staggering along until they dropped from drought, starvation, the lash, or their festering wounds. Women might elect or be selected to becomes wives of Muslims, thus gaining exemption but also requiring them to part with their children. The military was aided by surrounding Kurdish and Circassian tribesmen who looted and raped the women, kidnapping a few favorites and murdering many. For months, packs of bedraggled survivors wound through the deserts of western Asia until they fell or were slain. Toynbee, assessing all the evidence, estimated that two thirds of the 1,800,000 Armenians in the Ottoman Empire in 1914 were annihilated or deported to the desert.

The internment of civilian West Coast Japanese and Japanese Americans in World War II was not one of America's proudest moments. In the spring of 1942, through an Act of Congress, a series of evacuation orders was issued designating the western half of the states of Washington and Oregon, the entire state of California, and a portion of Arizona a military defense zone from which anybody of Japanese descent, even "one-sixteenth of Japanese blood," had to remove himself. Many Japanese were sent to barbed wire-enclosed internment centers. One Japanese-American, Gordon Kiyoshi Hirabayashi, convicted of violating the restrictions, appealed the conviction to the U.S. Supreme Court, where he lost. In his comment on the case, Justice Frank Murphy noted: "In this sense it bears a melancholy resemblance to the treatment accorded to members of the Jewish race in Germany and in other parts of Europe."

Instructions To All Persons of Japanese Ancestry

WESTERN DEFENSE COMMAND AND FOURTH ARMY
WARTIME CIVIL CONTROL ADMINISTRATION
Presidio of San Francisco, California
May 3, 1942
INSTRUCTIONS
TO ALL PERSONS OF
JAPANESE
ANCESTRY
Living in the Following Area:

All of that portion of the City of Los Angeles, State of California, within that boundary beginning at the point at which North Figueroa Street meets a line following the middle of the Los Angeles River; thence southerly and following the said line to East First Street; thence westerly on East First Street to Alameda Street; thence southerly on Alameda Street to East Third Street; thence northwesterly on East Third Street to Main Street; thence northerly on Main Street to First Street; thence northwesterly on First Street to Figueroa Street; thence northeasterly on Figueroa Street to the point of beginning.

Pursuant to the provisions of Civilian Exclusion Order No. 33, this Headquarters, dated May 8, 1942, all persons of Japanese ancestry, both alien and non-alien, will be evacuated from the above area by 12 o'clock noon, P. W. T., Saturday, May 9, 1942.

No Japanese person living in the above area will be permitted to change residence after 12 o'clock noon, P. W. T., Sunday, May 8, 1942, without obtaining special permission from the representative of the Commanding General, Southern California Sector, at the Civil Control Station located at:

Japanese Union Church,
120 North San Pedro Street,
Los Angeles, California.

Such permits will only be granted for the purpose of uniting members of a family, or in cases of grave emergency.

The Civil Control Station is equipped to assist the Japanese population affected by this evacuation in the following ways:

1. Give advice and instructions on the evacuation.

2. Provide services with respect to the management, leasing, sale, storage, or other disposition of most kinds of property, such as real estate, business, and professional equipment, household goods, boats, automobiles, and livestock.

3. Provide temporary residence elsewhere for all Japanese in family groups.

4. Transport persons and a limited amount of clothing and equipment to their new residence.

The Following Instructions Must Be Observed:

1. A responsible member of each family, preferably the head of the family, or the person in whose name most of the property is held, and each individual living alone, will report to the Civil Control Station to receive further instructions. This must be done between 8:00 A.M. and 5:00 P.M. on Monday, May 4, 1942, or between 8:00 A.M. and 5:00 P.M. on Tuesday, May 5, 1942.

2. Evacuees must carry with them on departure for the Assembly Center, the following property:

(a) Bedding and linens (no mattress) for each member of the family;

(b) Toilet articles for each member of the family;

(c) Extra clothing for each member of the family;

(d) Sufficient knives, forks, spoons, plates, bowls, and cups for each member of the family;

(e) Essential personal effects for each member of the family.

All items carried will be securely packaged, tied and plainly marked with the name of the owner and numbered in accordance with instructions obtained at the Civil Control Station. The size and number of packages is limited to that which can be carried by the individual or family group.

3. No pets of any kind will be permitted.

4. No personal items and no household goods will be shipped to the Assembly Center.

5. The United States Government through its agencies will provide for the storage, at the sole risk of the owner, of the more substantial household items, such as iceboxes, washing machines, pianos, and other heavy furniture. Cooking utensils and other small items will be accepted for storage if crated, packed, and plainly marked with the name and address of the owner. Only one name and address will be used by a given family.

6. Each family, and individual living alone, will be furnished transportation to the Assembly Center or will be authorized to travel by private automobile in a supervised group. All instructions pertaining to the movement will be obtained at the Civil Control Station.

Go to the Civil Control Station between the hours of 8:00 A.M. and 5:00 P.M., Monday, May 4, 1942, or between the hours of 8:00 A.M. and 5:00 P.M., Tuesday, May 5, 1942, to receive further instructions.

J. L. DeWitt
Lieutenant General, U.S. Army
Commanding

Kiyoshi Hirabayashi v. United States

SUPREME COURT DECISION

An Executive Order has given a military commander the right to designate a military area and make restrictions to govern this area. The Act of Congress of March 21, 1942, makes it a misdemeanor to knowingly disregard these restrictions. Gordon Kiyoshi Hirabayashi was convicted in the District Court (California) of violating the Act of Congress. The decision was appealed and the judgment of conviction affirmed.

The particular restriction presently being discussed states that all persons of Japanese ancestry residing in the military area must be within their place of residence daily between the hours of 8:00 P.M. and 6:00 A.M. It has been contended that the curfew order and other orders on which it rested were beyond the war powers of the Congress, the military authorities and of the President (as Commander in Chief of the Army). It is also being questioned whether the restriction violated the Fifth Amendment by unconstitutionally discriminating between citizens of Japanese ancestry and those of other ancestries.

Gordon Kiyoshi Hirabayashi (appellant) asserted that the indictment should be dismissed because he was an American citizen who had never been a subject of and had never pledged allegiance to the Empire of Japan. In addition, the Act of March 21, 1942, was thought to be an unconstitutional delegation of Congressional power.

The appellant was born in Seattle in 1918 of Japanese parents who had come from Japan to the United States, and who had never afterward returned to Japan. He was educated in the Washington public schools and at the time of his arrest was a senior in the University of Washington. It was also maintained that Mr. Hirabayashi had never been in Japan or had any association with Japanese residing there.

Gordon Kiyoshi Hirabayashi felt that he would be giving up his rights as an American citizen in obeying the curfew imposed by the military commander. For this reason he was away from his place of residence after 8:00 P.M. on May 9, 1942. The jury returned a verdict of guilty on both counts: 1) failure to report to the Civil Control Station on May

11 or May 12, 1942, to register for evacuation from the military area, and 2) failure to remain in his place of residence from 8:00 P.M. to 6:00 A.M. Hirabayashi was sentenced to imprisonment for a term of three months on each, the sentences to run at the same time.

Certain social, economic, and political conditions existed when the Japanese came to the United States. These conditions are believed to have caused the Japanese to stick together and prevented their assimilation as a part of the white population. In addition, large numbers of children of Japanese parentage are sent to Japanese language schools after public school is over. Some of these schools are thought to be sources of Japanese nationalistic propaganda, encouraging the children to pledge allegiance to Japan. Considerable numbers, estimated to be approximately 10,000, of American-born children of Japanese parentage have been sent to Japan for all or part of their education.

As a result of all these conditions affecting the life of the Japanese in the Pacific Coast Area, there has been little social intercourse between them and the white population. Because persons of Japanese ancestry have been faced with many restrictions while residing in the United States, they may have become more isolated from the rest of the population and more attached to Japan and Japanese institutions.

The Executive Order permitted establishment of military areas for the purpose of protecting national defense resources from sabotage and espionage. The Act of Congress ratified this Executive Order. Both were an exercise of Constitutional power to wage war. Once the Executive and Congress have this power, they also have the freedom to use their own judgment in determining what the threat is and how it can be resisted. A court should not decide whether the Executive and/or Congress did the right thing nor should a court substitute its own judgment for that of the Executive or Congress.

Measures adopted by the Government may point out that a group of one nationality is more dangerous to the country's safety than any other group. This is not entirely beyond the limits of the Constitution and should not be condemned just because racial differences are usually irrelevant.

Appellant, however, insists that the exercise of the power is inappropriate and unconstitutional because it discriminates against citizens of Japanese ancestry, in violation of the Fifth Amendment.

Distinctions between citizens solely because of their ancestry are hateful to a free people whose institutions are founded upon equality. For that reason, discrimination based on race alone has often been considered a denial of equal protection. These considerations would be in effect here were it not for the fact that the danger of espionage and sabotage makes it necessary for the military authorities to look into every fact having to do with the loyalty of populations in the danger areas.

MR. JUSTICE FRANK MURPHY CONCURRING STATEMENT

Distinctions based on color and ancestry are utterly inconsistent with our traditions and ideals. They are at variance with the principles for which we are now waging war. We cannot close our eyes to the fact that for centuries the Old World has been torn by racial and religious conflicts and has suffered the worst kind of anguish because of inequality of treatment for different groups. There was one law for one and a different law for another. Nothing is written more firmly into our law than the compact of the Plymouth voyagers to have just and equal laws. To say that any group cannot be assimilated is to admit that the great American experience has failed, that our way of life has failed when confronted with the normal attachment of certain groups to the lands of their forefathers. As a nation we embrace many groups, some of them among the oldest settlements in our midst, which have isolated themselves for religious and cultural reasons.

Today is the first time, so far as I am aware, that we have sustained a substantial restriction of the personal liberty of citizens of the United States based upon the accident of race or ancestry. Under the curfew order here challenged no less than 70,000 American citizens have been placed under a special ban and deprived of their liberty because of their particular racial inheritance. In this sense it bears a melancholy resemblance to the treatment accorded to members of the Jewish race in Germany and in other parts of Europe. The result is the creation in this country of two classes of citizens for purposes of a critical and perilous hour—to sanction discrimination between groups of United States citizens on the basis of ancestry. In my opinion this goes to the very brink of constitutional power.

Except under condition of great emergency a regulation of this kind applicable solely to citizens of a particular racial extraction would not be regarded as in accord with the requirement of due process of law contained in the Fifth Amendment.

. . . a denial of due process of law as that term is used in the Fifth Amendment. I think that point is dangerously approached when we have one law for the majority of our citizens and another for those of a particular racial heritage.

Nor do I mean to intimate that citizens of a particular racial group whose freedom may be curtailed within an area threatened with attack should be generally prevented from leaving the area and going at large in other areas that are not in danger of attack and where special precautions are not needed. Their status as citizens, though subject to requirements of national security and military necessity, should at all times be accorded the fullest consideration and respect. When the danger is past, the restrictions imposed on them should be promptly removed and their freedom of action fully restored.

In his excellent book, *Crisis in Black and White*, Charles E. Silberman, the distinguished journalist and teacher, draws an unsparing and cogent analogy between the traumas suffered by Africans at the hands of slave traders and the appalling experiences of prisoners in concentration camps. This selection speaks for itself.

The Greatest Trauma of All

CHARLES SILBERMAN

What happened to transform the heroic African into the submissive slave?

For one thing, the process of enslavement subjected the African to a series of traumas that tended to sever him from his culture and institutions and destroy his sense of identity. First, there was the physical torment of the long march to the sea from the point of capture: tied together by their necks, the slaves walked barefoot for weeks through the steaming jungles; those who wearied were abandoned to die a slow death by starvation. (The British abolitionist Thomas Fowell Buxton wrote of having seen hundreds of skeletons lining one of the caravan routes.) Arriving at a coastal trading port, the slaves were subject to the further shock of being exhibited naked to the European slave traders. The slaves who were bought were branded like cattle and, like cattle, herded on shipboard; those considered unfit or undesirable were abandoned to starve to death.

Then began the greatest trauma of all: the dread Middle Passage, a trip so brutal that only an age which has been debased by the existence of the Nazi crematoria could believe it really happened. Here is one description:

> ... The height, sometimes, between decks, was only eighteen inches; so that the unfortunate human beings could not turn around, or even on their sides, the elevation being less than the breadth of their shoulders; and here they are usually chained to the decks by the neck and legs. In such a place the sense of misery

and suffocation is so great that the Negroes . . . are driven to frenzy. They [the slave traders] had on one occasion taken a slave vessel in the river Bonny: the slaves were stowed in the narrow space between decks, and chained together. They heard a horrid din and tumult among them, and could not imagine from what cause it proceeded. They opened the hatches and turned them up on deck. [The Negroes] were manacled together, in twos and threes. Their horror may be well conceived, when they found a number of [Negroes] in different stages of suffocation; many of them were foaming at the mouth, and in the last agonies—many were dead. The tumult they had heard was the frenzy of those suffocating wretches in the last stage of fury and desperation, struggling to extricate themselves. When they were all dragged up, 19 were irrecoverably dead. Many destroyed one another, in the hopes of procuring room to breathe; men strangled those next to them, and women drove nails into each other's brains. Many unfortunate creatures, on other occasions, took the first opportunity of leaping overboard, and getting rid, in this way, of an intolerable life.

It is estimated that approximately one-third of the Africans taken prisoner died en route to the coast and at the embarkation station, and that another third died during the Middle Passage and the "seasoning" that followed. Most slaves were landed first in the West Indies, where they were "seasoned" or broken in to their new roles as slaves; only afterward were they transshipped to the United States.

Concentration camp prisoners went through an analogous series of shocks. The first was the shock of "procurement": Gestapo policy was to make arrests at night, to heighten the element of shock, terror, and unreality. A day or two later came the second shock, transportation to the camp, which "involved a planned series of brutalities inflicted by guards making repeated rounds through the train"; prisoners transported in cattle cars were sealed in, under conditions much like those of the Middle Passage. When they arrived at the camp, there were sham ceremonies designed to reassure the prisoners—so that the next round of terrors would have even greater impact. Those not marked for early extermination would go through "registration," filled with indignities, including inspection while naked. (Descriptions of this process in the concentration camps is remarkably similar to descriptions of the inspection of slaves in the 18th century.) In the concentration camp, registration ended with perhaps the most devastating weapon of all: being marked with a number—which symbolized the prisoners' loss of his name, hence of his identity. "Because he . . . had become a number," the psychologist Elie Cohen has written, "the prisoner belonged to the huge army of the nameless who peopled the concentration camp." Without question, the African slave's loss of his own name—slaves were given new names by the traders or by their new masters—was even more devastating, for in preliterate society, a man's name is considered an essential part of his personality. Surely it is significant that the Black Muslims insist on discarding their "slave names" and taking new names instead.

Ominous Signs

Does history repeat itself? *This selection, reprinted from The New York Times of September 17, 1976, describes the desperate plight of Indochinese (Vietnamese, Cambodians, and Laotians) seeking an escape from Communist rule. To people who know the history of the 1930s, these pathetic incidents call to mind vividly the situation of Jews who managed to leave Germany or other countries on board ships or even small boats, only to discover that no government would permit them to land. The best known of these episodes was the voyage of the St. Louis, which left Hamburg, Germany, in May 1939 bound for Havana, Cuba. Aboard were 937 Jewish passengers, all with American quota permits and special permits to wait in Cuba while their American visas were being processed. But the Cubans changed their minds, and the ship was forced to cruise aimlessly in the Atlantic while urgent pleas were sent to one government after another. Finally, after 35 days at sea, England, France, Holland, and Belgium agreed to share the refugees between them. Other ships, however, were not so fortunate; some had to return to their ports of origin; others, unseaworthy to begin with, went down at sea.*

Voyages of the Damned

THE ASSOCIATED PRESS

FLEEING INDOCHINESE OFTEN REBUFFED BY PASSING SHIPS

Bangkok, Thailand, Sept. 16—Ships on the high seas are tending to pass up boatloads of refugees fleeing Indochina as nations in the area become more reluctant to grant them a haven.

Over the last few months, ship captains have discovered that taking on refugees may well mean a great deal of time and money lost in trying to discharge them at one inhospitable port after another.

A Panamanian-registry freighter picked up 31 Vietnamese refugees in the South China Sea more than two months ago. The refugees, refused entry into Singapore and Yemen, are reported still aboard the freighter on their way to Japan after a journey of 16,000 miles.

A group of 33 Cambodians, after having fled to Vietnam in 1975, escaped recently aboard a fishing smack only to find Thai and Malaysian officials pushing them out to sea. The boat is now in Thai waters for the second time, its voyagers hoping for a change of heart on the part of the authorities.

Giving help to foundering vessels is required by international law, and refugee sources said some cases of ignoring refugee appeals on the high seas had led to violations of seafaring traditions and laws.

Twenty-two Vietnamese, cramped aboard a 20-footer, said they had been passed up by five vessels while limping toward Thailand in August. The refugees said that one of the ships stopped and towered over them, its crew staring down but ignoring their pleas.

Another refugee boat from Vietnam, later rescued, was waved away from an oil rig in the South China Sea. That rig's rope ladder was reportedly pulled up as the boat approached.

Explaining some seemingly callous acts, Western refugee officials said captains—under pressure from their companies to speed along the sea lanes and not delay in ports of call—must sometimes make a difficult assessment of just how badly off a refugee boat is. There are indications that some escapees may try to exaggerate their distress to get a safe trip to a distant port.

Sea escapes are increasing after a year and a half of Communist government in Indochina. Almost 2,000 refugees have been reported in various corners of Asia this year, with a sharp increase noted after the United States announced last May that it would accept 11,000 more Indochinese.

Singapore has taken the toughest stand and refuses entry to refugees unless a foreign government guarantees it will take them.

Except for refugees with relatives, Hong Kong does not allow Indochinese to come in and settle. The Government says the colony is already overpopulated.

Malaysia, the Philippines and Indonesia take a more flexible attitude, although all three generally will not give permanent exile to refugees. Malaysia, which refugee sources said had pushed some boats out of its waters, makes exceptions for Moslems from Indochina.

Japan does not allow refugees permanent asylum but permits them to stay temporarily and has taken in about 170. Thailand has adopted the most liberal policy and, despite some attempts to discourage refugees, has taken in more than 70,000 fugitives. Almost 600 of them came by boat.

The United Nations High Commissioner for Refugees appealed in July to all "first port-of-call" countries to grant refugees temporary entry on the understanding that the United Nations agency would do its best to resettle them. The agency also appealed to potential countries of resettlement, and some, notably United States, France, Norway, Australia and Canada, have responded.

EXCERPTS FROM A REFUGEE LOG

Following are excerpts from a letter logging the sea escape aboard a 20-foot fishing boat of 26 refugees from Vietnam to Thailand. The letter was written in English and made available by the group's leader, who did not wish to be identified.

Aug. 22: About 1700 I saw a merchant ship 20 kilometers away heading northeasterly. We tried to reach this ship with white flag and great hope to be saved. The ship changed course and increased speed. We were left behind in desperation.

Aug. 23: After a few cups of strong coffee into my empty stomach I regained alertness and kept the wheel till the afternoon so Bich could rest. The sea worsened and reached condition 6, which gave little mercy to our small boat.

At the worst time, the water pump broke down and water kept coming in the boat.

In such a situation we saw a weak light starboard side. Just as seeing heaven, we headed to the light hoping to find a rescue ship. It seemed like we never reached the light. Mostly all of us were on the verge of fainting.

Aug. 24: At daybreak, we found out it was an oil-drilling station. We again approached her with white flag and SOS light signal. Nothing could have been more discouraging when some people signaled for us to go away and when we neared, the rope ladder was pulled up. We were not let on the ship [near the rig] and nobody came down to offer any help.

Later, some arrangements were made and we were allowed to go alongside an oil ship. Food and drinks and other supplies were given generously. Not that receiving food did not make us happy, but the warm way in which the people on the ship had shown toward us made us believe there was still meaning to the word "humanity."

A daring and controversial experiment carried out by psychologist Stanley Milgram in the early 1960s revealed some startling facts about the behavior of "ordinary" Americans under stress, and perhaps helped explain why so many Germans blindly followed orders to commit immoral and inhuman acts. Milgram's work suggests that even in our free society, we are highly conditioned to do as we are told by authority figures, even to do things we know are wrong. This article is from *TV Guide*, August 21, 1976.

Obedience to Authority

STANLEY MILGRAM

Sometimes an event occurs during our lifetime that leaves an impression that is both indelible and puzzling. For me that event was the widespread participation of the German people in a system of death camps that destroyed millions of innocent men, women and children. The hapless victims were shot, gassed, and burned in ovens.

These deeds were carried out by a people who were as civilized as any people in the world. How was it possible for them to act so cruelly? Did their behavior reveal a potential that is present in all of us? As a social psychologist whose job is to look into the why and how of human behavior, I decided to explore the response of ordinary people to immoral orders.

In order to explore behavior, social psychologists often rely on an important tool, the experiment. Although experiments in chemistry and physics often involve shiny equipment, flasks and electronic gear, an experiment in social psychology smacks much more of dramaturgy or theater. The experimenter carefully constructs a scenario to focus on certain aspects of behavior, a scenario in which the end is unknown and is completed by the experimental subject. The psychologist tries to create circumstances that will allow him to look at the behavior very carefully, note what he observed, and study its causes.

The experiment I set up was relatively simple: a person comes to the laboratory and, in the context of a learning experiment, he is told to give increasingly severe electric shocks to another person (who, unknown to the subject, is a confederate and does not actually receive the shocks).

This arrangement gave me a chance to see how far people would go before they refused to follow the experimenter's orders. But a fuller scenario is needed to grasp the flavor of the experiment.

Imagine you had answered an advertisement to take part in a study of learning, and are arriving at the university at a time agreed upon. First, you are greeted by a man in a gray technician's coat; he introduces you to a second volunteer and says you are both about to take part in a scientific experiment. He says it is to test whether the use of punishment improves the ability to learn.

You draw lots to see who is to be the teacher and who the learner. You turn out to be the teacher, and the other fellow, the learner. Then you see the learner strapped into a chair and electrodes placed on his wrist. You are told that, when the learner makes a mistake in the lesson, his punishment will be an electric shock.

As teacher, you are seated in front of an impressive-looking instrument, a shock generator. Its essential feature is a line of switches that range from 15 volts to 450 volts, and a set of written labels that goes from slight shock to moderate shock, strong shock, very strong shock, and so on through XXX—danger, severe shock.

Your job, the experimenter explains to you, is to teach the learner a simple word-pair test. You read a list of words to him, such as blue day, nice girl, fat neck, etc., and he has to indicate by means of an answer box which words were originally paired together. If he gets a correct answer, you move on to the next pair. But if he makes a mistake, you are instructed to give him an electric shock, starting with 15 volts. And you are told to increase the shock one step each time he makes an error. In the course of the experiment the "victim" emits cries of pain and demands to be set free, but the experimenter orders you to continue. The question is: how far will you proceed on the shock generator before you turn to the experimenter and refuse to go on?

Before carrying out the experiment, I wanted to know how people thought they would behave in this situation, and so I asked them to predict their own performance. I posed the question to several groups: psychiatrists, psychologists, and ordinary workers. They all said virtually the same thing: almost no one would go to the end.

But in reality the results were very different. Despite the fact that many subjects experience stress, and protest to the experimenter, a substantial proportion continue to the last shock on the generator. Many subjects obeyed the experimenter no matter how vehement the pleading of the person being shocked, no matter how painful the shocks seemed to be, and no matter how much the victim pleaded to be let out. This was seen time and again in our studies and has been observed in several universities where the experiment has been repeated.

But there is more to the experiment than this simple demonstration of obedience. Most of our energy went into systematically changing the factors in this situation to see which ones increased obedience and which led to greater defiance. We studied the effects of the closeness of the victim, the importance of the sponsoring institution and how the sight of other people obeying or defying an authority affected obedience. All of these factors have a powerful effect on whether the subjects obeyed or defied the malevolent authority. This shows that how a person behaves depends not only on his "character" but also on the precise situational pressures acting on him.

When the experiments were published, opinion about them was sharply divided. On the one hand, the American Association for the Advancement of Science awarded the work its annual socio-psychological prize. At the same time, the experiments attracted fierce criticism, centering mainly on the ethical issues of carrying out the research. The experiments that I had hoped would deepen our understanding of how people yield to authority became themselves the focus of controversy.

But the problem of authority remains. We cannot have society without some structure of authority, and every society must inculcate a habit of obedience in its citizens. Yet these experiments show that many people do not have the resources to resist authority, even when they are directed to act inhumanely against an innocent victim. The experiments pose anew the age-old problem: what is the correct balance between individual initiative and social authority? They illuminate in a concrete way what happens when obedience is unrestrained by conscience.

The former Soviet Union was a prison; citizens of the U.S.S.R. could not leave it without permission, which was granted only in special circumstances. For Jews, who were discriminated against in jobs and education and denied cultural or religious institutions of their own (unlike the U.S.S.R.'s other ethnic minorities), emigration was their only hope of living a free life. Starting in 1971, and largely as the result of pressure from the United States, Soviet authorities permitted limited numbers of Jews to leave the country. (Between 1971 and the end of 1976, the total Jewish emigration was slightly over 100,000.) This selection, by David K. Shipler, is reprinted from *The New York Times*, February 6, 1975.

Visa Is Sweet Sorrow to a Soviet Couple

DAVID K. SHIPLER

Moscow, Feb. 5—Alekssandr and Lyudmila Lunts have packed their books in suitcases. They have begun to say goodbye to friends. They are finally going to Israel.

They are husband and wife, but are making this journey in contrasting moods and for sharply different reasons. He is a Jew; she is an ethnic Russian. The two facts are central to their definitions of themselves, pivotal in determining where they look to find their roots. For each of them, the sudden, surprising news that they would get their long-sought emigration visas set in motion great, contradictory currents of relief and sorrow, ecstasy and pain.

"It's not only a problem of tickets and visas," Mr. Lunts said. "Almost everybody who decides to leave has to cut out something from the soul."

Many Jews—Jews are officially considered one of the more than a hundred non-Russian ethnic groups in the Soviet Union—say frankly that they want to leave not simply because they are Jews or because they are burdened by the anti-Semitism or by the lack of religious freedom, but mainly because they find the political and educational system oppressive, stifling and hypocritical. They want to speak openly, read freely. And they are thinking of their children's future.

Mr. Lunts's motives are not so secular. "If I were not a Jew, I don't think I would leave the country," he said. "The bad features of this social system, for me, would not be enough to make me leave.

"Many years ago there were periods when I began to forget that I was a Jew. But pretty soon I had to remember it—I was forced to remember it. The word, 'Jew,' when pronounced in a trolley bus, is pronounced in a low voice. It is important, but not so important, this cursing in shops and in trolley buses and in stores. When simple people were cursing it was not so important, but when I saw that intellectuals were also anti-Semitic, I felt it very strongly."

Mr. Lunts sat in his sparsely furnished apartment in southwest Moscow, the disorder of moving surrounding him. "To be in your own country is very important," he said intensely. "This is why I want to go to Israel. I feel my country is there, not here."

But his wife's country is here, not there. She is not a Jew, and so she shares none of her husband's compulsion to search for a land that she can feel belongs to her. The forces that tug at her pull back, toward Russia.

He understands. "It is very difficult for her," he said. "It is a sacrifice for me."

In the beginning, it was simply because she loved him, Mrs. Lunts explained. He was a mathematician and computer specialist with a good job in a scientific institute. When he decided to apply for a visa more than three years ago, she agreed to apply also. She was his second wife, they had been married eight years and she did not want to be without him.

"When we began I was not so sure that we should leave the country," she said. "I thought that even here we could survive. But as time went on I realized we could not."

Simply put, she saw in those years the dark sides of the Soviet system, sides she said she never knew existed. Shortly after his application, Mr. Lunts was dismissed from his job, a common fate for those who ask to go to Israel.

She then felt she had to resign her post as a geologist to protect her friends and colleagues at the institute where she worked. They said they would welcome her back if she did not emigrate.

During the jobless years, her husband was jailed twice, for a few days each time. He was picked up on the street for questioning by the KGB—the Committee for State Security—perhaps 20 or 30 times. His apartment became a meeting place for other applicants and for those who had been turned down.

She saw what suffering the Government could bring on people, and now as she pads around the apartment in blue jeans, getting things ready, tears are never far below the surface. "I love the country—it is the system," she said. "The longer we are here, the stronger the feeling we should go as fast as possible."

"I was a geologist," she added. "I was on expeditions many times in Siberia, Central Asia. I like my land very much. I do not want to think that I cannot see this place again. I like this place very much.

"My parents remain here, my sisters and many, many friends. I hope that somewhere, somehow I will be able to come back."

Her husband harbors the same hope, but he dares to say what she must know is true, yet is afraid to put into words. He too leaves people behind. His 18-year-old son by his first marriage is going with them, but his older daughter, married and content, is not. Nor is his 84-year-old father.

"I know that I have no chance of meeting them again," Mr. Lunts said.

A sign now hangs in the corridor of his apartment, hand-painted on brown paper by friends during a party marking his 52nd birthday, just a day after he learned on January 21 that the visas would be issued.

It reads, "Visa—the best gift."

The defeat of Hitler did not spell the end of his particular form of madness. The world is still in danger. Other leaders have used, and are using, similar methods in order to achieve unlimited power, and to destroy groups and individuals they regard as undesirable, for whatever reason.

The final selections carry important messages about the future. In the first, taken from the book *The Destruction of European Jews*, Raul Hilberg warns us to beware of administrative measures directed against any one group; if not stopped in time, they can lead to measures of physical extermination. He points out, too, that destructive minds today have access to technological tools for killing large numbers of people such as Hitler never even dreamed of.

In the final selection, Elie Wiesel, the writer who has done more than any other to transmit the message of the Holocaust, asks, "Could it happen again?" He is referring specifically to Jews. The events he refers to were current at the time the article was written, in 1974, and undoubtedly influenced the writer's mood. Nevertheless, his basic feeling is one of uncertainty and fear.

The Occurrence Is Past; The Phenomenon Remains

RAUL HILBERG

Let us point out at once that the Germans have not been the only ones in history who have had a reason to embark upon a destructive course of action. When we examine the world historical scene, we may note that many times, in many countries, bureaucracies have launched the opening phases of a destruction process. Even now, in the Union of South Africa and elsewhere, specialists are selecting, exploiting, and concentrating new victims. Very often, seemingly harmless bureaucratic activities—such as the definition of a particular group and the exclusion of its members from office—contain the seeds of administrative continuity. Potentially, these measures are stepping stones to a killing operation, but as a rule insurmountable barriers from without and within arrest and disrupt the destructive development. Externally, the opposition of the victims may bring the process to a halt; internally, administrative and psychological obstacles may bar the way. The discriminatory systems of many countries are the leftovers of such disrupted destruction processes.

The German destruction of the Jews was not interrupted. That is its crucial, decisive characteristic. At the threshold of the killing phase the flow of administrative measures continued unchecked. Technocratic and moral obstacles were overcome. An unprecedented killing operation was inaugurated, and with the beginning of this operation the Germans demonstrated once and for all how quickly even large groups, numbering in the millions, could be annihilated . . .

As time passes on, the destruction of the European Jews will recede into the background. Its most immediate consequences are almost over, and whatever developments may henceforth be traced to the catastrophe will be consequences of consequences, more and more remote. Already the Nazi outburst has become historical. But this is a strange page in history. Few events of modern times were so filled with unpredicted action and unsuspected death. A primordial impulse had suddenly surfaced among the Western nations; it had been unfettered through their machines. From this moment, fundamental assumptions about our civilization have no longer stood unchallenged, for while the occurrence is past, the phenomenon remains.

Before the emergence of the 20th century and its technology, a destructive mind could not play in fantasy with the thoughts that the Nazis were to translate into action. The administrator of earlier centuries did not have the tools. He did not possess the network of communications; he did not dispose over rapid small arms fire and quick-working poison gases. The bureaucrat of tomorrow would not have these problems; already, he is better equipped than the German Nazis were. Killing is not as difficult as it used to be. The modern administrative apparatus has facilities for rapid, concerted movements and for efficient massive killings. These devices not only trap a larger number of victims; they also require a greater degree of specialization, and with that division of labor the moral burden too is fragmented among the participants. The perpetrator can now kill his victims without touching them, without hearing them, without seeing them. He may feel sure of his success and safe from its repurcussions. This ever-growing capacity for destruction cannot be arrested anywhere.

Since the end of the Jewish catastrophe, basic decisions have been made about the future. In the Christian world the remaining alternatives are gradually moving toward polar ends. After 2,000 years there is no defensible middle ground. The ancient compromise, with all its contradictions, is weakening day by day. To the Jewish community that growing dichotomy conveys unique opportunities and unprecedented vulnerabilities. Jewry is faced with ultimate weapons. It has no deterrent. The Jews can live more freely now. They can also die more quickly. The summit is within sight. An abyss has opened below.

There are people and groups who claim that the Holocaust never happened. A phenomenon referred to as "Holocaust denial" or revisionism of history has appeared in America and other parts of the world.

Deniers argue that the Holocaust never happened or that the extent of the killing has been greatly exaggerated. Their argument flies in the face of overwhelming evidence. And according to Deborah E. Lipstadt, author of *Denying the Holocaust, The Growing Assault on Truth and Memory* (New York: The Free Press, 1993), even to debate whether or not the Holocaust occurred is like discussing whether or not slavery existed in this country or whether the Earth is round. Walter Reich reviewed her book along with another book by Pierre Vidal-Naquet, translated by Jeffrey Mehlman, *Assassins of Memory* (New York: Columbia University Press, 1993).

In the following excerpt from his review which appeared in the *New York Times Book Review* on July 11, 1993, Reich points out that one of the main bases for denial of the Holocaust is the tradition of anti-Semitism or prejudice against Jews. Thus, even though the evidence of the Holocaust is overwhelming and includes detailed records that the Nazis themselves kept of their war on the Jews, the phenomenon of denial will likely continue as long as there is anti-Semitism.

Editors of several college newspapers have been approached by Holocaust denial groups seeking to publish ads stating that the Holocaust never happened and calling for debate on the issue.

Should editors accept these ads? Consider this question as you read the excerpt from Reich's book review.

Erasing the Holocaust

WALTER REICH

The primary motivation for most deniers is anti-Semitism, and for them the Holocaust is an infuriatingly inconvenient fact of history. After all, the Holocaust has generally been recognized as one of the most terrible crimes that ever took place, and surely the very emblem of evil in the modern age. If that crime was a direct result of anti-Semitism taken to its logical end, then anti-Semitism itself, even when expressed in private conversation, is inevitably discredited among most people. What better way to rehabilitate anti-Semitism, make anti-Semitic arguments seem once again respectable in civilized discourse, and even make it acceptable for governments to pursue anti-Semitic policies than by convincing the world that the great crime for which anti-Semitism was blamed simply never happened—indeed, that it was nothing more than a frame-up invented by the Jews, and propagated by them through their control of the media? What better way, in short to make the world safe again for anti-Semitism than by denying the Holocaust?

Remarkably, despite the existence of overwhelming evidence that the Holocaust really happened, and the repeated discrediting of the Holocaust deniers, they have managed to have their case presented in a variety of forums. To some extent, this success has been a product of an age that promotes the idea that every issue must have two sides, and that each should be accorded equal respect in the marketplace of discussion. This approach to ideas is fostered by a number of current assumptions, increasingly popular in academia, regarding the indeterminacy of truth, as well as by the modern phenomenon of television talk shows and the journalistic ethos that no news story is complete unless all views about it are aired, including the most absurd and discredited. This ethos is captured crisply in Ms. Lipstadt's account of her refusal to participate in a debate with a Holocaust denier on a nationally televised show. "In one last attempt to get me to change my mind," Ms. Lipstadt recalls, the show's producer "asked me a question: 'I certainly don't agree with them, but don't you think our viewers should hear the *other side*?'"

But the success of the Holocaust deniers is also the product of an age in which the freedom to express views is confused with an obligation to facilitate their expression. During the last two years, Holocaust deniers have managed to get advertisements promoting their views published in numerous college newspapers in this country on the ground, sometimes voiced by university officials, that to stop them from doing so would be to muzzle free speech. As Ms. Lipstadt observes, the same universities that have insisted on the right of Holocaust deniers to publish their ads have established policies that would block the publication of ads likely to cause pain to racial minorities or women, not considering the pain that Holocaust denial causes to persons who have survived the Holocaust or who have lost loved ones in it.

Finally, the deniers' success is also, paradoxically but very profoundly, the result of our need for good news. I realized, as I was reading these books, and as I was immersing myself in the arguments of the deniers, that I was, at some level of fantasy, hoping that the deniers were right—hoping that those millions of Jews had not been killed, that they were alive secretly in the United States or elsewhere. It would have made me happy to believe that the deep vein of sadness in my life caused by the knowledge that so many in my family had been gassed or shot, and that six million other Jews had been similarly murdered, was merely the product of a bad dream.

In a moment of reverie, and in the yearning to escape despair, one seizes on such a fantasy. But the devastating truth about the Holocaust is that is was a fact, not a dream. And the devastating truth about the Holocaust deniers is that they will go on using whatever falsehoods they can muster, and taking advantage of whatever vulnerabilities in an audience they can find, to argue, with skill and evil intent, that the Holocaust never happened. By being vigilant to these arguments we can all fight this second murder of the Jews—fight it, and weep not only for the victims' mortality but also for the fragility, and mortality, of memory.

Ominous Signs and Unspeakable Thoughts

ELIE WIESEL

I admit it sadly: I feel threatened. For the first time in many years I feel that I am in danger. For the first time in my adult life I am afraid that the nightmare may start all over again, or that it has never ended, that since 1945 we have lived in parentheses. Now they are closed.

Could the Holocaust happen again? Over the years I have often put the question to my young students. And they, consistently, have answered yes, while I said no. I saw it as a unique event that would remain unique. I believed that if mankind had learned anything from it, it was that hate and murder reach beyond the direct participants; he who begins by killing others, in the end will kill his own. Without Auschwitz, Hiroshima would not have been possible. The murder of one people inevitably leads to that of mankind.

In my own naïveté I thought, especially in the immediate postwar period, Jews would never again be singled out, handed over to the executioner. That anti-Semitism had received its death-blow long ago, under the fiery skies of Poland. I was somehow convinced that—paradoxically— man would be shielded, protected by the awesome mystery of the Event.

I was wrong. What happened once, could happen again. Perhaps I am exaggerating. Perhaps I am over-sensitive. But then I belong to a traumatized generation. We have learned to take threats more seriously than promises.

There are signs and they are unmistakable. The sickening spectacle of a diplomatic gathering wildly applauding a spokesman for killers. The scandalous exclusion of Israel from UNESCO. The arrogant self-righteousness of certain leaders, the cynicism of others. The dramatic solitude of Israel. The anti-Semitic statements made by America's top general. Anti-Semitism has become fashionable once more both in the East and in the West.

No wonder then that suddenly one hears discussions on a subject that many of us had thought buried long ago: Jewish survival. Can Israel—the country, the people—survive another onslaught? How many times must it sacrifice the best of its children? How long can one go on living in a hostile world? Is it conceivable that Hitler could be victorious posthumously?

For those of us who have lived and endured the human and Jewish condition in its ultimate depth know: at this turning point in history, the Jewish people and the Jewish State are irrevocably linked; one cannot survive without the other. As a community, we have rarely been so united. And never so alone.

And so, the idea of another catastrophe is no longer unthinkable. I say it reluctantly. In fact, it is the first time I say it. I have chosen until now to place the Holocaust on a mystical or ontological level, one that defies language and transcends imagination. I have quarreled with friends who built entire theories and doctrines on an event which, in my view, is not to be used or approached casually. If I speak of it now, it is only because of my realization that Jewish survival is being recalled into question.

Hence the fear in me. All of a sudden, I am too much reminded of past experiences. The enemy growing more and more powerful, more and more popular. The aggressiveness of the blackmailers, the permissiveness of some leaders and the total submissiveness of others. The overt threats. The complacency and diffidence of the bystanders. I feel as my father must have felt when he was my age.

Not that I foresee the possibility of Jews being massacred in the cities of America or in the forests of Europe. Death-factories will not be built again. But there is a certain climate, a certain mood in the making. As far as the Jewish people are concerned, the world has remained unchanged: as indifferent to our fate as to its own.

And so I look at my young students and tremble for their future; I see myself at their age surrounded by ruins. What am I to tell them?

I would like to be able to tell them that in spite of endless disillusionments one must maintain faith in man and in mankind; that one must never lose heart. I would like to tell them that, notwithstanding the official discourses and policies, our people does have friends and allies and reasons to advocate hope. But I have never lied to them, I am not going to begin now. And yet . . .

Despair is no solution, I know that. What is the solution? Hitler had one. And he tried it while a civilized world kept silent.

I remember. And I am afraid.

Is the United States immune to groups that are founded on hatred and bent on destruction? In this next reading from *The New York Times*, we learn about the behavior of the people in one American town, Billings, Montana, during the first months of 1994, when they faced hate and prejudice in the form of various kinds of attacks by skinheads against Jews and other minority groups in their town. Skinheads, usually young men with shaved heads who belong to neo-Nazi groups, believe in white supremacy and violence against minorities. Uniting against the skinheads, the town acted according to their belief that, "If you harass and intimidate one member of this community you are attacking all of us."

This reading raises the same question that we confront in so many of the selections in this book: that is, how to respond to evil. The response to prejudice of the people of Billings provides inspiration and instruction as our society, and all societies, continue to be tested and tried by "ominous signs." This article shows what human beings who refuse to be immobilized by fear can do when working together in a united way to stand up to evil in their midst. Would we all do the same?

Montana Outrage Stalls Skinheads

Billings, Mont., Feb. 19 (AP)—When swastikas appeared here in Montana's largest city, Chief Wayne Inman was determined to halt the hatred early. As a police officer in Portland, Ore., in the late 1980s, he had watched skinhead racism and anti-Semitism mushroom and turn deadly.

"Hate crimes are not a police problem," Chief Inman said. "They're a community problem. Hate crimes and hate activity will flourish only in communities that allow it to flourish."

So, he and others stirred the city to a level of outrage that at least for now appears to have cowed the racist groups.

The first signs of bigotry came last year, when fliers started showing up in mailboxes, on doorsteps, under windshield wipers, vilifying Hispanic Americans, Indians, blacks, homosexuals, lesbians and welfare recipients. The fliers reserved special venom for the 48 Jewish families among the city's 81,000 residents.

Then, in January, people attending a Martin Luther King, Jr., Day observance returned to find their parked cars papered with Ku Klux Klan material.

SKINHEADS IN BLACK CHURCHES

In the spring, skinheads began showing up in two and threes at Wayman Chapel African Methodist Episcopal Church, glowering in the back pews.

In August, a black swastika painted on white poster board was nailed to the door of Beth Aaron Synagogue, and tombstones were toppled in its cemetery.

In October, swastikas and racial slurs were spray-painted on the home of a husband and wife of different races.

Chief Inman recognized an emerging pattern: hate literature to intimidation to vandalism to personal attacks. In Portland that evolution culminated in the November 1988 beating death of Mulugeta Seraw, a young Ethiopian, by three skinheads returning from a meeting with recruiters from a white supremacist group.

"I saw the emergence of the hate groups and a community's denial, and I saw a wake-up call that was the death of a black man by baseball bat because he was black," Chief Inman said. "That's what it took to wake up Portland. We didn't have to go through that here to get the wake-up call."

The 100,000 people living in the Billings area reacted swiftly and in unison.

"There was not silence," Chief Inman said. "There was a community outrage, saying, 'If you harass and intimidate one member of this community you are attacking all of us.'"

And the resistance was more than bluster. Within five days of the spray-painted vandalism, 27 volunteers from Painters Local 1922 swarmed over the defaced house and obliterated the slurs in 45 minutes.

Bigotry resurfaced the next month. On Nov. 27, a beer bottle was hurled through a glass door at the home of Uri Barnea, conductor of the Billings Symphony. Five night later, a cinder block thrown through a window sent shards of glass flying over the bed of 5-year-old Isaac Schnitzer.

Both houses were decorated with Hanukkah menorahs, and in both houses babysitters were watching children.

SYMBOL OF RESISTANCE

The city reacted immediately. Christian churches distributed photocopies of menorahs. The Billings Gazette published a black-and-white picture of a menorah with an editorial, then a full-page version in color. Several businesses began providing paper menorahs.

Within days, the nine-candled symbol of Jewish perseverance and resistance was displayed in thousands of windows across the city.

The menorah idea started with the Rev. Keith Torney of the First Congregational Church and Margie MacDonald of the Montana Association of Churches.

"This was just getting to be too much," Mr. Torney said. "First the gays, then the black community, but it seemed to me they kind of hit their stride in the Jewish community. It's like they're searching around to get attention."

Civic leaders, churches and businesses declared their revulsion. The Universal Athletics Company replaced its billboard display on a busy thoroughfare with this message: "Not in Our Town! No Hate. No Violence."

But the hatemongers returned. Over two weeks in December, they broke windows at two Jewish homes and two churches that displayed menorahs, shot bullets through windows at Billings Central Catholic High School and stomped and battered six vehicles at homes displaying menorahs, telling two owners in phone calls, "Go look at your car, Jew-lover."

TOO MANY TARGETS TO HATE

The spasm of hate created more resistance. Many more people put menorahs in their windows.

"It became physically impossible for the hate groups to harass and intimidate thousands and thousands of Billings citizens," Chief Inman said.

On Dec. 10, about 100 people attended a Hanukkah service at Beth Aaron Synagogue. Outside, neighbors discreetly stood vigil in the dark.

The city is not proclaiming victory, but Chief Inman thinks the hate groups have backed off. No vandalism has occurred since the incidents in December, and the literature and anonymous calls have diminished.

"I would hate to predict we have stopped the influence and impact of hate crimes, but something appears to be working," he said.

A number of Nazi war criminals have been brought to justice since the Nuremberg Trials of 1945–46 because of individuals like Simon Wiesenthal, the Klarsfelds and other Nazi-hunters. M.E. Kerr's novel *Gentlehands* raises the question of how to respond to aging war criminals who are suddenly exposed after having successfully entered the United States with new and respectable identities. In Kerr's novel a working class boy, Buddy Boyle, tries to impress his girlfriend by bringing her to meet his wealthy German grandfather who for years has been estranged from his family but with whom Buddy has become friends. When an "article"—reproduced below—appears in the local paper indicating that his grandfather may, in fact, be a Nazi war criminal, Buddy refuses to believe the story. On the other hand, as revealed in the excerpt below, Buddy's father and brother are prepared to face the difficult truths of his grandfather's hidden past. The reader comes to realize the agonizing dilemma facing family and friends of alleged war criminals who have escaped accountability for their behavior. Although many of these former Nazis have died, there are still several living in neighborhoods throughout America which means this question remains relevant: Should aging Nazis be arrested or be allowed to live out their days in peace?

Excerpt from *Gentlehands*

M.E. KERR

MONTAUK MAN ACCUSED OF BEING NAZI

In this Wednesday's *New York Record*, Seaville summer resident, Nicholas L. De Lucca, in a front-page article, will accuse Frank O. Trenker of Montauk, of being a former SS officer at Auschwitz, notorious for his acts of cruelty and murder.

De Lucca, 57, a free-lance investigative reporter and occasional stringer for *The New York Record* city desk, has a personal interest in forcing an investigation into Trenker. His cousin, Roselina De Lucca, died at Auschwitz. De Lucca never met his cousin. She was 15 when she was among the Roman Jews transported from Italy to the infamous Polish concentration camp, in 1943.

Information concerning her treatment and death was documented by one of the few Jewish survivors from Rome.

367

On the basis of information provided by an Austrian Nazi-hunter, De Lucca has been in pursuit of Trenker through many countries, for three years. According to De Lucca, there is no statute prohibiting the admittance of a war criminal, but all immigrants upon entrance to America must sign a statement declaring that they did not participate in the persecution of a minority because of race, creed or national origin. De Lucca's intention is to stimulate official action against Trenker on the basis that Trenker falsely signed this statement, and is subject to denaturalization and ultimate extradition to West Germany.

The New York Record alleges that Trenker was known by the ironic nickname "Gentlehands" at Auschwitz, because of his habit of playing often an aria from the opera *Tosca*, "O dolci mani," to torment the homesick Italian females.

The article describes a day when young Roselina De Lucca sneaked the collar off a dead guard dog, thought to be poisoned by a prisoner. ("The raggedy, ill, cold and hungry inmates had learned that everything was useful: string to tie up their shoes, old rags to wrap around their frozen feet anything with which to barter for something to help them stay alive, and this child had found a way to secure the collar of the dead dog.") After she was forced to stand naked in the snow, as an example, for two hours, Trenker then offered her a warm coat and hot soup. On her way to get them, according to the article in *The Record*, Trenker, a member of the SS, sicked the surviving attack dog on her.

Little is known about Trenker in Montauk. A shopkeeper described him as a good-hearted man who loves animals and always has a smile and a friendly word for others. Many spoke of his strikingly handsome appearance, and the article mentions the fact that Trenker was one of the youngest SS officers at Auschwitz, known for his imposing good looks.

Most citizens interviewed asked not to be named, but the overall feeling exists either that it could not possibly be Trenker ("Not that man—he wouldn't hurt a fly"), or that if indeed Trenker was an officer in the SS, and all that the article claims, "It was a long time ago. The past is over. Let the poor man be. He's not hurting anyone."

I was still standing on the sidewalk, finishing the article, when my father pulled up in the Toyota.

"Get in!" he said. He reached across and opened the door for me. Streaker was in the backseat.

"I've got three more hours, Dad."

"Get in, Buddy!" He pounded the empty seat beside him with his fist.

I still had on my apron, and my sweater was hanging up in the employees' room, but I got in, and my father took off. I'd left the copies of *The Citizen* outside Sweet Mouth, except for the one I had in my hand.

"Did you read it?" my father said.

"It's a mistake, Dad." I started to explain that I couldn't just walk out on Kick, either, during the lunch hour, and my father cracked his fist down on the steering wheel this time, and told me to keep my mouth shut.

"*We* haven't been mentioned," my father said, "yet. But your mother's a wreck!"

"It isn't Grandfather," I said; I almost laughed at the idea, but my father punched the steering wheel again and barked, "The hell it isn't!"

"That damn Nazi," Streaker said.

"Shut up, Streaker!" my father said.

I had to look out the window to get control of myself. I had to try to talk to myself the way Grandpa would talk something through with me, staying cool, figuring it out rationally: it was a fact people were often unfair and mean, and my father was certainly a person who leaned far over in that direction, so what did I expect him to react like after he read that article? And now I just had to concentrate on keeping *my* head.

"What do you think of your grandfather now?" my father said, as though he'd never heard me say it was a mistake, it wasn't him. "Are you proud of him?"

I knew he wasn't really looking for answers to his questions.

"Did you take his jeep this morning, Buddy?"

I nodded.

"Answer me, Buddy!"

"You're not interested in my answers," I said. "You listen because you want to hear that you're right, so you can't hear that you're wrong."

"Did - you - take - his - jeep - this - morning?" my father said, very slowly, his eyes bugging out with rage.

"I take it every morning."

"You used to take it every morning!" said my father.

"You stop taking it," Streaker said.

"Leave it where you left it," my father said.

"Leave it where you left it, Buddy," Streaker joined in.

"I won't need any transportation after today, anyway," I said. "I'll be fired for this little number, leaving Kick during the lunch rush."

"That story just breaks my heart," my father said. "After what I just read in *The Citizen*, your story just breaks my heart."

I said it very softly. "It's not Grandfather, Dad. Don't you think I know Grandfather by now?"

"No I don't think you know Grandfather by now, or anything else! You were interested in producing a fancy relative to impress Miss

Gottbucks from Beaublahblah, well, you produced one for her, didn't you?"

"We can't talk," I said.

"You're damn right we can't!"

"Is Buddy going to live with us again?" Streaker asked.

"Buddy is going to stay home from now on," my father said, "whether Buddy likes it or not!"

TREATMENT OF NATIVE AMERICANS: MASSACRE AT WOUNDED KNEE

Native Americans are referred to as "native" because they inhabited the Americas prior to the settlement —some would say the invasion— by Europeans during the 16th and 17th centuries. Eventually United States policy supported that settlement resulting in the forced removal of these natives from lands on which they had lived and hunted for hundreds of years to reservations in areas that lacked many of the resources that had once enabled them to be self-sufficient. While the story of the official treatment of Native Americans, which included not just removal from their lands but also death by hunger, war and disease, is too complicated and lengthy to be shared here, there is one individual and one episode that effectively symbolize that story. The individual is Sitting Bull and the episode is the massacre at Wounded Knee (1890) in what is now South Dakota.

Sitting Bull, or Tatanka-Iyotanka, is best known to non-Indians as the Hunkpapa Sioux chief who masterminded Custer's defeat at the Battle of Little Big Horn, a temporary and rare victory for the Indians. But Sitting Bull's fame among his own people rested on his spirituality as much as his military reputation. As American pressure to secure Sioux lands and destroy Sioux culture intensified, he came to personify his people's struggle for freedom. Sitting Bull and his people were ultimately defeated and rounded up onto reservations against which Sitting Bull continued to protest. He was placed under house arrest, but even two years as a prisoner of war did nothing to deter his devotion to the way of life he had fought to defend. When the Ghost Dance religion—which authorities viewed as a threat—took hold among the Sioux in 1890, the assumption was that the Sioux would look to Sitting Bull as their spiritual leader. Authorities concluded that he had to be removed. On December 14, 1890, the Indian police went to his cabin to arrest him and there was a shootout in which Sitting Bull was killed, some accounts saying he was shot in the back. "But killing Sitting Bull did not stop trouble on the Sioux reservations; instead, it proved to be only a prelude to greater tragedy. Two weeks later, amid continuing tensions occasioned by the spread of the Ghost Dance religion, soldiers of the Seventh cavalry slaughtered some two hundred Miniconjou people at Wounded Knee. The event marked the end of the armed conflict between Plains Indians and the United States Army and came to symbolize the end of a way of life" (Calloway, 1996, 196).

The following is an account of the massacre at Wounded Knee given by Black Elk, an Oglala Sioux holy man, who was a young man at the time. In his old age he shared these reflections. (From John G. Neihardt, "Black Elk Speaks: Being the Life Story of a Holy Man of the Oglala Sioux" Lincoln: University of Nebraska Press, 1988 ed., 253–62, 270; in Colin Calloway, ed. Our Hearts Fell to the Ground, Plains Indians Views of How the West Was Lost. New York: Bedford Books, 1996, 200–4.)

Massacre at Wounded Knee–1890

BLACK ELK

It was now near the end of the Moon of Popping Trees, and I was twenty-seven years old (December, 1890). We heard that Big Foot was coming down from the Badlands with nearly four hundred people. Some of these were from Sitting Bull's band. They had run away when Sitting Bull was killed, and joined Big Foot on Good River. There were only about a hundred warriors in this band, and all the others were women and children and some old men. They were all starving and freezing, and Big Foot was so sick that they had to bring him along in a pony drag. They had all run away to hide in the Badlands, and they were coming in now because they were starving and freezing. When they crossed Smoky Earth River, they followed up Medicine Root Creek to its head. Soldiers were over there looking for them. The soldiers had everything and were not freezing and starving. Near Porcupine Butte the soldiers came up to the Big Foots, and they surrendered and went along with the soldiers to Wounded Knee Creek where the Brenan store is now.

It was in the evening when we heard that the Big Foots were camped over there with the soldiers, about fifteen miles by the old road from where we were. It was the next morning (December 29, 1890) that something terrible happened.

That evening before it happened, I went in to Pine Pidge and heard these things, and while I was there, soldiers started for where the Big Foots were. These made about five hundred soldiers that were there next morning. When I saw them starting I felt that something terrible was going to happen. That night I could hardly sleep at all. I walked around most of the night.

In the morning I went out after my horses, and while I was out I heard shooting off toward the east, and I knew from the sound that it must be wagon-guns (cannon) going off. The sounds went right through my body, and I felt that something terrible would happen....

[Black Flk and his companions rode toward the sound of the shooting.]

In a little while we had come to the top of the ridge where, looking to the east, you can see for the first time the monument and the burying ground on the little hill where the church is. That is where the terrible thing started. Just south of the burying ground on the little hill a deep dry gulch runs about east and west, very crooked, and it rises westward to nearly the top of the ridge where we were. It had no name, but the Wasichus sometimes call it Battle Creek now. We stopped on the ridge not far from the head of the dry gulch. Wagon guns were still going off over there on the little hill, and they were going off again where they hit along the gulch. There was much shooting down yonder, and there were many cries, and we could see cavalrymen scattered over the hills ahead of us. Cavalrymen were riding along the gulch and shooting into it, where the women and children were running away and trying to hide in the gullies and the stunted pines....

By now many other Lakotas, who had heard the shooting, were coming up from Pine Ridge, and we all charged on the soldiers. They ran eastward toward where the trouble began. We followed down along the dry gulch, and what we saw was terrible. Dead and wounded women and children and little babies were scattered all along there where they had been trying to run away. The soldiers had followed along the gulch, as they ran, and murdered them in there. Sometimes they were in heaps because they had huddled together, and some were scattered all along. Sometimes bunches of them had been killed and torn to pieces where the wagon guns hit them. I saw a little baby trying to suck its mother, but she was bloody and dead.

There were two little boys at one place in this gulch. They had guns and they had been killing soldiers all by themselves. We could see the soldiers they had killed. The boys were all alone there, and they were not hurt. These were very brave little boys.

When we drove the soldiers back, they dug themselves in, and we were not enough people to drive them out from there. In the evening they marched off up Wounded Knee Creek, and then we saw all that they had done there.

Men and women and children were heaped and scattered all over the flat at the bottom of the little hill where the soldiers had their wagon-guns and westward up the dry gulch all the way to the high ridge, the dead women and children and babies were scattered.

When I saw this I wished that I had died too, but I was not sorry for the women and children. It was better for them to be happy in the other world, and I wanted to be there too. But before I went there I wanted to have revenge. I thought there might be a day, and we should have revenge.

After the soldiers marched away, I heard from my friend, Dog Chief, how the trouble started, and he was right there by Yellow Bird when it happened. This is the way it was:

In the morning the soldiers began to take all the guns away from the Big Foots, who were camped in the flat below the little hill where the monument and burying ground are now. The people had stacked most of their guns, and even their knives, by the tepee where Big Foot was lying sick. Soldiers were on the little hill and all around, and there were soldiers across the dry gulch to the south and over east along Wounded Knee Creek too. The people were nearly surrounded, and the wagon guns were pointing at them.

Some had not yet given up their guns, and so the soldiers were searching all the tepees, throwing things around and poking into everything. There was a man called Yellow Bird, and he and another man were standing in front of the tepee where Big Foot was lying sick. They had white sheets around and over them, with eyeholes to look through, and they had guns under these. An officer came to search them. He took the other man's gun, and then started to take Yellow Bird's. But Yellow Bird would not let go. He wrestled with the officer, and while they were wrestling, the gun went off and killed the officer. Wasichus and some others have said he meant to do this, but Dog Chief was standing right there, and he told me it was not so. As soon as the gun went off, Dog Chief told me, an officer shot and killed Big Foot who was lying sick inside the tepee.

Then suddenly nobody knew what was happening, except that the soldiers were all shooting and the wagon-guns began going off right in among the people.

Many were shot down right there. The women and children ran

into the gulch and up west, dropping all the time, for the soldiers shot them as they ran. There were only about a hundred warriors and there were nearly five hundred soldiers. The warriors rushed to where they had piled their guns and knives. They fought soldiers with only their hands until they got their guns.

Dog Chief saw Yellow Bird run into a tepee with his gun, and from there he killed soldiers until the tepee caught fire. Then he died full of bullets.

It was a good winter day when all this happened. The sun was shining. But after the soldiers marched away from their dirty work, a heavy snow began to fall. The wind came up in the night. There was a big blizzard, and it grew very cold. The snow drifted deep in the crooked gulch, and it was one long grave of butchered women and children and babies, who had never done any harm and were only trying to run away....

[Black Elk and other warriors wanted to fight the soldiers, but Red Cloud persuaded them to think of the women and children and submit.]

And so it was all over.

I did not know then how much was ended. When I look back now from this high hill of my old age, I can still see the butchered women and children lying heaped and scattered all along the crooked gulch as plain as when I saw them with eyes still young. And I can see that something else died there in the bloody mud, and was buried in the blizzard. A people's dream died there. It was a beautiful dream.

And I, to whom so great a vision was given in my youth—you see me now a pitiful old man who has done nothing, for the nation's hoop is broken and scattered. There is no center any longer, and the sacred tree is dead.

Si Lewen:
The Man and His Art

THOMAS YOSELOFF

When Si Lewen completed his first book of drawings, *The Parade*, in 1950, Albert Einstein wrote:

> I find your work, *The Parade* very impressive from a purely artistic standpoint. Furthermore, I find it a real merit to counteract the tendencies toward war through the medium of art. Nothing can equal the psychological effect of real art—neither factual description nor intellectual discussion. It had often been said that art should not be used to serve any political or otherwise practical goals. But I could never agree with this point of view. It is true that it is utterly wrong and disgusting if some direction of thought and expression is forced upon the artist from outside. But strong emotional tendencies of the artist himself have often given birth to truly great works of art. One has only to think of *Gulliver's Travels* and Daumier's immortal drawings directed against the corruption in French politics of his time. Our time needs you and your work.

The Parade and its sequel, *A Journey*, spring from Lewen's past and emotional experiences. Si Lewen was born as the First World War was coming to an end, in 1918, in Lublin, Poland. Soon after, his parents fled with him to Berlin. In Switzerland, at the age of five, he decided to become a painter. Returning to Berlin, he received his first art lessons from Max Adron, a student of Paul Klee and the Bauhaus, and from Klaus Richter of the Berlin Academy. The political and cultural ferment of the Weimar Republic, and especially German Expressionism and the work of Kaethe Kollwitz, George Grosz, and Frans Masereel, added their influence.

In 1933, when Hitler came to power, young Lewen, then 14, fled to France. Here, he was fascinated by the modern French school, especially Cubism. Two years later he came to New York and continued his studies at the National Academy of Design. When the United States entered the Second World War, he joined the American Army and took part in the European campaigns from Normandy to Germany.

Back in New York after the war, he resumed his art studies and began work on his long series of continuously related drawings and paintings. The publication of *The Parade* in 1957 was the culmination of this phase of his work. In 1968, Lewen and his wife, Rennie, left New York City and settled in New Paltz, New York, where he has been working on the "Millipede"—a multimedia multiptych project of "continuous progression, procession and transformation." Already 1,000 feet long and still growing, it appears to Lewen to have no end in sight.

Si Lewen's work reflects a world of step-by-step progression of often tragic events and images. For him everything is but a step, a transition to the next stage. All of his work is a part of a procession, a migration, an Odyssey. In *A Journey* the "visitor" travels through the nightmare of the concentration camp, where the camp serves as the ultimate expression of the nation state.

Einstein found Lewen's work "impressive." Other distinguished critics have expressed their own reactions on seeing his work. August L. Freundlich wrote in 1962:

The work of Si Lewen is the work of a forceful giant with the sensitive conscience of the artist...

Lewen's paintings are unusual in these days of abstract and wildly expressive art. He combines emphasis on precise design with an often scathing comment on the events in our lives. He is both artist and child of our century. Lewen's artistic world shows the grimness and horror which exist in war and its aftermath, in the slums of the city, and in the changes which man has made detrimentally to his environment.

Meyer Levin, in writing about *The Parade*, said it was "so powerful that when I first looked through it I felt I could not write about it." It was, he said, "created with a fury that can only be compared to Goya's in the 'Horrors of War'."

The Parade and *A Journey* may be unique. Lewen acknowledges, however, that they were inspired and influenced by the "novels without words," the books of woodcuts by Frans Masereel, published in the 1920s. Lewen has written of his own motives in creating *A Journey*:

I wanted to record graphically what I have seen and what I see, to bear witness—to a world often beyond rational comprehension. This is, I believe, the most valid aesthetic commitment a contemporary artist can make. The drawings represent my concern with the graphic image as a superior reflection of visible reality, a recognition of reality

as a continuum, a step-by-step evolution. Everything and every event inevitably follows another and leads to another.

Of the "plot" and the symbolism in the work, he has written:

A Journey graphically describes, by means of its 72 drawings, the journey of a man. He enters a forest. The forest grows darker. Deep in the forest another man behind a barbed wire fence beckons and directs him to the entrance of a camp. Here the traveler encounters the inmates of the camp.

The visitor meets a gardener, who offers him a severed hand. He rejects this and moves on. He looks into the window of one of the buildings, and is invited in for dinner. Dinner consists of a butchered man, and the traveler is offered the victim's heart. He runs out and vomits, and is nearly drowned in his own effluence.

He emerges and encounters processions of inmates and victims. In one building a guard invites him to participate in the torture of other men. He refuses and runs out, encountering another guard, who directs him to the Palace of Justice. After emerging from a maze, he is taken before a tribunal of three judges. For his refusal to participate in the affairs of the camp, the visitor is condemned to die, and is hanged. A parade passes the gallows, proclaiming Justice, Freedom, Fatherland and God. The dead visitor is dragged to the crematorium and burned.

Out of the ashes a hand emerges. It is that of the visitor, and out of his scream a bird emerges. Clutching the bird as it flies from his throat, the visitor is flown out and beyond the camp. The traveler once again resumes his journey.

A Journey is at once a graphic masterpiece, stark, beautiful and moving in its simplicity, and a searing emotional experience, bringing forcefully to the viewer the pain, the frustration, the inhumanity of the concentration camp. It is the realization of a total Kafkaesque quality, rarely experienced in art. The viewer will become immersed in Lewen's world, a Kafka world of brutal bureaucracy, of dehumanization, of the total destruction of the human spirit. Unlike Kafka, however, Lewen in *A Journey* insists upon resurrection, survival and redemption.

THE DRAWINGS OF SI LEWEN

The drawings in this section were produced by artist Si Lewen and are among the 72 works of art in his book, *A Journey* (Associated University Presses, 1980). A powerful commentary on man's inhumanity during the Holocaust, their impact moved Albert Einstein to say, "I find it a real merit to counteract the tendencies toward war through the medium of art."

In *A Journey*, Lewen portrays "a visitor" traveling through the horrors of the concentration camp. The images are beautiful and touching in their simplicity, and bring forcefully to the viewer the pain, anger and nightmares experienced by victims of Nazi persecution.

Born in Poland in 1918, Lewen grew up in the political and cultural ferment of the Weimar Republic but fled to France at the age of 14 when Hitler came to power. He came to the United States where he studied at the National Academy of Design. He saw war firsthand when he served with the United States Army during the Second World War. These works of art, taken from *A Journey*, reveal how an artist confronts subjects like the Holocaust that defy authentic representation.

Excerpts from *A Journey*

Epilogue

Dear Teacher:

I am a survivor of a concentration camp. My eyes saw what no man should witness:

> Gas chambers built by **Learned** engineers
> Children poisoned by **Educated** physicians
> Infants killed by **Trained** nurses
> Women and babies shot and burned by
> **High School** and **College** graduates

So I am suspicious of education.

My request is: Help your students become human. Your efforts must never produce learned monsters, skilled psychopaths, educated Eichmanns.

Reading, writing, and arithmetic are important only if they serve to make our children more human.

CHAIM GINOTT
1972

Glossary of Terms

Anti-Semitism prejudice against Jews; dislike or fear of Jews; discrimination against or persecution of Jews.

Aryan has no validity as a racial term. It has been used by the Nazis to mean a superior, Nordic-type Caucasian Gentile.

Auschwitz a city in southwestern Poland where there was one of over 100 Nazi extermination camps.

Bismarck, Otto von Prussian prince and chancellor (1815–1898) who unified Germany; later called the "Iron Chancellor."

Demagogue a person who obtains power by means of appeals to emotions and prejudices.

"Final Solution" the term used by Nazis to mean the mass physical extermination of the Jews.

Genocide the systematic killing and annihilation of a whole people or nation.

Gestapo the German internal security police organized in 1933 under the Nazi regime to operate against political opposition.

Holocaust complete destruction of people or animals by fire; the destruction of European Jews 1933–45. From the Greek "burnt whole."

Juden "Jews" in the German language.

Kristallnacht "night of broken glass," (November 9, 1938) when the Nazis instigated a pogrom, or organized attack, on Jews and Jewish-owned businesses in Germany. The Gestapo had been rounding up thousands of Polish Jews who were living in Germany, since neither government recognized them as citizens. The son of one of the first couples to be arrested showed his anger by assassinating a German official in Paris on November 7, 1938. Two days later, the official died and Nazis had an excuse for beginning the pogrom. More than 7,000 businesses were destroyed, 100 Jews murdered, and thousands arrested and taken to concentration camps. It was soon after this attack that the most severe laws were passed and the genocidal activities that came to be known as the Holocaust began.

Nationalism devotion to one's nation; excessive patriotism; doctrine that national interests are more important than international considerations.

Nihilism the general rejection of customary beliefs in morality, religion, or, loosely, any violently revolutionary movement involving some use of terrorism.

Nuremberg city in Germany where the Nazis held large rallies, and later where an International Military Tribunal held trials of Nazis accused of War Crimes (1945–46).

Pogrom an organized massacre of, or attack on, the Jews or other minority groups. Term used in Eastern Europe. From the Russian "like thunder; devastation."

Prejudice a judgment or opinion formed before the facts are known (prejudge); a preconceived idea, usually unfavorable, of intolerance or hatred of other races, creeds, religions, etc.

Prussia a former state of Germany regarded as militaristic.

Racism program or practice of discrimination, segregation, persecution, and domination on the basis of race. Scientists claim that there is no such thing as "race." "Race" has generally been used to recognize three major groups of mankind as Caucasian, Negroid, and Mongoloid. The Nazis considered non-Aryans (Jews, Gypsies, Poles, and blacks) as "racially" inferior and undesirable.

Revisionists refers to individuals who are attempting to deny that the Holocaust ever happened in spite of the overwhelming evidence provided by survivors, liberators of the camps, bystanders, and extensive Nazi documentation. Anti-Semitism is thought to be the basis for their revisionism or denial of the Holocaust.

Righteous Gentile refers to any non-Jew who rescued, hid, or attempted to help Jews in danger of being rounded up and killed during the Holocaust. Many of these Righteous Gentiles, who risked their lives for others, are commemorated by trees planted in their honor at Yad Vashem, the Holocaust Museum in Jerusalem, Israel.

Scapegoat a person, group or thing that bears the blame for the mistakes or crimes of others.

Skinhead a person, usually a young adult, who maintains a shaved head and wears symbols of neo-Nazi, prejudiced, pro-violence beliefs.

Stereotype a fixed image or notion of a person or group; having no individuality; to assign the characteristics observed in a few members of that group to the whole group.

Third Reich the Third Republic, referring to Hitler's administration in Germany (1933–45).

Totalitarianism a government or doctrine in which one political party or group maintains complete control and makes all others illegal.

Treaty of Versailles the Treaty which was signed at the end of World War I that stripped Germany of her lands, treasury, and pride.

Treblinka a Nazi concentration camp. Extermination center northeast of Warsaw, Poland.

Weimar Republic the German Republic from 1919 to 1933. Its constitutional assembly met in the city of Weimar in 1919.

Yad Vashem the Holocaust museum that sits atop a hill in Jerusalem, Israel, and which contains, among other things, the documentation of over two million Jews who died in the Holocaust.

Yom HaShoah the day set aside each April to memorialize the six million Jews and millions of others who perished in the Holocaust. The day is meant for remembrance, ceremony, and lectures, both in America and in many places around the world.

Index

About the Authors

Roselle K. Chartock, Ed.D., is professor of education at the Massachusetts College of Liberal Arts. She taught social studies for fifteen years at Monument Mountain Regional High School in Great Barrington, MA, where she resides. Her most recent publications include *Educational Foundations: An Anthology* and a chapter in *Including Music in a Study of the Holocaust*. She continues to write, lecture, and offer workshops on the subject of the Holocaust.

Jack Spencer has been part of the Berkshire Hills Regional School system in Great Barrington, MA, for 30 years as a social studies teacher, principal, and assistant superintendent. He lives in Stockbridge, MA.